TERMINATING
HOPE

TERMINATING
HOPE

BASED ON A TRUE STORY

KERRY HERNANDEZ

author
ready

For information contact:
kerry.hernandez@hotmail.com

Published by:
Author Ready

Copy Editor: Kim Autrey • Content Editor: Debbie Rasmussen
Cover design by Melt Project
Interior book design by Francine Platt, Eden Graphics, Inc.

This book based on true events. It reflects the author's present
recollections of experiences over time. Some names and
characteristics have been changed, some events have been
compressed, and some dialogue has been recreated.

Paperback ISBN 978-1-958626-36-8
Ebook ISBN 978-1-958626-37-5

Library of Congress Number: Pending

Manufactured in the United States of America

First Edition

*I dedicate this book
to all the voices unheard.*

ACKNOWLEDGMENTS

Firstly I would like to thank my friends and family who have listened and supported me through this journey; I would not have made it here without you. I would like to express our deepest gratitude to the many individuals and organizations who have contributed to the advancement of the field of domestic violence and the legal system. Their dedication, hard work, and passion for the subject matter have been invaluable.

I would like to acknowledge Dr. Daniel Saunders of the University of Michigan, whose significant research on the response of court officials to domestic abuse cases, titled "Child Custody Evaluators' Beliefs About Domestic Abuse Allegations: Their Relationship to Evaluator Demographics, Background, Domestic Violence Knowledge and Custody-Visitation Recommendations," has made a significant contribution to this field. His work has provided important insights into the ways in which court officials respond to domestic abuse cases and has helped to improve the legal system's response to domestic violence.

I would also like to extend my appreciation to Professor Geraldine Stahly of California State University San Bernardino, whose research article "Protective Mothers, Endangered Children: Quantifying System Failure" has shed light on the failure of the system to protect victims of domestic violence and their children. Her work has been instrumental in identifying the gaps in the system and has contributed to the ongoing efforts to improve the legal response to domestic violence.

I am deeply grateful to Joan S. Meier, J.D., for her significant contributions to the field of domestic violence law. As the Founder and Executive Director of the Domestic Violence Legal Empowerment and Appeals Project (DV LEAP) and Professor of Clinical Law at George Washington University Law School, Ms. Meier has become a leading voice in the domestic violence legal community. Her work has been instrumental in ensuring that victims of domestic violence receive the legal representation they deserve and has helped to shape the legal response to domestic violence.

Ms. Meier's expertise in this area is particularly noteworthy, as she has specialized in custody and abuse cases and has litigated hundreds of domestic violence cases at both the trial and appellate levels. In addition to her impressive legal career, Ms. Meier has been an influential advocate for domestic violence issues at both the national and local levels. She has served on the Mayor's Commission on Violence Against Women (VAW) and has been a member of numerous other local and national bodies. Currently, she serves as the "lay" member of the American Psychological Association's Board for Advancement of Psychology in the Public Interest.

Ms. Meier's scholarship on domestic violence, custody and abuse, and parental alienation syndrome has been widely published and praised. She has also delivered numerous trainings and workshops for lawyers, judges, advocates, and mental health professionals, helping to advance knowledge and awareness in these critical areas. For her significant contributions to the field of domestic violence law, Ms. Meier has been recognized with numerous awards and honors, including the American Bar Association Commission on Domestic Violence's Sharon Corbitt Award for "Exemplary Legal Services to Victims of Domestic Violence, Sexual Assault, and Stalking."

I would also like to extend my gratitude to Barry Goldstein, one of the leading national and international experts regarding domestic violence, for his invaluable insights and expertise in this field. His work has helped to raise awareness about the complex nature of domestic violence and has contributed to the ongoing efforts to improve the legal response to domestic violence.

I would like to acknowledge the California Protective Parent Association for their unwavering commitment to making child safety a first priority. Their work has been instrumental in ensuring that children are protected from domestic violence and that their safety is always the top priority.

Finally, I would like to express my sincere appreciation to all the survivors who have shared their stories and experiences. Your courage and resilience have been an inspiration to me and your contributions to this field are immeasurable. To all of the strong advocates out there thank you for boosting their voices. Your voices have been essential in raising awareness about the devastating impact of domestic violence, post separation abuse, child abuse has on the children, families and communities.

1

I SHOULD HAVE SEEN THIS COMING

NOVEMBER 15, 2017

t's a little past 10 a.m. as I stared down at the daunting pile of dishes in my sink. The screech of tires outside shattered the still air. I looked out my kitchen window to see Moe's SUV buck to a stop.

It's a month before Christmas, and the holidays put him in an ill temper. As usual during exchanges, I walked out to help unbuckle the girls from their car seats; Kay was four, and Anna was two. Moe was already screaming and ranting. Moe jumped out, and before his heels hit the asphalt, he ripped open the back driver's side door and yanked Kay out of her car seat.

What is he doing?

I was on the other side trying to get Anna out when Moe screamed, "Get the f*** away from my car!"

What?

He flew around the back of the SUV holding Kay, waving his right arm in the air still screaming, "Get the f*** away from my car! Get the f*** away from my car!"

What is wrong with him?

Moe charged straight at me. I was still trying to get Anna out of her car seat. Instinctively, I shielded Anna closing the gap between my left shoulder and her car seat to protect her and braced for impact. He shoved me against the open door.

Kay was still clinging onto his left hip as he continued to push me with his right hand. Using my back as a shield, I frantically tried to get the bottom latch unbuckled.

I dropped my elbow down to protect the baby growing inside my belly. All I could think about was getting the girls safely inside my house. Anna was now in my arms, her little blonde head tucked under my chin; we had no escape. I was now wedged tightly into the inside corner of the door.

He continued to shove me trying to get to Anna. The entire time he kept screaming, "F*** you! Don't touch my car! Get the f*** away from my car!"

"It's okay, it's okay, baby," I repeated. I wasn't sure if I was saying it out loud or just in my head.

Moe used his whole body to push us tighter into the wedge of the door. I continued to use my back as a buffer.

Still holding Anna, I put my other hand up against the door, trying to create a pocket of safety for her. I sunk my head next to Anna's ear and curled into a protective ball. Staring at my hand pushing against the door, my freckles began to blur as Moe pushed harder.

My baby squirmed inside me, and the danger of our situation became a stark reality.

I was terrified that Anna or Kay would get hurt, but I couldn't fight back… I couldn't move. Panic started to seep in. I was pinned so tightly in the door jam, I couldn't breathe. It felt like my throat was closing.

"Hey! What's going on here?"

Moe spun around creating an opening for us to escape, and as we did, Kay's terrified green eyes through her auburn bangs stopped me in my tracks. I'm not leaving without her, too.

The man who yelled was Tony, my boyfriend, and my unborn child was his first baby. Moe looked feral.

Tony approached Moe cautiously and calmly. He gestured for Moe to put Kay down slowly.

Tony asked Moe to give Kay to me. For whatever reason, Moe complied.

I ran into the house with the girls, and I heard Moe yell, "You gonna fight me right here in front of the house?"

Once inside the house, I locked the door and put the girls down. The girls were scared, and I began kissing their faces. I scooped them up and took them to their room in the back of my house, so they wouldn't hear their dad yelling. I don't know why I waited to call the police. I guess I thought it would be easier if Moe just left. The girls were safe inside, and Tony could handle himself.

Tony worked in construction and was stronger in stature than Moe, who had a slim build.

Later, Tony told me that he had asked Moe to take a walk down the street to get him away from the house. Tony said Moe was acting insane, jumping up and down in the street.

At one point, Tony asked Moe, "Are you okay?" Moe ripped off his glasses and yelled, "Do I look like I'm on drugs?" That's not what Tony asked.

Tony said Moe's eyes were dilated, and before he could say anything, Moe yelled, "Everybody thinks I'm on drugs!"

Tony said Moe ranted on and on, but then Moe jumped back into his SUV and sped away before the police arrived. I had no idea that this was just the start of things.

2

PEANUT BUTTER AND JELLY SANDWICHES

got used to comments from new people, usually said with a slight inflection of disgust.

"You two were married?"

"How did you end up with him?"

"I can't picture the two of you ever together."

It wasn't surprising the questions came. Moe now had a thin and gaunt face. To hide his sunken cheeks, Moe had grown a long, unkempt beard that he frequently stroked. Sometimes he would decorate his beard with miniature Christmas tree ornaments, or he attempted to braid it into two forks. Eventually, once your eye moved up the monstrosity that hung below his face, your eyes were met with a narrowed gaze and furrowed brows. His face had been beaten by the sun and gave the appearance of a constant scowl. He had also lost a significant amount of weight, causing his legs to become like those of a frog. His belt had to be cinched tightly to hold up his pants.

My responses were usually the same.

"He's a completely different person now... I don't know this person anymore" or "Did you know he graduated with a bachelor's with honors from a prestigious university?"

Friends were shocked to see Moe's before and after.

Sorry—I realize I haven't introduced myself. My name is Seraphine Soyla, and I probably ask more questions than I should. I grew up in a small town and always felt a strong desire to see more of the world and explore new places. When I was seventeen, I left for college. I had a passion for art, which led me to a university to study the subject more formally. The plan was to also double major in pre-med; however, I graduated before I finished my last course; organic chemistry. Eagerly, I traveled to different countries, immersing myself in different cultures and continued to learn as much as I could about the world around me. I continued to follow my instincts and pursue my passions, even if that meant going against the expectations of others. Despite my adventurous spirit, I managed to achieve stability by finding a job that I was passionate about. Throughout my journey, I embraced the chaos and always tried to live on my own terms. Always grateful for the experiences and lessons I have learned along the way.

I met Moab Malvado, in college during the spring of 2007. His friends called him Moe.

My pencil had slipped off my desk, and Moe handed it back to me. Black hair, green eyes, and a clean-shaven face.

We began talking before and after class, and it turned out we were both finishing our undergraduate prerequisites.

Moe wanted to be a respiratory therapist, and I wanted to be a nurse. He was interested in history, enjoyed simulating conversations, and could deliver speeches that enthralled listeners. Before I met him, he had served in the army for four years, he had been stationed in Germany, deployed to Iraq, and had been awarded a Purple Heart.

Moe laughed when he told me he was so enchanted by the wonders of German cathedrals and museums that he received a letter from the Red Cross reminding him to contact his mother back home.

He was open about his experiences there, telling me how his convoy was hit by an improvised explosive device (IED) and the obstacles he had to overcome consequently. He was discharged in 2005.

Moe was forthright about his weaknesses. I was reassured because it seemed like guys I talked to before suppressed their faults.

After the quarter ended, we went our separate ways and didn't see each other for a while. We ended up running into each other on campus about two years later. I invited him to go hiking, expecting him to decline.

At that time, I was training for a half marathon and running on average fifteen miles a week. He was a smoker and strenuous activity wasn't really his thing. He agreed to go "as long as it's not like an eight-mile hike." I assured him it was only about two miles.

The day of the hike we arrived at the trail, and standing at the base, Moe looked up toward the summit. "We're hiking that?"

I put on my backpack. "Yup, let's go."

He seemed to regret his decision immediately but said nothing. On the way up, he verbally communicated he was fine, but his face told an entirely different story.

While we continued up the trail, I would look back. Moe stopped frequently, he claimed to admire the view. "Such a nice view here, don't you think?" He leaned back with both hands pressed into his lower back, sweat pouring from his forehead.

He pointed to the valley, but quickly, his hand shot to his knee. Hunched over he was out of breath.

I laughed in my head but said, "I packed a lunch. This looks like the perfect spot to rest. Do you want some water?"

He nodded, and I handed him a bottled water. I had made peanut butter and jelly sandwiches, but the baggies they were in embarrassingly got smashed by my water bottles. I handed him a crumpled sandwich, but he made it seem like it was the best sandwich he had ever eaten.

We didn't make it to the summit but headed back down after lunch.

I joked with him. "Now that you've conquered this trail that eight-mile trail should be no problem."

He just stared at me. "No more trails."

I laughed. "Do you need a cigarette?"

He glared at me. "I hate you."

I thought he was funny, endearing, and a good sport for attempting a hike he was clearly not prepared for. As my half marathon date neared, I continued to joke with him, "It's not too late you can sign up with me if you want."

I laughed when he gave me this dead pan stare.

After a long pause, he said, "I'm not running no half marathon, but I'll go with you and hand you water."

He did exactly that as he cheered me on.

My best friend was the social queen bee, always having an event or party. I invited Moe and slowly he began coming out to everything wih me, and my friends really started to like him. He was kind, thoughtful, smart, and he won over my friend's seal of approval.

Moe took me to meet his parents. His dad, Lot Malvado, had a red face and light blue eyes. He was a pastor at a small Christian Baptist church. Moe also had two older sisters and one younger sister. Their Hispanic last name originated from Spain; however, no one in the home spoke Spanish. His mom, Edith, was easy to talk to. She embarrassed Moe when she showed me baby pictures of him. Moe was afraid she had blown any chance he might have at a relationship with me, and that I would never speak to him again.

I laughed at that, and we began dating shortly after. He was humble and slow to anger.

His family was open and inviting. He had one sister who seemed a little crazy, but what family doesn't have at least one bad apple.

Moe's large family was close knit; something I longed for since a large portion of my family had passed, and the few remaining seemed to have scattered to the wind. Our family gatherings slowly dwindled creating a larger desire for family connection. I have always been inquisitive and slightly rebellious, but what I desired the most was family.

Although Moe and I had different journeys, it seemed like our goals were strongly linked. As fate would have it, we were both accepted to the same university. Because the nursing school provided entrance classes every semester, I was able to start right away, whereas Moe had to wait until the fall to begin his respiratory therapy education.

For two years, both of us were devoted to school. To escape our studies, we talked about the future and where we wanted to travel together. We decided to take my last summer and fly to England to visit my best friend who was stationed at Lakenheath Air Force Base.

When we got back since I had a prior degree, I was able to take my NCLEX exam early. I was hired onto an adult intensive care unit (ICU) and began working full-time on night shift. At that time, if you worked full-time, they would pay for ten units of school per year. So, I took advantage of that and slowly completed the last part of my BSN.

But before we graduated together, Moe and I had been dating for nearly three years, naturally, the next step was marriage. We were married on December 20, 2012. We went to New Zealand on our honeymoon, and I ended up getting pregnant.

A few of my friends had struggled with fertility issues, so I had stopped taking my birth control thinking it might take us awhile, too.

Nope. Fertile myrtle here got pregnant immediately, and Kay was born nine months later. Four months before Kay arrived, Moe graduated from his respiratory therapy program with honors, and I was officially done with school.

With the stress of school, our new baby, and everything leading up to this summer, Moe wanted to take some time off before completing his board exams, and I understood.

Moe was 70 percent disabled with PTSD, so he received VA disability. The hospital gave me eight weeks paid maternity leave. We were renting a tiny house, so financially we were okay. I took a few additional months off since I had a third-degree tear after Kay's delivery, which made walking painful. My OB-GYN doctor told me the only way to fix the muscles that I assumed healed improperly, was to have another baby. Good thing we planned on having more.

Kay was that perfect baby that slept through the night and ate all her food with no fuss. Moe doted over us. "No don't get up. I got it."

Everything was perfect. We dreamed of moving to Hawaii. I was all in. Let's do it. So, I applied to The Queen's Medical Center intensive care unit in Honolulu on the island of Oahu.

3

WHITE VINEGAR AND PALM TREES

November 2, 2013

If everyone's dreams of moving to Hawaii came true, the islands would sink into the ocean. That was our plan... but it didn't happen; I didn't get the job.

Now we might have put the cart before the horse because we had already hired a moving company, and all of our belongings were on a container in the port of Long Beach. Moe was snoring next to me, and I was staring at the ceiling contemplating our stupid impulsive ambitions.

How would we get all our stuff back? How much would this cost us? I looked at Kay asleep in her nest in the middle of our bed.

Typically, I didn't get up in the middle of the night and walk around because Kay was right there. However, I couldn't sleep, and I was thirsty.

I wandered into the kitchen and flipped on the lights and screamed.

The kitchen walls seemed alive, from floor to ceiling the walls seemed to move.

Moe ran into the kitchen. "What's wrong?"

"The walls moved!" I screamed. I covered my mouth with one hand and pointed at the walls with the other. "Are those cockroaches?"

Moe said they were water bugs and led me back to bed. He promised to deal with it first thing in the morning.

Our tiny house was infested. I had never seen so many bugs in my life! How had I not seen them before?

Moe wanted to bug bomb the kitchen, but I was worried about the chemicals and poison getting into Kay's things. The house was too small anyway, and all our stuff was already packed in a container. The only solution was to find another place. As I envisioned roaches crawling in our ears while we slept, I packed an overnight bag, and we drove to Moe's parents' house the following night. We insisted we pay them something while we lived there until we found a new place to rent.

His mom was elated and began flipping through catalogs, excited she was going to get a new dishwasher. Theirs had been broken awhile but they didn't have the extra money to fix it. Edith began planning all the dinner get-togethers she was going to have afterwards.

Family gatherings are one of my favorite things, yet, I discovered that each home has its own set of rules. At Moe's parents,' we were told to hide our purses from his cousin who might steal money. At my parents' house, we couldn't talk about anything medical because my dad was squeamish. But the home that had the most rules was Moe's oldest sister.

She had given birth to five children, but one died from a rare heart defect less than a month after birth. Their house was a shrine to his memory. Most of the year no one was permitted to visit. Moe described it as a hoarder house, and their neighbors frequently turned them in to the city claiming their weeds were too high and posed a fire danger. Moe said her house was so bad at one point, they found a dead squirrel inside, and that he personally had called CPS (Child Protective Services) several times on her. Moe told me how his oldest sister went to culinary college, but she never used it. He laughed that she wasted her college education by working at Pablo's Tacos, making minimum wage.

Moe instructed me there were two rules when inside her house but really there were three. For the holiday, we celebrated at their home. Everyone's eyes avoided the large picture of their lost baby that loomed over the room from the mantle. A large fake tree stood to the left of the mantle covered in dust so thick it made my throat itch. Rule one: do not sit on the furniture, it's filthy.

No one talked to her husband; Moe's parents hated him and ignored him. I don't think I ever heard him speak. He looked like a sad, worn-down turtle with dark, negative energy. There was just something off about him. Rule two: the family was not permitted to walk down the hall, and no one was allowed to open any closed doors.

The carpet had so many stains that they seemed to blend, making the light carpet appear brown. When I stood in the living room, I noticed their attempt to paint the walls, but the new paint stopped a few feet from the ceiling.

No one mentioned it or even looked up. They seemed to try to ignore the room while making small talk with each other. Which brings me to the unspoken rule three: ignore everything and always pretend everything is okay.

"Did you try the lemon cake? It's very good."

"Timmy got scarlet fever again, so he can't play soccer this week."

"Oh, how dreadful... the heaven in a bowl is delightful. Did you try it?"

It was an awkward observance of conformity shaped into polite banter while consuming tarts on dishes of denial.

Back at his parents' house, Edith recited righteously recalling the time she had slapped her oldest daughter's husband so hard across the face it tumbled him backward. He had called her daughter a whore when she told him she was pregnant with their first child and accused her of cheating.

Edith lingered in the memory for a moment. I supposed the story was to portray what a good mother she was for defending her daughter. Yet, they continued to have more children together and things didn't…

My thought was cut off by Moe asking, "Hey, I have to go down the hill. You coming?"

Moe looked tense and serious. I grabbed my purse and followed. I asked him if everything was okay, and he just sighed and slightly rolled his eyes.

"Yeah, it's my sister… I'll tell you about it on the way." I already knew the dramatic story would take the whole hour drive. Moe had a fire and ice relationship with his other sister, the second oldest. Best friends one minute, not speaking the next.

She worked as a pharmacy technician at a psychiatric facility. She worked so many doubles I often wondered when she slept. Caffeine diet pills were easy to come by over the counter, and she took so many her lower jaw seemed to move constantly. She took any and every pill that had a side effect of weight loss. She seemed to consume them by the handfuls.

How she got them I was never 100 percent sure, but the rumor was she had multiple doctors prescribing her multiple things. She was apparently very good at convincing people to give her the things she wanted.

Every couple of months she was either in an eating disorder clinic or in the hospital for attempted suicide. Through all of it, she was financially successful and owned two houses. Moe proceeded to tell me his sister and her husband were probably going to get a divorce. She was currently married to a sous chef.

He was very nice and always invited Moe and me over for dinner to show off his skills. We happily obliged his requests. At dinner, she used to tell us how much he spoiled her. But now she's claimed he didn't love her enough, and that he never supported her when she would go away to an eating disorder rehab. She also accused him of beating her. Apparently, we were driving down to help support her for the latter, but Moe pointed out that all her other relationships ended with them beating her.

Moe said he didn't buy it, but he must be her brother and defend her. It was a long night.

The next morning with breakfast I started searching through the rental listings again. Some of the rentals were insane. One had a flight of rickety stairs to a two-bedroom loft where I couldn't even stand-up straight. Another, the previous renter had punched holes in the walls. I was grateful Moe's parents were housing us, but I couldn't stand the smell of vinegar. Edith would clean the entire house with white distilled vinegar—counters, bathrooms, floors—everything.

After scouring for weeks, I found a house. No low ceilings and no holes in the walls, it was already better. The house was on a hill near a sea of HOA houses. Each had perfect palm trees, topiary bushes aligned in a row, and pristine green grass. The rental stood tall with two stories.

The master bedroom on the top level overlooked the west valley. It had that high ceiling trend that swept through all the track houses in the nineties. They all just made me want to construct a loft to make use of the wasted space. How do people clean those high windows anyway?

The house was stunning and impractical, nothing we would want to live in forever but to rent for a while seemed exciting.

Moe said it's too expensive. It's seven hundred and fifty dollars more than the tiny bug infested rental. It was fine—we could cover the rent, and the smell of Edith's vinegar made me feel like I was starting to pickle.

We signed the lease.

Moe's family came over oohing and aahing when they went through the house. They seemed excited, but Moe was less enthused. I didn't know if he was embarrassed because of the reason we moved, or if he just thought the house was too big because he seemed discontented about it all.

My maternity leave ended shortly after we moved in. Transitioning back to the night shift was proving difficult. Moe was critical that I was always tired and forgetful since going back to work. I quickly realized the night shift was too demanding with a new baby in the house, so I applied to move to day shift.

I tried to brush off Moe's critiques because I was aware of the fact he was displacing some of his frustrations. He was struggling to pass his third respiratory therapy exam. He initially failed the exam by 3 percent, he tried again and failed by 1 percent... literally, probably by one or two questions.

The third time he failed by 6 percent, and his aggravation and disappointment grew. But he didn't want to talk about it, and words of encouragement only seemed to upset him more.

I suggested we take a cruise to Alaska over the summer. I thought it could help him regroup then he could take the exam study course he had been talking about when we got back. He liked the idea, so I started to plan. Kay was nine months old, and my mom offered to watch her. I added every extra excursion offered, including a small plane ride into the fjords.

I have always hated small planes and helicopters and spinning amusement rides and boats. Including cruises, because I have terrible motion sickness, but Moe had always talked about going to Alaska. I wanted him to have a hedonistic experience. Carpe diem.

4

CRUISING NEXT TO ICEBERGS NEVER ENDS WELL

July 15, 2014

Once on what felt like a Ford Pinto with wings, I quickly regretted ever getting onboard. I was sitting in the front next to the pilot while flying between the Misty Fjords of nauseating doom. It was everything I expected it to be. The pilot looked over at me; I must have been fifty shades of green because he landed on the water in between the two mountain cliffs.

I've always preferred walking. It maintains a degree of solace that no matter the incline of the trail, you will eventually get to your destination unencumbered by nausea and vomiting. Yet, there I was, standing on a plane on top of the water trying to swallow down the acid fumes expelling from my stomach. Proud I kept it together, I tried to enjoy the beauty. My stomach churned the entire time. I wished I could tell you that things improved dramatically following that unpleasant experience, but we might as well have been on the Titanic.

Does he seriously not get it? My mind quickly went over all the facts.

He was with me on shore as I searched for that particular bottle of local wine specific to Alaska, and he thought it was okay to just exchange it for what... a bottle of two-buck chuck?

My mind went back to a previous argument over wine when he gave one of his teachers one of my expensive bottles I had purchased in New Zealand. I guess he thought all wines were the same, but we already had this discussion. There was no way he could think that I was going to be okay with any of this, and *this* was entirely different... this was like him handing another girl a drink at a bar while I was in the bathroom but not just any drink, my birthday drink.

My head was spinning. I paid for this cruise. I did this for him. Then some woman he doesn't know asked him to get her a drink. Instead of saying "no" or "sorry I'm married," he snuck in while I was sleeping, took the bottle, and gave it to HER!

I tried to calm down, but I was so angry, I don't even remember him really trying to apologize to me, he just kept repeating "but she said she'd buy another bottle." "You should have said, 'No, I'm married' and walked away!" *How did he not get it?*

Then I started to wonder if maybe I was blowing things out of proportion. I took some deep breaths and asked for more details; "How many people were there?"

He claimed one other guy was there. *Okay, maybe that guy wanted a drink, too.* "Was the other guy drinking the wine, too?" That would have been better, for whatever reason.

But Moe said no, that the other guy didn't drink any. "So, you're now telling me you were drinking alone with *her?*"

More questions flooded out, "How long were you there? What time did you come back?"

Moe didn't say anything. He just looked at the floor.

I didn't want to say anything that I would regret, so I left the room and didn't speak to him the entire day. When I eventually came back to the room, he had ripped off a corner of a piece of paper and wrote "sorry," folded it up, and left it on the bed. The tiny corner of paper almost made me madder. We were mid-cruise, so I had two options. I could be mad for the remainder of the cruise or move on and deal with it later.

I got over it.

When we were back home, I remember telling my girlfriends what had happened. They were shocked. "He did what?" It seemed so out of character for him and truthfully, I was still seething mad because of "the apology"—really? A ripped corner of paper—it was so pathetic, it was insulting.

A month later, I found out I was pregnant with baby number two. But this time, Moe seemed indifferent. He was pulling back and hiding away. I would walk around the house looking for him, but I couldn't find him.

I'd call his cell phone, then suddenly he would magically appear. It was like an annoying game of hide and seek. When I asked where he had been, his voice would trail off. He never really answered me.

This began happening more frequently; it was so weird.

Moe's good, close-knit, Christian home wasn't what it was five years earlier. Trouble moved through the whole family like a sieve exposing larger complexities not previously visible to outsiders. His parents may have still been married, but most of the time, Moe's dad was staring at the TV from his recliner. He was apathetic to everyone. Edith, who initially appeared generous and welcoming, was simply incapable of saying no.

She had no boundaries, avoided issues, made excuses, tolerated problematic behaviors, and sacrificed her own needs by saying yes to all her children's desires, without concern of hers, or their, personal welfare, health, or safety.

This was her idea of love, and his dad couldn't be bothered. Moe's oldest sister found out she was pregnant with their sixth child. The problem was her doctors had warned her many times not to get pregnant again. They told her that she and the baby would be at considerable risk for serious complications, possibly death due to her weight and medical conditions.

She poorly managed her health issues and was frequently noncompliant about taking her medications. Some days when she walked into her parents' house, she was barely able to speak. She would ask Edith for one of her blood pressure pills, claiming either she forgot to pick up her prescription, or the pharmacy couldn't refill due to insurance issues. They were both on the same medication, but sharing with her daughter would leave Edith short at the end of the month, forcing Edith to go to the emergency room for a hypertensive emergency.

Edith had an irrational fear that her daughter would withhold her grandchildren from her if she didn't give her what she wanted. The fear wasn't even plausible because her daughter didn't have the financial means to be independent from her family.

Moe's grandfather owned the home they rented and charged them five hundred dollars a month, but they were years behind in payments. Moe told me the doctors advised her to end the pregnancy while she was in her first trimester. Not only could she die and leave her four living children motherless, but the ultrasounds were also showing signs that the fetus either did not have kidneys, or that they were not going to be functional. They told her the baby would most likely need a kidney transplant at the age of two *if* he lived to two years.

A lump sat in my throat when I thought of the difficult decision she had to make. A choice between knowing the challenges ahead and risking her own life leaving her other four children motherless or ending the pregnancy on the heels of grief from just losing her last child.

She chose to take the risk and asked for prayers on social media.

5

TOXIC FAMILY AFFAIR

September 2, 2014

Moe's second oldest sister swallowed a bunch of pills attempting suicide again. Moe's whole family drove to the emergency room. I walked in to see his mom sitting at the side of the bed holding her hand. A get-well balloon was tied to the end of the bed.

His sister was looking around at us from her bed like she expected more sympathy from everyone.

Her heart rate was abnormally fast. Upset that the nurse wasn't properly pampering her daughter, Edith yelled, "She could have died!" The nurse responded professionally but the roll of her eyes as she left annoyed at the whole scene said, "not to be unsympathetic but she does this every four to six months."

It's a bizarre relationship between Edith and her daughter. Her marriage with the sous chef dissolved, her now ex-husband claimed he couldn't do it anymore. Between the mental manipulation and physical assaults after her drinking binges, he said the final straw was when she told him to choose between his daughter or her.

He had also served in the military, and a year ago, a girl messaged him on social media "were you in such in such town during this year?"

He learned that he had a daughter who just had a baby, so he found out that he was not only a dad, but a grandfather, too, all in one day. Moe thought it was hilarious.

The joy and excitement he must have felt to meet his only child and her baby quickly became something else when he found out her boyfriend had given her a black eye. So, he bought her a plane ticket to come and live with him for as long as she needed.

Moe's sister couldn't handle that someone else was getting attention. She accused her husband of cheating on her and then told him to choose between his daughter or her. In the few short months they had been separated, she had already fallen in love with someone new, and they were engaged. I'm not sure how long they dated before getting married, but it wasn't long.

All her husbands were great guys, and this one was no exception. He stood on the other side of her bed. He was nice and pleasant. As we left the hospital, Moe said he felt bad for him.

When we got home, Moe told me, "I don't have enough to cover my auto insurance this month."

"Oh okay, how much do you need?" Even though we were married, we still had separate bank accounts, we just hadn't had time to sit down at a bank. Later that same month, "I need money for the electric bill." Next month same thing.

The V.A. gave him around $1,500 every month, and he also borrowed $500 a month from me. When the mail came, we got an urgent notice. The yellow letter read, you have by this date to pay the water, or it will be turned off.

I asked Moe about it, and he told me this long story that he couldn't get the water switched in his name.

The bill was over $800, and with the threat of having our water turned off, I had to pay it. But then it hit me, if he hadn't been paying for water or the other utilities, and had been borrowing money for his car payment, then where was $2000 a month going?

He yelled at me saying it all went to groceries and diapers, but that didn't add up either because I bought most of the groceries.

Then he accused me. "You're the one that wanted to move into this big house!"

I yelled back, "So, you would rather we stay and raise Kay and our new baby in that tiny house infested with roaches?"

Moe was quiet but still wanted to blame all our current financial problems on me. Moe still could not pass his exam. As the weeks went by, I felt like I was drowning trying to keep the bills afloat. I told Moe he would have to get a job, any job, before baby number two arrived.

My student loans would be coming out of deferment soon, and I would need help. I was so stressed over the thought of not being able to cover rent, groceries, utilities, his auto expenses, auto maintenances, student loans, and caring for Kay while entering my third trimester of pregnancy.

I helped him put together a résumé and cover letter, but at this point, Moe was hardly around. We rarely slept in the same bed. Not because we had two bedrooms, but because I went to bed with Kay by 9 p.m., and he would stay up to who knew when. When I woke up at 5 a.m. he was already awake making coffee in the kitchen. On the days I worked, the minute I got home, Moe had dinner ready. Kay would be staring at me bouncing up and down with her tiny fingers gripping the top of the side rail with a movie on in the background. I soon figured out that when he did something for me, he expected something in return.

Moe handed me a plate of food and would ask if he could go to his friend's house. If I said no, he would throw a fit and tell me that I never let him hang out with his friends. He would pout and stomp around like a teenager. It was easier just to let him leave, then Kay and I would hang out in peace and get ready for bed.

A few days later, Moe joined us for breakfast. He was energetically telling me his sister was now hellbent to get pregnant because she was jealous of all the attention her older sister was receiving. The problem was her new lover had been married, divorced, had two older kids, and had gotten a vasectomy to prevent more. But now the only thing that was going to make her "better" was having children of her own because adoption was not an option given her history. So, she now had an insatiable need to get pregnant despite her severe irrational fear of gaining weight. To solve her conundrum, she took to craigslist and put out an ad. Moe told me she found some guy in Los Angeles County that would help her.

Unbelievably, their mom agreed with the entire plan and accompanied her daughter to the hotel. Despite his sister's multiple efforts, her plan didn't work. Eventually, she found a doctor in Texas to surgically undo her husband's vasectomy, and later they had twins.

I would never understand any of this or how everyone seemingly went along with her risky and mentally unbalanced plans.

6

ADDICTED TO DENIAL

December 13, 2014

By November, Moe still did not have a job, and I knew I could not renew the lease because I couldn't keep up the charade. I knew the only way we were going to make it financially was to move back in with our parents and put all our stuff in storage. Moe had become even more distant, and our marriage began to feel like a roommate situation. He came and went as he pleased.

With our new baby swiftly approaching, I thought I needed to do something drastic to light the fire under him. Maybe separating and going to counseling would spring him into action. But with the way Moe had been acting, I knew telling him this would render him useless. I also knew I was not physically capable of moving a two-story house into storage by myself.

So, I waited until after all our stuff was moved into storage, then I told him I thought it was best if I lived with my parents and he lived with his parents for the time being. As I expected, he acted like I had manufactured a huge conspiracy against him. I tried to reassure him that I did not want a divorce and told him that I would be signing up for marriage counseling.

I don't think he heard a word I said. We still had a week or so before the final home inspection, and he was still sleeping inside the house while I had been staying at my parents. I asked if he could just do the last little cleanup around the house before the inspection, but instead, the day before the inspection, he had all of his friends over for a bonfire in the backyard. They totally trashed the house.

Cinder wood scattered everywhere… empty cans and black soot all over the cement patio. Trash and more empty cans were all over the living room floor, and open food containers piled on the kitchen countertops.

When I confronted Moe, he just kicked a small burnt piece of wood around the backyard. He continued to kick things and sulked around like Eeyore. I walked back inside the house.

Combating my large belly, I leaned down and angrily began picking up the bits of trash in the house. Who *is* this person?

When I was pregnant with Kay, he was never like this. He wouldn't let me do hardly anything, and if I even said anything like "it's okay, I got it," he refused saying, "No, you're pregnant, it's my job to do this."

Where was *that* guy? After going up and down the stairs, bending over trying to pick up all of the trash, I stopped abruptly and leaned against the wall. My belly and back throbbed. I knew I couldn't complete the task of cleaning the two-story house alone. I was so mad while trying not to be mad, I tried to focus on a solution.

I called a family friend that ran a cleaning company, and my parents helped me pay for the cost. I told Moe he was going to pay my parents back half of the cost it took to clean up his little party.

The final day on the lease was December 14, 2014. I don't remember much else about what happened that month, but I know Moe and I spent that Christmas together, and we got pictures with Kay at his dad's church.

His dad, Pastor Lot, relished in the limelight of his Christmas sermon yet remained silent about Moe. He offered no guidance to us. I thought he might have known that we were going to attend counseling and thought it was better to leave it to the professionals.

In January 2015, we started therapy. The lobby was small with a tiny reception window made of thick plastic with a hole cut awkwardly low. Immediately to the left was a locked Dutch door. To the right was another door against the far wall and around the corner of the entryway was a single bathroom.

There were four chairs pushed up against the wall opposite the reception window. At the end of the narrow isle of chairs was a small table that had an array of teas that were all caffeine free. Beside the cups and sugar, the water dispenser offered one of two options: hot or cold water.

I checked in with the receptionist then grabbed some cold water and sat down. Moe came in as the therapist opened the door in front of us and asked, "You ready?"

I stood up, and we walked back to his office. He motioned us to two chairs in front of a large window with a tall, tiny table between us. His chair was across from ours. On the other side of the small room was his desk with his computer and beside it, a tall bookshelf that stretched to the ceiling.

The first session did not go well. Moe was mad the therapist told him that he needed to change some things. He pointed at me and yelled, "Well, she needs to change, too! She doesn't tell me she loves me enough!"

"So, what I'm hearing is you want the cake and icing of the relationship, but you don't want to help bring any of the ingredients to help make that cake?"

"I always have to say I love her first! She should come up to me and say it every once and awhile, too!"

"Is this something that has changed over the course of your relationship?" asked the therapist.

"No, she's never been the first to say it, I always have to be the one."

"Okay, so from what I've heard so far, what behaviors are you engaging in that would facilitate her wanting to tell you she loves you?"

Moe folded his arms tightly across his chest. "I was just saying she needs to tell me she loves me more, that's all, cause she's terrible at saying it."

I told the therapist that it felt like we were more like roommates, and Moe got even angrier when the therapist pointed out that even roommates pay half the costs of where they live.

Moe was a hot mess between crying and yelling. He couldn't seem to regulate any of his emotions. Moe was sure I was the only problem.

We continued to go, but every time, Moe wanted to blame me and wanted me to do "homework" as well.

"She doesn't do anything!"

"She wanted to move into that big house."

The therapist pointed out that I was now in the third trimester of my pregnancy and had other duties to attend to at that moment. Moe acted like a child, crossed his arms angrily and pouted.

"Oh, so because she's pregnant, she doesn't have to work on anything?" Whenever possible, I drove myself to the sessions because when we drove together in his SUV, he would speed over 80 mph and weave in and out of traffic even with Kay strapped in her infant carrier in the back.

I told the therapist that he scared me when he drove like that.

Moe's only response was "Well, what is she gonna work on, you know she's not perfect."

The therapist pointed out "if your wife is telling you something scares her, or makes her feel unsafe, shouldn't you address that and correct that behavior?"

Moe avoided answering. Instead, he just continued to yell and argue with the therapist.

From January to April, Moe had only seen Kay sixteen times, and it was mostly because I went to his parents' house to help Edith's mother who was home in hospice.

Moe's grandparents lived in the house to the right of his parents' home. His grandma was in a hospital bed in their living room. Across from her bed was a long sofa with a small sofa to the left and a TV to the right.

The family would gather around on the sofas and talk. I asked Edith how she was doing and if she needed any help around her house. She never asked about the elephant in the room.

I also avoided issues in an attempt to create a bubble around myself for the sake of my pregnancy. Conflict washed off my skin like water off a duck's back. I didn't want any of the unpleasant things whirling about me to be absorbed into our new baby girl.

With only a few weeks until my delivery date, I was physically unable to pick Kay up. I asked Moe if he could temporarily move in to help.

It seemed like a practical idea, except Moe wasn't useful. He would stand in the bathroom for hours and pick at his face. When the day finally arrived, Moe sat in the corner of the delivery room. *Was he really playing video games on his phone?*

When I had Kay, Moe was holding my hand and putting cool rags on my neck. This time, my mom and his mom were standing on either side of me when I delivered. He was too consumed by his phone to notice our baby's head crowning.

Maybe it was the epidural, but I just felt numb to it all.

After Anna was born, I was wheeled to the antepartum unit. I was relieved when Moe left. Not angry, and I was a little surprised by that.

The room hummed with chatter of friends and family replacing Moe's absence, but slowly, one by one, they all left. It was quiet now, and my eyes drifted closed as I cradled Anna tightly in a swaddling blanket.

A pink and blue beanie kept her head warm, and a sense of peace swept over my body. I was not thinking of tomorrow or of events past. With each of her tiny sleepy breaths, I relaxed deeper, sinking into the cotton sheets.

7

PUSHING THE BUTTON

A hand touched my shoulder, I opened my eyes to see a nurse in purple scrubs standing next to my bed.

"Good morning, did you and baby sleep okay? Do you have any pain? Do you want to order breakfast?"

I looked down at the small bit of milk on Anna's lips. Still fast asleep, her face was pressed against my left breast, her tiny fist clenched.

Yes to all three. The nurse made small talk as I tried to mentally prepare for our discharge into reality.

A week later, Moe was still "assisting" me at my parents' house and asked if he could go to his friend's mom's house in Oceanside. I was spoon-feeding Kay and breastfeeding Anna. I just looked at him. "Really?"

He started again with the teenage "you don't let me do anything, I never get to see my friends."

I didn't argue. Instead, I reminded him Anna had just been born, but I told him I wasn't going to tell him what he should or shouldn't do. By now, he should know what his priorities should be.

He showered, packed a bag, and left. If it wasn't clear before, it was noticeably clear now. We were obviously not his priority.

I waited an hour for him to reach his destination then texted him not to return and that his stuff would be bagged up and waiting outside whenever he chose to come and get it. Two days went by. He didn't respond, call, or text.

Finally, when Moe called, he said he had to tell me something. "You have the right to know."

"The right to know what?"

Moe explained he had been using methamphetamine but heavily emphasized that he wasn't addicted, that he was only "chipping." Whatever that meant.

He swore he only started after I left him in December. He said it helped to kill the pain he felt from me leaving him. He told me he was ashamed, that he hadn't been good to me, but he hoped I could forgive him.

That Zen bubble I had tried to create around myself to deflect all the negative had just popped. When I started looking back on his behavior, I felt dumb that I hadn't seen it.

He told me that after he got out of the military in 2005, he used meth for a couple months because of his PTSD, but he checked himself into a rehab program. He said he never desired to use it again, and I believed him. After he excelled in school, graduated with honors with a degree in respiratory therapy, had a home, a family, two babies, and with nine years sobriety, why would he throw it all away? For what?

Moe already knew my stance on drugs, especially methamphetamine. Living in Southern California, I have seen the effects of meth; it will literally destroy your life. I saw kids after high school abandon everything and for what? So they could feel like they had eight shots of espresso and stay up for days?

No thanks, that sounded terrible to me. I'd rather be able to take a nap and keep my teeth.

He kept telling me he only did it a couple times, but frankly, it sounded like he was trying to convince himself more than me. He had abandoned me, our girls, and ignored the risks and consequences. Now he was minimizing and denying he had a problem? That's literally the classic behavior of a person addicted to drugs.

An avalanche of details suddenly filled my mind. Moe never did get a job. He admitted he never went to an interview because he hadn't applied for a single job. He made zero effort.

When I looked back, he never tried to make things work. He was augmentative every time we went to couples counseling. He barely saw Kay, and he didn't contribute anything that would have shown me he wanted to make our family, a *family*.

What was I doing?

I looked back over our pictures of our life and cried. I found our picture from last Christmas. I noticed how skinny he was in the photo, and then it dawned on me. I searched through my photos to find our Christmas picture from last year.

I compared them side by side. In our Christmas picture from 2013, Moe's face was full and round. He was wearing a brown plaid button up shirt, and his belly hung over his jeans.

This last Christmas picture, his face was thin, his white button-down shirt was baggy and loose, poorly hiding his skinny frame. How did I not notice how much weight he lost? We separated December 14, 2014, and there was no way he lost seventy to a hundred pounds in eleven days.

He was still lying!

When I asked him about it, he doubled down and denied he ever used prior to December 14, but the picture showed otherwise. I was living with him. He wasn't going to the gym, and he wasn't dieting. But he was always at a friend's house and coming home late. Is that why he was always gone?

Is that where the missing $2000 went? I wondered how much he was really using. How much is meth? How much meth could he get with $2000? This whole time he was blaming me for renting such a big house. But now I knew he had been using while I was a work, and he was supposed to be taking care of Kay.

What had been going on while I was at work for twelve hours? Kay was always in her play pen when I got home, and how long did he leave her in there? I wondered if he had been ignoring Kay all day by putting her *safe* in her playpen, so he could get high.

I tried to rationalize, maybe he had started to use because he was trying to stay up and study? But obviously, he hadn't been studying at his friends' houses to pass his exam.

I thought about him picking his face at my parent's house, how did I not see it? Did he bring meth to my parents' house?

I started to freak out. What if a piece fell out of his pocket? What if one of the girls put it in their mouth?

OMG! He could have killed them! I couldn't stop thinking about Kay possibly being left for hours alone while I was at work. What was she doing and thinking all day? Where's my mommy? Where's my daddy? When she cried, was he around or did she cry alone?

I couldn't get over the *what if* something tragic had happened to the girls, and he brought that danger into our home. These things were unforgivable. Now he was expecting me to forgive him while he was still lying to me.

8

FAMILIAL PATTERNS

May 1, 2015

Did you know that the average length of marriage in America is approximately eight years. I wondered if Moe and I should have thought of moving to the Maldives instead of Hawaii. It's known for its crystal-clear waters, it's genuinely expected to sink due to climate change, and divorce is as common as coconuts. We would fit right in.

C'est la vie.

Instead, we were living in the Inland Empire; an aggressive and heathenistic community with only an arid climate to cool our tempers.

Its namesake points to its own hubris, and like most empires, over time, they become arrogant which leads to complacency, breeding bureaucracy that induces corruption.

If left unbridled, its insatiable and avarice appetite can result in a society of injustice.

Maybe I should think of moving. Denmark, Finland, and New Zealand are said to have the lowest levels of corruption. Finland and Denmark sound a bit cold. New Zealand is nice this time of year.

I was pulled out of my thoughts when the phone rang.

"Hello?"

"You are going to be the reason my brother doesn't get better if you don't take the girls to his rehab and support him through this!" It was Moe's second oldest sister... the unhinged one. Moe had checked into a drug rehab after I told him I wanted a divorce. Guess she doesn't have that much faith in her brother. Was she really trying to blame me for the potential outcome of Moe's recovery?

This family was so good at displacing accountability. Now they were shifting the blame to me. I wasn't surprised. There was no sense in arguing with her, so I responded with some variation of, "I disagree. I'm sorry you feel that way, but I will not be taking our two babies to a drug rehab facility."

She lashed back. "You're selfish, I hate you, and I'm never going to speak to you again!"

Oh no, what ever will I do now? Her tactics didn't work on me. Driving to San Bernardino to a drug rehab with a toddler and newborn was not something I was going to concede to.

She kept yelling incomprehensibly before she hung up on me. She never spoke to me again.

I later discovered the enrollment into the drug rehab was just a ploy, anyway. Moe's friends asked him if he really needed rehab or if I was making him go. He told them that "the truth" was that he didn't need to go. He told them that since I was probably going to file for custody, he needed to show that he was trying to get sober, and that he was being pushed in that direction.

It was all for show, so he could appear that he was doing the necessary corrective steps for other people. He was in rehab for about one month. When he got out, his *friends* advised him not to give me a penny until he was forced to. What kind of advice is that? I never cared for his friends. He took their advice and disregarded any sense of duty or responsibility for the two lives that contained half of his DNA.

He sent me a sad text or two, but he made no genuine effort. He stopped by for about an hour over the next couple months, maybe five times, maybe. Again, he demonstrated we were not his priority. All of this just solidified my decision.

Managing two babies alone was challenging enough, but the thought of trying to figure out what paperwork was needed to file for a divorce was overwhelming. I wasn't even sure where to hire an attorney, but people helped navigate me through it.

When Moe heard that I had hired an attorney, he was furious and accused me of going behind his back. He thought he would beat me to the punch and filed first. The attorney explained that she had seen this a lot, that the other party thinks they are winning if they file first.

Well, give him his trophy then. My imagination reeled like a scene from a movie of a boy clenching his trophy he just won for "participation," while shouting in a high-pitched tone, "You're not leaving me! I'm leaving you!"

I imagined the girl walking away from him didn't even break a stride, look back, or flip him the bird. She just continued on until she was out of sight.

His friend served me the divorce papers at my parents' house. I read the paperwork, he had filed for divorce and alimony. Alimony? He had been siphoning off money from me for over a year and had the audacity to ask for alimony while leaving me solely responsible for our two babies?

Anger consumed my sorrow, and any lingering sadness I may have felt was gone.

9

BOXCAR FAMILIES

The Family Court System was explained to me like a train. Each court hearing would be a stop, the passengers or information would get aboard or stay behind, and whatever happened during that stop would stay at that stop.

Once the train left the platform, there would be no going back. Basically, don't bother the conductor, a.k.a. the judge, by bringing up what happened at previous stops because they have already moved on.

So, there would be nothing they could do about what happened in previous towns. You lost your wallet twenty miles back? Oh well. It is what it is.

Your experience will be based on what type of conductor you are handed to. Once you are aboard that train, you would not be permitted to leave.

I imagined there would be four different types of train conductors: the golden conductor, the incompetent conductor, the robot conductor, and the evil conductor. Each train passed through the communities with passengers, staff, and prisoners aboard.

The golden conductor was well-educated and knowledgeable on how to operate the train while ensuring the safety of their surroundings as well as the passengers on board. The staff had open dialogue with the conductor that is constructively utilized to improve services. As they pass through towns, they proceed slowly and cautiously as there might be children playing around the tracks. The prisoners aboard would be in the rear of the train and secured with around-the-clock guards.

The incompetent conductor doesn't know how to fully operate the train because they were never professionally trained, so they cannot ensure the welfare of the passengers. The staff's knowledge varies from person to person, qualifications are overlooked, and operations are disorganized because the conductor is too preoccupied managing the engine. The frustrations of the staff are not heard. The conductor will claim they did not see the child playing on the tracks. But even if they did, they lacked the knowledge to stop the train from killing the child. The conductor would feel awful. They would grieve the child and strive to be better. The prisoners in the rear of the train would be secured and guarded by one officer. Things would often slip through the cracks; there would be no safeguards in place.

Things about the robot conductor would be greatly unknown because essentially, they would be the man behind the curtain. The train would be programmed to run nearly automatically to get from point A to point B per the system manual with minimal staff. The system is incapable of visualizing anything other than what is written in the manual. If a child stumbled onto the tracks, the train would not stop and would feel nothing because, after all, it would be performing within its parameters. The prisoners in the rear would be secured and would be monitored. Any complaints or concerns from passengers and/or staff could be addressed by formally writing to the main branch. Responses could take a minimum of eight to twelve weeks and generally read, "the appropriate actions were taken."

Finally, the evil conductor has been well taught how to operate a train. They didn't care about the passengers and would use a train intended for animal transportation rather than humans. Their only concern would be to get to their destination. They would see the children playing on the tracks ahead, but they would not stop because everyone should know that it would be dangerous. They would not be to blame because their parents should have been supervising. Besides, they wouldn't be the ones who killed the children, the train did, and they would claim no fault. The staff would not be held to any standards, and they would be treated poorly. The prisoners would have escaped due to malfunctioning locks and not enough security, but the conductor would claim it was not in the budget to fix. The conductor would be indifferent to the bodies that may lie dead in the cabins. If everyone had just followed their rules, none of this would have happened, they deserved whatever happened to them.

10

MONSTERS DEVOUR
FROM THE INSIDE OUT

Moe wrote in his court testimony, "I did inform her that I was using amphetamines... I have never been arrested nor had any legal violations. The petitioner was never cognizant of my use of amphetamines, until I informed her. It was I who realized that my use of amphetamines was getting out of hand, becoming a definite deterrent to my functioning."

'*I* informed her, it was *I* who realized'... pride had taken the wheel. Was he really trying to explain to the court that because he informed me of his drug use, this was an achievement deserving of alimony? Was he also trying to rationalize and minimize that his drug use wasn't that bad because he had never been arrested or had any legal violations directly for drugs? His ego was blinding him from the truth because the truth was Moe had already received three traffic tickets this year alone for speeds over twenty-six miles over the limit and another for speeding over seventy miles per hour and had no proof of insurance, but he wasn't making the correlation.

"Denial is the ultimate comfort zone." – David Goggins

Moe wrote to his friend, "She's going around making me look like a monster. Yeah, I did drugs behind her back. But I came clean to her, I wasn't caught, I was full of guilt and wanted to get clean for myself, my kids, and for her. So, I just flat out told her what I was doing and went to rehab. She makes it seem like I was doing it in front of the girls. I would get high after everyone went to bed. I do feel like a piece of s*** about it, but I'm no monster by any means. A monster wouldn't have told the truth, go to rehab, check into after care, fight this custody battle so I can have them. A monster would have continued to choose drugs over their children. I've got almost three and a half months clean. I don't even drink anymore. Not that drinking is bad, but for me, it leads me to drugs, so I don't do it. I do love to have sex when I'm high, though. Man, it's great."

The friend responded, "Hell ya I love that s***, too."

Moe wrote back, "Ya, it's the one thing I miss about it. Anyway, lol, no I don't judge you, if your kids weren't safe, it's a problem, but it sounds like you got it under control. Besides, if you're out of control with that then there is no way to hide it. It's obvious."

But he didn't tell the full truth; he didn't stop using. He continued to choose drugs over the girls. I didn't need to say anything, his subconscious was already devouring him. Whispering in his head at night, "You're a monster. You are a monster." Waking up, I imagine Moe saying, "I'm a monster. No, it was just a nightmare. I didn't do drugs in front of the girls. Their eyes were closed. They didn't see me. I'm not out of control. I hid it. Only drug addicts aren't able to hide it. I didn't get caught. Only drug addicts get caught. They didn't see me. I didn't get caught. I'm not a drug addict. I told her I was bad, therefore, I'm good. I'm good. I'm good. I'm a good dad. I'm not out of control. She's just making it seem like I'm the monster. I'm not the monster. She's the monster."

Round and round his mind would spin. Loss can feel like a dark pit, but guilt can sear the soul, and sometimes, it seems easier to flip that hot ember onto someone else.

Maybe it was a moment of clear self-reflection or maybe he was just high, but Moe told the court mediator he thought the girls would be better off with me and gave me sole legal custody, which the court granted. They also issued child support in the amount of six hundred and eighty-eight dollars, deviating lower from the recommended amount due to the fact Moe was still unemployed.

11

THE CRASH ON THE WEST OUTER HIGHWAY

OCTOBER 2, 2015

Moe's friend, who served me the divorce and alimony documents, got Moe a job washing dishes at the bar where he was employed. About a week later, Moe contacted me about an hour into my shift at work. I wondered why he would be calling me that early.

"Hello?" His voice was trembling. "I got into a car accident." He started crying. "I, uh, fell asleep and hit a pole." He was sobbing. "They had to airlift me to the hospital… they're… they're going to be taking me into surgery." He was crying so hard he couldn't speak.

"It's going to be okay, what hospital are you at? I'll be right there." My charge nurse looked at me and immediately asked, "What's wrong?"

I explained what just happened. "Okay, go, I'll get the runner to cover your list. I hope he's okay."

"Thank you." I grabbed my bag and headed to the elevator. Luckily, the hospital where Moe had been taken was close by. I parked and ran into the hospital.

"Where's the surgery section?" I asked the man sitting behind the information booth. He showed me on the map.

"Thank you," I said and hurried down the long beige corridors. I made it just before they took him into surgery. He was on a gurney with a white sheet over his body.

He looked at me then down to his leg. "I broke both my legs and some ribs, and they said I lacerated one of my organs." Tears were streaming down his face. His terror mounted with every breath. "They're taking me into surgery."

The nurse stood at the foot of the gurney. She pointed to his left leg and explained what they were going to do. His left femur had snapped, and he had a fracture in his lower right leg.

Later, I saw a picture of his truck. It looked like a smashed tin can, the whole front was gone. Moe had claimed he fell asleep and hit a pole. His truck had flipped, and they found him dangling behind his driver's seat by his seatbelt. It was assumed that if he hadn't been wearing his seatbelt, he would have been thrown out of the vehicle and would not have survived.

It was an awkward position to be in when I was still upset at him. But I wanted to ease his fear. "It will be okay." My eyes welled up. I told him I would call his family and let them know what's going on as they wheeled him away to the operating room.

I called his family and close friends to let them know what had happened, where he was, and what the nurse told me. I waited for his family to arrive while he was in surgery. Hours went by. Where were they? I'm in the middle of a divorce with him, I just started dating someone else, and I'm the only one here.

What could they possibly be doing that was more important? They rushed to the hospital for his sister every few months, but when their son literally almost died in a car accident, they're MIA? I can't leave and let him come out of surgery and wake up alone in a room.

The surgery took over six hours, and his family was nowhere to be seen. Once he got out of surgery, the medical staff rolled him onto one of the units. About four hours later, his parents finally showed up. It took them ten hours before they finally sauntered in. Unbelievable. They lived less than an hour away from the hospital. I didn't even know what to say to them, so I just left. I never told him, what good would that do? I brought the girls in to see him later. A week or so later Moe was discharged.

With his hospital stay now behind him and a white paper bag full of legal narcotics in hand, he took up residence in the warm and welcoming arms of his enabling parents. The pendulum of Moe's emotions quickly shifted back into distortion. He claimed I only went to the hospital to see if I could get his drug results, and that I *never* brought the girls to see him in the hospital.

His mom called on his behalf to tell me they would look after the girls if I would allow them to stay for a couple of nights every week.

But, alongside our personal drama, his family seemed to be imploding. His parents' house was a circus after the death of his grandma. His parents had to move Grandpa in to care for him and Moe's oldest sister had separated from her husband and needed a place to stay. One of the reasons she left was her husband had been giving her a monthly allowance so small it wasn't enough to feed her and the children for one day. So, she also moved in with her four children. They were preparing the home for child number five who was still in NICU on dialysis.

Moe had rods and pins in his leg and couldn't walk.

Moe's parents only had a three-bedroom house. They had their bedroom, Grandpa was in the second, and the oldest daughter was in the third. Moe, who couldn't walk, was propped in the middle of the living room, and the four kids were sleeping on sofas or wherever they could find space.

I tried to be polite and explain that I thought bringing two more babies would be too much. She disagreed, of course. But I thought it was way too high of a risk for a potential accident to happen.

She was simply incapable of saying no to any request from her children, even if it posed safety issues. She didn't see them. I finally had to plainly say no. She took it like I was personally insulting her ability to care for our babies, but she refused to see or understand any of my concerns. She never spoke to me again. I was starting to notice a familiar pattern.

When Moe found out I was dating, he had a meltdown worthy of an Oscar. Accusations of infidelity rained down like confetti. He went so far as to claim he didn't think Anna was really his. I responded to his accusations with all the enthusiasm of someone being served a salad with no dressing. Moe was spiraling downward faster than the Hindenburg. Moe and I went to court again after his accident.

12

THE CHAMELEON WITH THE WHITE PAPER BAG

November 18, 2015, Court Orders

Temporary sole legal custody of children shall be with mother. Sole physical custody with mother. The parents shall communicate all pertinent information regarding the children through text message.

1. Phase One

   a. Mother shall transport the minor children two times per month in subsequent months for a minimum of 3 hours with transportation provided by mother with days and times as mutually agreed.

2. Phase Two, commencing at such time father is able to operate a vehicle:

   a. Every Monday and Thursday from 10:30am until 4pm

b. One additional day visit for three hours as arranged between the parents.

c. Father shall submit to a random drug test as requested by the other parent. The requesting parent shall pay for the test. If the test is positive, the requesting parent shall be reimbursed.

d. Father may petition the court for more contact at such time as he has established and maintained positive and consistent contact with the minor children for a minimum of 6 months.

Phase One was exceedingly short because maybe a week later, Moe bought a new vehicle and within a week of owning it, got into another accident. This time, of course, it wasn't his fault. Moe got his mom or dad to drive him every Monday and Thursday, using them like chauffeurs, while his new vehicle was getting fixed.

One day in my front yard, Moe started yelling and cussing at me over a queen bed that I bought while we were married, that he felt entitled to. His dad stood there while Moe carried on.

I asked his dad, "Are you going to stop this or are you going to continue to let him cuss at me?"

Lot didn't say anything. He was as useful as an expired coupon.

I said to Moe, "You will not cuss or yell at me. You can have the bed, I don't care. I'll buy another one. Anything else?"

Moe apparently needed the last word. "The bed is mine and you f**** know it. Come on, Dad, let's leave."

Moe's dad turned and left with him. I stood there and watched them leave. *He calls himself a pastor?*

While living with my parents, I saved every penny I could for a down payment on a house. I wanted a solid foundation for the girls to call home.

The realtor promised the un-finalized divorce would not be an issue. However, while trying to close escrow, this initial non-issue was an issue with the underwriter, and Moe took this opportunity to... I'll let him tell you...

"She is buying a house. Mind you, in the middle of a divorce. She is in escrow and needs the divorce to be finalized before she can close on the house. Well, Wednesday, I picked up divorce papers. There's no time frame in which I need to have them in. So, I'm not signing them. I told her if you want me to sign these, so your house doesn't fall out of escrow, then you're gonna have to let me have my daughters two nights a month. Not a huge request. She also wants me to sign a quitclaim. Basically, saying I have nothing to do with the house nor do I want it. I told her I'm not signing s*** unless you let me have my daughters overnight twice a month. She refuses and says I'm blackmailing her. I'm just trying to get more time with my daughters. It's not my fault she is stupid enough to try and buy a house in the middle of a divorce. She gave me all the leverage I need."

Note: When you are going through a divorce, change your shared passwords. Apparently, Moe had been doing a lot behind the scenes.

In July, Moe reached out to a female named Lizard; she was an active drug user. Moe wrote to her ever so romantically. His entire vernacular had shifted to what can only be described as a drug-induced porno scene that I don't care to repeat. Fast forward to after the accident, being without a vehicle didn't stop him. He just took his parents' vehicle.

Moe messaged Lizard. "Well, let me know when you're up to getting down. My car is in the shop right now getting worked on. I got hit in my new car on Sunday. So, for the time being, I am borrowing my parents' van."

Lizard disappeared for a few days. When she finally sobered up enough, she admitted to Moe that she was frapped. (Frapped apparently means high on methamphetamine.)

Moe told Lizard, "I don't care if you're frapped."

Moe consoled her and let her know he didn't judge her. Moe said, "I'm always at my cousins. She's always smoking." And not cigarettes or weed. Nothing good happened at his cousin's. She was what I called a career drug addict, when someone has been using illicit drugs for ten to twenty plus years.

Moe had told me about how his cousin had left her three sons in his care for over two months without saying a word. She just left. Her oldest was severely disabled, non-verbal, non-ambulatory, and needed around-the-clock total care. The second oldest fathered a baby at the age of fourteen, and the youngest seemed to be Pastor Lot's scapegoat for every problem when he visited.

The conversations between Moe and Lizard changed after this. He started to offer her pills, dangling them in front of her like a carrot. She had no reason to leave him when he could get her all the drugs she wanted.

When Moe was running low, he claimed that his cousin's son "has a bunch of Tylenol with codeine."

Lizard was taking so many drugs. It was hard to tell what she was talking about, "Cops we r e at my girls pad for 5 f*** hours today found a f*** wax lab and yep all b@d.com. I cant f*** stand this shot anymore im over it frill doe." Moe flew right alongside her. "I'm a little buzzed on southern comfort and 40mg of norcos." "Are you smoking out (Moe's cousin's son) or is he smoking you out?" They continued on about dabbing and the conversation trailed off.

The part that bothered me the most was when he brought our girls into their conversation. "I get to see my babies tomorrow. I kinda got tipsy tonight. Had a couple norcos and tequila shots. Made me very horny."

Moe talked about our innocent babies in the same breath with getting wasted and hooking up. Disgusting.

Lizard replied, "Luuuucky... wishing I could see my babies."

Moe continued. "I have to wait five months before I can petition for joint custody. I just got my supervised visitation lifted. I had forgot I took the norcos, cuz it's nothing for me to take norcos or Percocet after my accident. So, when am I going to see you?"

I felt sick. I had been working, taking care of the girls, saving up to get a house, and Moe texts, "Gonna get ready and head down to 'town' and pick up my lil ones for the day. Ex is being a bitch as usual. But she can't stop me from taking them. It's in the court orders that I get unsupervised day visits. I wanna see you. I'm going to do mushrooms tonight."

Moe sent Lizard a picture of Kay double fisting two sippy cups right before he told her that he had downed a handful of psychedelic mushrooms. How can he speak of petitioning for joint custody while at the same time taking getting wasted, taking fists full of narcotics and eating mushrooms?

What Lizard didn't know was that Moe had been talking to many other women, casting his net wide trying to snare as much easy game as he could get.

To Kassandra, he wrote, "My divorce is almost finalized. She's fighting me for custody. She filed for divorce and custody when I was honest and told her I got high on dope."

Her response. "Oh s***, I'm so sorry. I relapsed, too."

Another addict.

Moe continued. "I was honest, and she used it against me. I've already went through the supervised visitation, I'm unsupervised now. She had a boyfriend since way before I told her I relapsed. We were in couples counseling when she started seeing this guy. I'm okay. I made my mistakes in my marriage. I was trying to right them. I did not want the divorce, but at least, I know I tried til the end. I'm living up here at my parents now. It happens. I have eight months clean now."

Literally, what was he talking about? He's lying out of both sides of his mouth. I didn't have a boyfriend when we were in couples counseling. He claimed he tried to the end. He made zero effort. Zero effort is what he called trying? He also claimed he had been clean for eight months. From what? Gluten? Because it's definitely not drugs or alcohol.

Kassandra: "I'm so sorry."

The sympathetic response he craved.

"She's a c***," Moe said then stepped it up a degree: "Ya, my heart was ripped out of my chest. My daughter was a week old when I just broke down and told Seraphine the truth about my relapse. My daughters have stayed the night with me once in eight months. I'm fighting tooth and nail for them."

She replied, "You keep fighting, and if you need a character reference, I've got you. She's a c***. I'm sorry."

Eventually in the conversation, Kassandra told Moe she had a boyfriend, but right now, she was telling him she had an achy back, and he pushed her sexual boundaries and made a comment on her chest.

Moe attempted to entice her with pills. "I went to the ER, and they give me oxycontin like three weeks ago. And I got a new bottle of Norco 5's yesterday."

It didn't work because she had her supply. "I've gotten down to two perks a day. When I get my script, I may just go bananas for a day."

"I like bananas, lol," said Moe.

To Nicki, he wrote: "First off, I think you are and always have been awesome as f***, your fun to be around, your always bubbly, and make me laugh and smile. I know we get along great, and I want to spend more time with you and get to know you, you're absolutely stunning, and I like to look at you, lol. But your just f****** awesome I wanna see you."

Love-bombing her with compliments, a slightly different approach. Maybe this one was not a drug addict.

She replied, "I'm at work, and I just found a bunch of riggs. I feel weird."

To her rescue, Moe said, "I know how you feel. U okay?"

"I'm good it's the first time I seen them since I got clean."

My mistake, another drug addict.

To Linda he wrote: The only one that actually may not have been an addict, Moe made sure to tell her he had a Purple Heart, a BS in respiratory care, that he was a Certified Respiratory Therapist, and that he paid child support. "I got two kids and pay a lil under $1000 a month, court order or not, I'm not one of those guys who doesn't take care of my own." (Objects that come out his mouth may appear 32% larger than they are; child support was $688.)

Linda told him, "I had a kid at sixteen, was married at seventeen, second kid at nineteen, divorced at twenty-four. Lol, he was an abusive a******, physically and mentally. Took a long time to recover from that and still working on the recovery part. Got remarried in 2011 to my best friend and am now getting divorced again. I think that I am not meant to be married."

There were many women, and like a chameleon, he changed his approach to cater to each one. All of these women had one common thread. He was exploiting vulnerable women of either low levels of education, poverty, or had a substance abuse issue.

Was this who he always was underneath? Or was it the drugs? After five years, you would think you knew someone, but I had no idea who this person was.

With the time frame of escrow soon to be closing, Moe forced the matter to be heard in court, which now had attached the reason why he refused to sign in his own words.

March 14, 2016, Court Orders

The father shall have supervised visits with the children as follows:

Times/days: Monday & Thursday 10am - 12 noon, commencing 4/9/16

Location: Determined as arranged mother and the monitors.

The parents shall return to Family Court Services for a review of the parenting plan in 5 months to assess father's progress in sobriety, participation in his recovery program, and the appropriateness of father sharing more liberal time.

Father shall, by 4/13/16 provide the court with a progress report from his substance abuse counselor.

Father shall follow all recommendations for aftercare upon discharge from outpatient treatment, including 12-step meeting attendance at least 3 times per week. At the time of the review mediation, father shall provide a sponsor letter.

Father shall attend outpatient substance abuse treatment groups twice per week at STAR program or at a court approved agency local to his community.

Father shall maintain regular communication with his sponsor.

Father shall continue in the recommended treatment for PTSD and provide a copy of this report to his therapist and sponsor.

The children shall have no contact with father's cousin.

I couldn't process the phonebook sized stack of messages I just read. It bothered me that he was aggressively grasping and manipulating vulnerable women in attempts to sleep with them. He was like a lion isolating his target from the herd. I knew a solitary hyena couldn't fend off a lion. Coincidentally, each hyena stumbled into a group chat with receipts of everything the lion said, and united the hyenas now had a fair chance. The lion, now so far behind the opponent's line, found himself ensnared by his own traps, and he was in grave danger of becoming dinner. They encircled him and ripped at his flesh. It's impossible to fight them all at once, but he narrowly escaped, fully aware he'd been in a fight, he retreated back to his lair to lick his wounds.

13

MINOR INCONVENIENCE

MARCH 14, 2016

Uncomfortably seated in a small room, a court mediator sat across from us listening to Moe as he shouted about how he was entitled to joint custody.

My stomach churned as my mind trailed off recalling his comments. Comments about the girls, sandwiched between describing how horny he was, and how many drugs he had just ingested.

She interrupted my thoughts. "You said you had concerns?"

It was like my brain suddenly pinched myself, you're in mediation, she's the mediator, and she is asking you a question. Tell her your concerns!

"Yes." I informed her of the conversations.

Moe interrupted, stuttering out, "I only said those things to sleep with those women, I wasn't really doing drugs."

That doesn't make it better, nor is that true.

The mediator pulled her glasses down to the end of her nose and stared at him. "If that was true, then why would you converse with active drug users? Because either way leads me to believe that you are not committed to your sobriety."

Moe doubled down that he was just trying to get sex, that he really was sober. He cried I was just out to destroy him, and that he was the victim. The messages seared into my memory banks. I recalled the one he wrote to his cousin's son.

I exploded. "You bragged about your sexual conquests to your cousin's son! You are like the only father figure to that boy. And you sent him a vagina picture saying that's the fatty I don't tell anyone about? You are not a victim. You're disgusting!"

Moe just looked down guilty, and in that moment, I instinctively knew I missed something. "Wait, how old is he?"

Moe said, "He's fourteen or fifteen."

I flip out. "Wait, what? You said those things to a…."

Moe interrupted and stammered out, "After playing hours of video games with him, I guess I just viewed him as an adult."

I lost it. "He's a kid! You said those things to a child?"

The mediator was just looking at us wide eyed. "If what you're saying is true, I'm going to have to report this."

Moe seemed apologetic in that brief moment but only because he was caught because the conversation spanned over months. Never once did he stop and think that maybe he shouldn't say these things to a child. The fact the line between right and wrong was so blurred was jarring. It's nonexistent and carried its own disquietude. Some things you wish not to know about a person, these where those things.

I don't remember the rest of the mediation, but I can call back every nauseating thing Moe said to that boy.

(For the full conversation between the boy and Moe see "The Conversation" at the end of this book. *(warning graphic)*

Moe didn't view him as an adult. He knew he was a child when he asked if his girlfriend's friend wanted to hook-up with someone older, and then followed it up with if he did, he would be behind bars. "Stat rape is stat rape." Moe added. "I just want to taste virgin p**** again," and laughed as he joked he'd fiercely rape her. Or when he asked for her nude picture, he knew she was underage "if she was 18...," and when the nude picture was sent, Moe replied, "That's kiddie porn." Yet, even that didn't stop him from commenting, "they're nice" about the young girl's breasts.

The scariest thing to me was there was no moral line. Not even with our own babies. He had no problem bringing them up to acquire false empathy for his sexual gain. Again, I felt queasy thinking back.

I never thought to question how old the prostitutes were in Germany he claimed he slept with between 2003 to 2005. I don't have time to deconstruct why I thought it was the norm for military men to have slept with at least one prostitute while overseas. There were other matters at hand. I filed an ex parte hearing after the mediation, his whole family showed up. Their eyes burned hate at me as I sat alone waiting to go in. I know they were talking about me as their eyes kept darting at me, and their hands came up to shield their mouths as they pointed. The bailiff called us in, and they piled into the back rows. Despite the facts they heard, they were infuriated after the court but not at Moe, at me. They claimed that I was just as much at fault as Moe, if not more so, because I decided to bring this matter to court and make it public. I will never understand their convoluted way of thinking... the complex mental gymnastics they had to do to reach that conclusion were Olympic level. These are children. You protect kids at all costs, no matter what, no matter who.

The orders read as follows:

September 29, 2016, Court Orders

Sole legal custody of the children shall be with mother. Sole physical custody with mother. Father shall have the children as follows:

1. Tuesday & Friday from 10am until 4pm, commencing 10/21/16.

2. The father shall, by 11/20/16, participated in individual counseling MSW regarding boundaries with minors, recognizing factors that could place children at risk of emotional harm and coping skills for a minimum of 12 sessions.

3. Father shall provide counselor with a copy of this report and the April 2016 FCS report.

4. The matter shall be re-referred to FCS for a CFS collateral only.

5. All other orders not hereby modified shall remain in full force and effect.

They can hate me all they want right now because they haven't read what I have read. I mean I'm not making this up. Moe wrote it. The conversation was printed out in front of me... there were screenshots. They should know, they should read for themselves, after all, the boy is a member of *their* family. Surely, they will protect him. His parents usually always drive with him when he comes to get the girls. I assume because they want to see them, as he has limited visitation time, and they refuse to communicate with me.

His mom had this nervous energy about her like she thought someone was always going to hit her or something. I got it. I'll walk out holding a plate with a sandwich. No one would think they're going to be punched by a person holding a sandwich.

They pulled up, I walked out with sandwich in hand, and they got out.

Edith was already clutching her purse straps tightly with both hands, oh geez.

Moe was blabbing away, so I picked up my sandwich and took a bite. Ignoring Moe, I swallowed my bite then said, "Edith, can I talk to you for a second?"

She looked at Moe giving him these lost puppy eyes.

"It will be short… I promise." I raise the sandwich up. "And I'm not going to hit you, so you can stop worrying." Her cowardliness annoyed me.

Moe blurted, "She ain't talking to you anywhere without me."

"That's fine, I don't care… you already know what you've said."

I motioned to my backyard table, and they both walked back.

It's fitting that Edith owned a Chihuahua because she was shaking harder than her dog in December. On the table was the stack of messages.

I said, "Your cousin's son is a part of *your* family, so you might care what your son said to him or what he said about your granddaughters and not just ours. It's all printed right here. I'm not saying anything untrue. You can read it for yourself, here, you can even have a copy."

She was about five feet away. Still clutching her purse with both hands, she leaned over just enough to get a better view. When she saw the screenshots, she flipped out and almost leaped into the air. "I'm not looking at those lies!"

She ran from my backyard and jumped into the car. She'd rather live in willful denial and refuse to read something that her son said, so she can go on pretending there are no issues. I should have seen this.

A few days later, a fist knocked on my screen door late in the afternoon.

"Hello?"

It's CPS. I know here in California they want to be called DCFS (Department of Children and Family Services) to reflect a more family-centered practice, but they will always be CPS to me. Before I could even invite her in, she pushed her way into my house. The house was still pretty empty as we had just moved in. She walked into the living room; her eyes darted around the room.

She asked me about the boy, but she never made eye contact with me.

I acknowledged the conversation I had read between Moe and the boy. I watched as she moved toward my dining table; she wasn't listening. She bent over and looked under the table. What was she doing?

This woman was not incredibly old or tall. She was maybe five feet and maybe in her late twenties.

The table was a bar height that stood almost four feet high. There were no obstructing views. Why was she bending over? What was she looking for? Did she think there was a child under the table clinging to the under-side like *spider-man*?

Puzzled, I asked, "Who are you looking for?"

She muttered a vague response that I could barely hear.

I asked, "What?"

She was looking for the boy.

"He doesn't live here."

I explained to her that she was at the wrong house, and that he wasn't my son. "I don't have any boys."

She did not seem to believe me and looked upset.

"I can give you their last known address."

She kept looking around, and I wrote it down on a piece of scrap paper.

She took the piece of paper, said nothing, stared at it, then she left.

That was weird.

The next day, I decided I had better call just to make sure the confusion was cleared up.

A woman answered the phone, and I explain what happened. "I am just calling to ensure the mix-up was straightened out."

"The investigation looks closed to me," she said.

I asked, "How can it be closed when she had the wrong house?"

Instead of answering, she asked me, "Would you like to open a new investigation?"

I asked again, "How could she close an investigation that never happened? She had the wrong address."

She repeated, "Would you like to open a new investigation?"

I was so confused. She was just at my house yesterday afternoon, and she had the wrong house. How could the investigation be closed if it never happened?

Like a robot, the lady asked a third time, "Would you like to open a new investigation?"

Well, this isn't going anywhere, so I conceded replying, "Yes."

To this day, it is unclear if they did any investigation at all based off my communications with law enforcement.

Law enforcement said my number was on their list, and apparently, I was also the only one who would answer. A deputy asked me if I had any other phone numbers, or if I knew where the boy went to school. They claimed they called his mom's number, but no one answered. This was not surprising.

She was no stranger to them. They told me the all alias they had for her and asked me if I knew if she went by any other names.

Next, he asked if I knew the high school where the boy was supposed to be attending. Apparently, he was no longer enrolled.

Moe's cousin had been kicked out of her dad's house again for doing drugs. She took her boys and was living in a place off-grid in Lucerne Valley.

"Can you bring the boy into the station?"

What?

He asked again if I could go and get him.

"I'm pretty sure taking a kid that is not mine is kidnapping." I was so confused at this point.

I started to wonder if he assumed I was friendly with the boy's mother. I was not, but maybe that's what he thought?

I called about a week or so later to follow-up.

The officer sighed and said he couldn't find the boy, and his mom wouldn't call him back.

Of course, his mom wasn't going to call them back. She did meth and she's not going to want police poking about.

He told me they had picked Moe up for possible drug charges with a minor but released him the same day and dropped all charges because they didn't have enough evidence.

When I asked if they also filed any charges in regard to the sexually inappropriate things he said to a minor, the officer explained that he didn't think Moe really broke any laws. "I mean, he wasn't really trying to have sex with the boy."

I kind of snapped. "So, it's okay to ask if a minor for nude pictures? It's okay to ask a minor if his girlfriend's friend would be interested in him as long as you perceive it as 'he was just kidding'? It's okay to send pornographic pictures to a minor as long as I intend not to sleep with them?"

He cut me off and asked, "Look, does the minor own or have access to a computer?"

"What? I don't know, probably, why is that relevant?"

The officer then explained to me that a boy his age would probably look up porn and pictures like that anyway on the internet. What was this officer saying? That the conversation Moe had with the boy was okay? He ended the phone call. Again, disgusted and while still mad, I thought that just must be the way it is up in his town where meth was as common as dirt, and roads were more like suggestions that no one bothered to follow.

Basically, no harm, no foul, just a *minor inconvenience*. If neither CPS or police care, and his own family was unwilling to help.

What could I do?

14

I'M THANKFUL FOR...

We were court ordered to complete a parenting class—because that would fix all the issues. I was still upset that Moe had no line between right and wrong.

They called it solutions for co-parenting; it was two hours each week over six weeks.

One mom sat at the end of the table staring down into her cup like she was reliving scenes from a war movie. That father never appeared in the class.

During a break, the teacher pulled her aside, and they had a private conversation.

She never came back after the second night.

Another couple divulged all their deep-seated hatred for one another, and then they explained they were now best friends. They were the most obnoxious annoying couple at the table because it all seemed so fake, like they were brown-nosing for points.

Couples sat in awkward tension at a table writing fake cards of gratitude while sipping coffee from Styrofoam cups. After the course was done, they gave everyone a certificate with a huge gold star and congratulations in large font.

Maybe things would get better. I mean it can only go up from here, right?

It's December 8, 2016, two and half years since Moe and I separated on December 14, 2014, and our divorce was finally finalized. **Final completion of Dissolution,** it read:

Should I take that to mean the closing down of a partnership, if we can call it that, or the process of dissolving... decomposing... the final end to a dissipated living?

The relationship I was in last year ended some time ago, and with new changes brought new hope and new relationships. For a moment, there seemed to be a change in Moe; he got a job driving for Uber.

I had been working on projects around my house. I built a chalkboard wall for the girls, drew up plans to build them a cool bunk bed with a hideaway space, and I was currently making a brick pathway alongside my house.

My mom came by every now and again to critique my work. "It doesn't look level. If you're going to do it, do it right."

She asked around and someone gave her a number. She called the number and gave him this sob story like I'm just this poor helpless single mother.

"Mom, you said what?"

"Well, he's coming over Tuesday."

"Hi, my name is Tony Malta."

I think my first words to him as he stared at my brick pathway were, "Hi my name is Seraphine. Sorry, but I don't really need your help."

"I can see that." He laughed.

He looked over at the fifteen foot long by eighteen-inch-deep hole that I dug. "What's that?"

"I'm going to put a pond there." He walked over to the trench and pointed at the roots from the neighbor's tree that I had carefully dug around.

"What are you some kind of archaeologist?" He laughed. "I've never seen a trench dug so precise."

"Well, I don't have a saw, so I couldn't cut the roots, so I just went around them."

He adjusted his hat, laughing as he looked on.

He pointed to my chalkboard. "Did you make that?"

"Yes." I then told him my plans to stand it up against the wall of my property.

"Why don't you just hang it on the brick?"

"You can do that?"

"Sure, it's easy."

"I didn't know you could screw into brick. That would be much easier than what I was planning."

He grabbed some screws and a drill from his truck, put it up, then stood there like what else you got? I told him about other issues that, in all truth, I had googled how to solve but really had no idea how to pull off. He explained how to fix it, and he quoted me a price.

"Okay," I said.

"I'll need to be paid before I start," he said.

"Not a problem," I reply.

He's testing to see if I'm good for the money.

After I handed him his payment, he began working.

Mid-project, I was glad I hired him; it was a lot of work that I had no interest in doing myself.

After he was done, I thanked him, and he said, "I'm taking you out tomorrow."

I laughed. "Your funeral."

The court had scheduled another hearing to track Moe's progress, and with nothing from CPS or police in regard to his cousin's son and the completion of their co-parenting class, the court expanded his time.

February 7, 2017, Court Orders

Sole legal custody of the children shall be with mother. Sole physical custody with mother. Father shall have the children as follows:

Tuesday from 10am until Wednesday at 10am

Friday from 10am until 4pm

All holidays shall be shared between the parents by mutual agreement.

Father shall provide all transportation for exchanges of physical custody or visitation except as otherwise agreed to between the parents.

Tony kept coming by. "Let me see those drawing you did for the bunkhouse. I can help you build that." One dinner turned into two then three. Tony eventually met Moe one day when Moe dropped off the girls.

Moe walked up to Tony. "Who are you?"

Tony stretched his hand out. "My name's Tony, nice to meet you."

Moe shook his hand, mumbled something, then left.

"He didn't seem so bad," said Tony.

I laughed, "Just wait, you'll see."

Moe quickly began to backslide into reckless habits, faster this time.

He started missing child support payments, and by the summer and in June, he missed three weeks of visitation.

At the exchanges, Moe would over share information about himself just to make conversation. He also was dating, and he also got into yet another car accident, again not his fault. It was a hit and run. How on earth they hit him on both sides was a mystery. It looked more like he tried to squeeze through two cement poles judging by the marks.

By this point, I think he had been in four or five car accidents in the last three years with multiple speeding tickets. His car insurance was now over $250 a month. Plus, he had to pay to get his SUV fixed all the time.

I had a feeling this Uber job wasn't going to last long. One day at the exchange, I noticed he had plastered the back of his SUV creating an arch of army military stickers. One or two stickers I totally get, but this was overkill and all at once was kinda cringe.

He also installed a new Purple Heart license plate and frame. For him to go full hog all at once felt more like he was just trying to avoid tickets than anything else. This ploy effectively worked as he abruptly stopped collecting speeding tickets, but his driving did not improve. A month later, he claimed he got rear-ended by someone in a parking lot, again not his fault.

It's now fall, and the girls were entering into preschool. Kay just turned four years old, and Anna was two years old.

Despite the inconsistent summer, I still had hope that Moe was turning around; he put on all the weight he lost plus more.

The preschool was every Tuesday and Thursday from 9 a.m. to noon which clashed with our court orders Tuesday from 10am until Wednesday at 10am, so I suggested he pick them up Wednesday at 9 a.m. and drop them off at preschool Thursday at 9 a.m.; one day less I had to see him, too.

I was doing my best to try to co-parent with Moe, trying to be agreeable and accommodating with the schedule because, after all, that's what the courts wanted us to do, right, be more mutually flexible? That was the whole point of the co-parenting class we took. If you follow the court too stringently, you were viewed as rigid, difficult, and inflexible. Yet, being flexible also backfired as well.

If you were even a margin outside of the court orders, law enforcement could not help you and would not help you. They had to follow the court orders by the letter. The courts also viewed any deviation from their orders as a breach or violation of the court orders. You're damned if you do and damned if you don't.

As time went on, Moe's behavior was starting to become erratic, showing up to the preschool unannounced, having confrontations with the staff, and yelling at me at the exchanges. I had just found out that I was pregnant with Tony's baby when the school called to inform me after Moe dropped the girls off that they require the girls to be potty trained or wear pull-up diapers.

"Yes, I am aware of your policy. Was there an issue?"

They explained that when Moe dropped off the girls, Anna had soiled herself in a diaper. When they asked him to change her and explained their policy, this upset Moe. Moe told the preschool staff that he did not have the funds to pay for pull-up diapers, and that the school should be happy with whatever he decided to dress them in, meaning baby diapers.

He also refused to change Anna before taking her to class and told the teacher that it was her duty to change her because that was what she was paid to do. Perhaps they were just still extremely frustrated with him but in a way, they made it seem like they might kick her out of the preschool if I did not resolve these issues.

I thanked them for notifying me. I assured them that I would handle the issues even though they were completely out of my control.

Moe had missed many holidays over the past couple of years, and he now believed he was entitled to the girls for *all* of the holidays to compensate. When the matter of holidays came up, it sparked an argument caused by his unreasonable expectations.

Moe was holding the girls while voicing his complaints, he knew I wouldn't argue in front of them, and I was forced to listen until he decided to hand them over at exchanges. I didn't argue over Halloween, but he was still demanding both Christmas Eve and Christmas Day. The conversation was going nowhere, so he eventually exchanged the girls over to me and left.

He called me well into the late afternoon on November 8, 2017, to argue more over the holidays. I explained that I was already scheduled to work on Christmas Eve, but I had Christmas Day off. He could have the girls Christmas Eve, and I could have them on Christmas Day, then next year we could switch.

Moe yelled, "Who gives a f***, Seraphine. Listen very closely, I don't give a s*** about your work schedule. I'm getting them for Christmas."

Again, I tried to explain to him that I could not change my work schedule because everyone was expected to work different holidays; it was mandatory.

Moe yelled, "Shut the f*** up."

Matching his energy would go nowhere, so I found the lowest calmest voice I could trying to invoke any resemblance of reason.

"You know I cannot simply change my schedule, so why are you acting like this, what's going on?"

Moe said, "You're acting like a f****** retard that's what was going on. You know I don't care about Thanksgiving you can have them, whatever, I don't give a f*** but I'm getting them for Christmas Eve and Christmas Day."

"You're acting unreasonable."

Before I could say anything else, he told me I could suck a **** and threw the phone. I could hear him screaming for a long time. I could tell he was pacing back and forth.

Moe picked up the phone again. "You're a real winner, Seraphine, great for you."

He was screaming so loud on the phone that everyone in a mile radius would be able to hear him. There was no way anyone could sleep through his ranting in his parents' house.

He screamed, "You witch," and he hung up.

I started to panic. He had the girls. There was no way they had not hear him. Were they scared right now? If they say something, was he going to yell at them? Would he hit them? He's going to be up all night ranting.

It was Wednesday, and he was supposed to drive them to preschool early tomorrow. What if he got into another car accident tomorrow morning with the girls in his car?

I did not feel that the girls were safe with him in the state he was in.

I jumped in my van and drove to his house. When I got there, I remained calm and asked if he would please let the girls come with me, so he could calm down.

Of course, he refused. "I'll only let them go with you when police arrive to my house!"

He slammed his parents' front door, so I called the police.

Moe's father got home from work.

I tried to talk to him, explain that the police were on their way, that I did not want to be here at his house, but I was concerned for the girls' safety because Moe was belligerent on the phone.

Pastor Lot said, "He's a grown man, and he can say whatever he wants."

I was shocked. Really? You're a pastor? That did not sound like wise godly wisdom. Was that what it said in the Bible?

Instead of saying that, I said, "Yes, you're correct, and while he may be a grown man, he is living under your roof. I cannot and will not tolerate being screamed at or being cussed at. Again, I am here because I do not feel the girls are safe right now with the behavior he is displaying."

He didn't budge. "Well, he's an adult, and he can make his own decisions."

"Those are your grandchildren, and I'm trying to keep them safe. Can you reason with him?"

"That's between the two of you." Again, he was about as helpful as a dysfunctional GPS navigation system.

I re-routed back to my van, upset by his obtuse remarks.

He is no man of God... I guess he only reserves his "Christian wisdom" for Sunday.

The deputies who arrived at Moe's parents' house looked like they were just out of high school and fresh from the academy.

I briefly told them why I was here before Moe and his dad had a chance to notice their lights and walk out.

Pastor Lot started going on and on about how he used to volunteer with the citizen patrol talking about the graphic details of accidents where he prayed over families that just lost their loved ones. His volunteer days were way before I started dating Moe.

Did he really think these deputies who were probably in middle school at that time, would remember these graphic accidents he's weirdly boasting about? It took thirty or forty minutes before the female deputy must have realized how much he merely enjoyed the sound of his own voice before asking to go in the house to see the girls.

The deputy walked back out to me with her pad and pencil ready. Nervous and in a quiet voice she explained that if Moe said no, because we were outside the court order, there was nothing she could do.

Luckily, Moe let the girls leave with me. He just wanted to make a production out of it. I learned that night to follow the court orders letter by letter because the police cannot assist you if you don't.

I requested Moe to take a drug test the next morning. It was already paid for. He just needed to show up, but he never did.

Since this was the first time Moe was a no-show for his drug test, I was waiting around for results that were not coming.

A week later, on Tuesday November 14, 2017, he pulled the girls out of preschool at 10 a.m. because he said it "cuts into my time."

The following day, he drove the girls to my house a little after 10 a.m. to drop them off. Which brings me to where we began, getting shoved into the wedge of his car door holding Anna while trying to protect the baby inside me.

15

NOVEMBER 15, 2017

Moe was gone before the police arrived. One officer left in an attempt to pursue him.

The police advised me to file a restraining order online in the county where the incident occurred, which was Riverside County. So, I did, and I also believed I needed to file an ex parte with the court in San Bernardino where our custody case was.

We proceeded to the ex parte first. A temporary judge who was standing in for the day explained that another judge had already made a decision pertaining to custody in the restraining order.

I said, "We haven't seen any other judge yet on this matter. How can a judgment already have been made?"

He explained that when another judge has already made a judgment on a case, he can't overturn their decision.

I didn't understand. We had never seen any judge on this matter. What was he talking about?

He repeated the same thing. "A judge has already made a judgment on this." Am I stuck in the twilight zone? I was getting frustrated at this point. Repeating the same thing was like just talking louder to someone that doesn't understand the language you're speaking.

"I can't overturn a decision that another judge made."

What judge? The last time we were in this court was nine months ago.

"A judge has already made a judgment on this."

I've died, that's the only logical explanation here. I've come back as Bill Murray in 1993. I am a cynical TV weatherman. This was going nowhere.

I sighed and brought up that Moe was a no-show for his drug test. The judge explained there was nothing written in the old orders stating any consequences if he didn't.

Does anyone have a toaster so I can take a bath?

He ordered us to go to mediation then stated that Moe must drug test today, and if he tested positive, he would have no visitation until the next custody court hearing. Moe was skinny as a bean stalk again; probably lost at least fifty pounds since July.

Fun fact: hard drugs like meth or heroin only stay in a person's system for three days, maybe five. So, any scheduled court date is ineffectual if they're just smart enough to see a drug test coming.

Moe knew I was frustrated, and after the judge said his final words to us, we existed into the court hallway where his whole family and the new girlfriend were waiting for him.

He started yelling, pointing, and laughing at me. "She f***** up the paperwork!"

His parents stood by watching as tears of frustration ran down my face. He was still pointing as he tossed his head back laughing, and I ran for the stairs.

Moe's test results came back positive for 8404 ng/ml of tetrahydrocannabinol, or THC.

The following week on December 7, 2017, we had our restraining order hearing in Riverside County. Tony came with me this time. I didn't have to ask him after he heard what happened outside the courtroom last time.

Moe's mom, dad, and second oldest sister were already there as we made our way into the exceedingly small courtroom. I wondered if any of them worked. Why are they all here again?

I tried to ignore their sideways glances during the cases ahead of us.

The judge was thin, dark, and seemed to take her time to truly listen intently. Leaving no areas unturned, she questioned everything, pointing out things along the way. I listened as she commented on the cases. "Does he always speak in scripture like this?" or "Sir, can I see your phone…" He handed it to her. "Yes, I see the message here… but I also… Sir, did you change her name to 'F*** that B****' in your phone?"

She asked a lot of questions, and I liked that. Once it was our turn, I told the judge the details of the incident and what unfolded prior to that day. Based off my testimony, she granted a restraining order and stated that she found there to be sufficient evidence of domestic abuse, and she was concerned for the probability of future abuse occurring. She scheduled a follow-up hearing in six months' time.

Moe's new girlfriend's name was Cecilia. She's five years younger than Moe, yet, apparently, they went to high school together. She said she always had a crush on Moe. Weird, she married a guy after high school that looked remarkably similar to Moe now. Her now ex-husband and she have a daughter, Mallory, who was two years older than Kay.

It's unclear why they divorced, fell out of love maybe. Cecilia grew up without a father, so her viewpoint was any father is better than no father at all, and her mom did or does drugs.

Cecilia was now a single mother, receiving less than $100 in child support, currently on welfare, in section eight housing, no job, and no car. The perfect mark; to her Moe was a hero. She was all in. She was even filling out Moe's court paperwork for him. Moe quit working for Uber. He either couldn't keep up with the auto repairs needed to maintain his position, or he knew he couldn't pass a drug test.

On December 20, 2017 Moe got a job at a warehouse moving boxes.

For the entire month of December, Moe texted me on my cell phone despite the restraining order and court order stating no visitations will take place if his drug test came back positive.

Moe messaged over and over "When can I FaceTime with my daughters?"

Friends advised a cease and desisted letter that Moe took to mean persist and continue. This is when the perverse accusations of "parental alienation" began. He accused that I unjustly kept the girls from him. He didn't consider that any of his own actions might have been a factor in this period of separation.

Later discovering my mistake and my overall lack of knowledge with filing the ex parte alongside the restraining order was embarrassing, and the humiliation I felt after was something I never wanted to feel again. So, again I set out to find a lawyer because I knew crying about it was not good for my pregnancy, and I obviously needed assistance navigating through this legal system.

It's a cumbersome process to select the *right* lawyer. You pretty much have to be a lawyer yourself to know.

A friend of a friend of Tony had used Attorney Joseph Benson, and they seemed satisfied with his service, so, I set up a consultation. During the consultation, I explained why I needed support in filing the proper court paperwork, and also the stress of these responsibilities was not healthy for me or my pregnancy. He said that he would help me and that he was a family man and faithful to his church. He then informed me of his fee and asked that I sign and return his retainer agreement.

I walked out sighing with relief thinking, okay this will soon be past me, now I can relax and prepare for the big day fast approaching.

16

CAREFUL CONSIDERATION

January 31, 2018

Unable to find parking, Tony and I parked near Meadowbrook Park. We walked across the bridge. I mentally recalled the patient I had that was said to have drowned in the river behind the courthouse.

It is true you can drown in an inch or two of water, that's all this *river* could offer; however, her demise was probably more tied to her urine drug test that lit the screen up like a forest fire and why she drowned in an inch of water.

The sky over the courthouse was grey like the suit I was wearing. I held my belly with both hands while I waited to pass through the metal security detector.

Directly past security was a grand, bifurcated stairway; one broad flight up leading to a generous landing where two smaller switchback flights to the left and right lead us up to the next floor. Our scheduled courtroom was on the third floor, and it was no shock when I saw his parents were there.

Mr. Benson waved us over from a table down the hallway.

When we approached him, he said, "Good morning, it looks like we have Judge Mazle Dina." He sighed. "She's the worst for your case, I'm hoping maybe we can see if we can get your case transferred."

Moe glared at me when he walked by wearing a long-sleeve blue flannel shirt, jeans, and chucks. He stood near us looking at the list of cases taped outside the courtroom door.

He turned around and eyeballed Mr. Benson.

Mr. Benson asked me, "Is that your ex?"

I sighed. "Yes."

Moe looked like he had lost more weight. Even his longer beard couldn't hide his sunken cheeks. The courtroom door swung open, and the bailiff said, "If you're in court fifty-three line up. Tell me your name and the number you are on the list. Then make your way into the courtroom where you will be sworn in."

Mr. Benson went over a few more details with us before we went in. After we were sworn in, Judge Mazle Dina slowly walked out of her chambers with a cup of coffee in hand. She had two deep furrow lines and a pronounced wrinkle across the bridge of her nose. Only her broad forearms extending down to her plump hands and short fingers were visible under her long black robe.

Her secretary sat to the right across from the court bailiff, and the court reporter sat to the left at her desk.

A courtroom is divided into two sides; the side where the judge and other legal officials sit, and the side where the audience and people awaiting to be heard sit. The lawyers sit in a row of chairs along the aisle separating the room. The cases that required interpreters were first, then the people whose lawyers were present. They fight to see whose case is going to be the quickest; and then everyone else is eventually heard.

When I was called up, I was required to stand on the right side near the bailiff.

After the legal pleasantries, Judge Mazle Dina pointed out she didn't know I was expecting as she stared down at my belly. Bold but gauche move since I didn't announce that I was, nor did she ask, she just blurted it out. It's a good thing I was six months pregnant, or this could have gotten really awkward.

Attorney Joseph Benson changed the topic. "Your Honor, if I can mention a few things. Is the court aware there is a domestic violence restraining order currently in effect?"

"It was mentioned in the mediation report," said Judge Mazle Dina.

Mr. Benson responded. "And that's what is so concerning because the mediator, while she did mention that she was aware of that (DVRO), she also indicated that there was a positive drug test as recently as November and said that the Father admitted to smoking marijuana for his pain, as well as PTSD because the Father indicated he had PTSD, which is concerning because the Father was in the military. He gets treatment at the VA. The VA does not prescribe medical marijuana ever. And so, I don't know where that marijuana is coming from, and I don't know if that is really something that should be utilized for pain. He also, in the mediation report in his own words, indicated that he yelled at the Mother on two separate occasions. One he said, 'Get the F*** away from my car,' at one of the exchanges and another time he yelled at the Mother at night. Now, we have the DV. All of these concerning issues, and these are the petitioner's own words that he has indicated these things. There is no mention of Family Code Section 3044 whatsoever. With this DV that is currently in place, there has been no rebuttal by the petitioner at all. Therefore, the presumption is sole legal and sole physical custody to the protected person who is the respondent. There hasn't been no discussion of the 3044 presumption and, obviously, there has been no rebuttal in 3044 subsection B by the petitioner. And I don't even know why the mediator would not mention that. So that's a problem. Now, we also have in the mediation recommendation it indicates that Father had admitted that he used meth two to three years ago. That's probably one year ago in the best scenario. We have all of those concerns. And if we look on the mediation report on page 11 and 12, the mediator's language is concerning. It says, *'The main issues are the alleged domestic violence and Father's use of substances.'* This is not alleged. There was a finding of domestic violence, a domestic violence restraining order issued." He continued. "After there is a rebuttable—the presumption is rebutted by the petitioner, we can come back and look at those things, but now that hasn't been done. Also, my client would request that Father, the petitioner, be granted four to six hours every Saturday supervised visitation due to the fact that Father has even admitted that he, number one, has a problem with the marijuana. Number two, he's yelled at Mom. And number three, he has PTSD in his own words. I think this case screams for professional monitor, and that's what this Court should order."

Judge Mazle Dina said, "Okay. I know I noticed that the restraining order was a little confusing." She continued. "It's from Riverside County?"

Moe shouted out, "Yeah. It's a no negative contact restraining order."

Judge Mazle Dina just looked at him then asked, "Were you arrested for domestic violence?"

Moe replied, "No, Your Honor. I was not."

"Okay," she said. But the way she said it was like "okay, good enough for me."

That made Mr. Benson's words trip out of his mouth. "And the minute order, if I can direct the Court's attention, it says, 'The Court finds sufficient evidence of domestic abuse and the probability of future abuse. The restraining order is granted.'" He continued. "Your Honor, even the mediator indicated, 'It's difficult to determine if Father's behaviors are a result of substance abuse or the inability to remain calm and rational when frustrated and stressed. Once again,

I think that is a very good indicator for this Court to grant supervised visitation in that regard.' Again, reiterating the mediator's statements, 'Clearly, Mother frustrates and upsets him. So, I recommend he take an anger management class.' "The mediator made all of these things happen and that 3044 mandates happen; however, she didn't make the correct recommendation, and she didn't invoke the 3044 presumptions. That is what was so concerning about her recommendations and the findings that she made."

Moe angrily said, "I don't think I've had a chance to really defend myself completely against her as far as the domestic violence."

Judge Mazle Dina shut him down. "This is not the forum for that because the restraining order…"

Moe interrupted her. "I understand that. But this is a…"

Judge Mazle Dina cut him off. "Please don't interrupt me. The restraining order is with Riverside County. So, there's really nothing to say about that."

She added, "It will expire eventually. In the meantime, the recommendation for you is anger management classes. If you do have PTSD, then you should be engaging in therapy."

Moe changed his tone to a higher pitch with a false sense of earnest and said, "I see a therapist regularly, your Honor." He exaggerated the words *Your Honor*. "I see one bi-weekly. I am on medication. I do have PTSD."

They carried on a bit.

Moe's voice cracked as he spoke, but she ignored it stating, "And the judge pro tem sitting here in November said that you're ordered to submit to a urine drug test. Failure to do so or a test positive, visitation will be suspended until further order of the Court. And you took a drug test that day, correct?"

Moe's words dragged out slow. "Your Honor, I did. And I had my medical marijuana card in hand in court."

"Okay. So, it's positive for marijuana," said Judge Mazle Dina.

"Yeah, I have both right here. I have two positive marijuana drug tests that I took for her," Moe said flatly. California had just legalized marijuana thirty days earlier, January 1, 2018.

Judge Mazle Dina said, "Okay. Well, I would not suspend visitation for a positive marijuana as long as the parties are aware that they cannot use marijuana at least twelve hours before they have custody of the children. My concern is the argument at the car. You went over the edge, sir. She came out to get the children from the car, and you went crazy on her."

Moe denied any wrongdoing and claimed, "I didn't even get a chance to give my side of the story. I had no idea she was pregnant!"

Judge Mazle Dina scoffed. "From what I can see, she's been pregnant for a while."

There was an awkward silence before the court said she's going to move away from all this talk about marijuana and domestic violence restraining orders, and she's just going to order a minimum twelve-week anger management class.

Mr. Benson attempted to circle back. "Your Honor, if I may, I talked to my client about this. The problem that we have is that he says he needs marijuana for his PTSD to remain calm. That's his own words. And if the Court is going to say he can't smoke marijuana around the kids, then he's going to show up at the exchanges and with the children with full blown PTSD and have another outburst like he did."

She looked at Moe. "Is that right?"

Moe started crying like he usually does to gain sympathy when he feels the tables are against him. "No, that's not right. Your Honor, I have kept my cool with Seraphine for eight years. I blew up once on the phone. And the other incident with the car, completely separate. I didn't lay hands on her. I didn't put not a single hand on her. She pushed her body weight onto me while reaching into my car."

Dumbfounded by the ball of lies Moe just vomited, Mr. Benson threw his hands up. "Your Honor." As if to say *you can't really allow this to continue.*

Moe's emotions then turn into anger, and he blurted, "I see a therapist—I'm speaking!"

Ignoring Moe's outburst, Judge Mazle Dina asked, "How often do you see a therapist?"

Moe was shouting at this point. "Twice a month!"

She asked, "What's your prescription?"

"Right now, it's Depakote."

"Okay," she said.

Words just tumble out of his mouth. "I'm doing everything that I'm supposed to be doing for PTSD. I have a corporal Purple Heart."

Moe liked to interject this fact, that he had a Purple Heart, into every conversation with anyone in authority. Police, mediators, etc. I've heard it dropped so many times in the past few years it's obscene. That, right alongside, "My dad is a pastor!"

Which sounds to me like, "Do you know who the f*** my father is?"

Today it's a *corporal* Purple Heart, which isn't even a thing.

Judge Mazle Dina said, "I get it, but I can even tell from today you're really worked up."

Spit was flying out of his mouth. "I am. I have PTSD, and I am in court. I am nervous. I am agitated. He's trained for this! He's been to college for this!"

Moe attempted to shift the focus off him.

Judge Mazle Dina said, in that professional patronizing voice every nurse knows, "Okay. So, let's try and calm down. How are you going to handle your symptoms if you're not allowed to use marijuana?"

Moe tried to calm down as his chest kept rising and falling like he just finished the performance of a lifetime. "Your Honor, my daughters bring me right out of everything."

Judge Mazle Dina looked confused. "I beg your pardon?"

Moe continued. "My daughters make everything go away. I will explain."

"That doesn't help me," said Judge Mazle Dina as she waved her hand over the papers in front of her.

Moe was undeterred and was now speaking like he was mimicking a therapist... almost robotic. "Your Honor, I have learned all my coping skills and everything. I went through six years of PTSD therapy with the VA. I have methods. I slipped once. I got angry at her and yelled at her once. Nothing was ever violent."

Yup, he is definitely trying to pull the wool over her eyes. How dumb does he think she is?

The judge cocked her head to the side and looked up at the ceiling. "Okay. That's hard for me to believe you. She wouldn't have filed a restraining order if it was just one time."

Moe tried to validate his points.

Mr. Benson jumped in. "Well, he's saying one time, one time, one time. If you look at the mediation report on page nine, his own words, he admits that he yelled another time. It says, 'Father states he did yell at her one night when she came to his house and took the children.' This is in addition to the car incident. And it's very concerning, Your Honor, we were unaware of the psychiatric medication prescription Depakote. And it's very telling that there is a use of marijuana with that psychiatric medication Depakote. I am very aware that the VA is not going to prescribe marijuana. And his psychiatrist who is prescribing the Depakote is not going to give him Depakote if he was aware that he routinely uses marijuana."

How many separate times does Mr. Benson have to describe Moe was less than truthful?

Moe attempted to beg. "Your Honor..."

The judge then stated, "You know, I don't want to get into all that with your medication. You know, I am willing as long as you enroll in anger management, and I see the certificate. I'm willing to let you have time with the children. So, I am going to work with you here. What the mother is saying is that basically any time you have the girls, you should be supervised. That's what she's saying. And she's got some facts to back up that request."

The conversation veered into pick up and drop off locations, when we work, etc.

When she started talking about the first, third, and fifth weekends, I said, "But I don't think he should be allowed with the kids without a supervisor at this time because his behavior over the last like half of the year has been slowly unraveling into chaos. And he's even lost, it looks like about sixty-five pounds, in a matter of a few months, and he's not running, you know. He's not doing that. So, I have high concerns that because of his aggressive and erratic behavior lately, that even my daughter has been affected because both instances were in front of the children. And he was holding our four-year-old while he was shoving me."

Judge Mazle Dina said, "That was also mentioned in the report. Have you had a significant weight loss?"

"Yeah," said Moe.

With a quick little nod of her head, she extended her chin and raised her eyebrows.

Moe stood motionless, and the judge asked, "Is it due to drugs?"

Moe said, "It's due to the fact that I broke both my legs in that car accident two years ago, and my leg is starting to heal. It started to heal about seven months ago. I went on a diet. I had to lose weight so I can have second and third—a second and third surgery. I have a torn ACL and a torn PCL on my left leg. And my left femur is starting to heal. It was broken. I work a job now where I probably walk fifty thousand paces a day. I am going back and forth sweating bullets. I work hard."

Why would he need to diet if he's working Monday through Friday sweating bullets averaging 50,000 paces a day? Let's do the math really quick. At 5'7" at an average pace of three miles per hour? He's claiming to average twenty-two miles a day. Fifty thousand paces times five days is 110,000 miles a week and with both of his legs still broken, a torn ACL with PCL, and while maintaining a calorie deficit... well, he should have lost almost three tons! Amazing. Truly amazing.

Judge Mazle Dina said, "Okay."

Okay? She said it like that's plausible. She's not going to point out the absurdity. I mean 110,000 miles a week! He's a medical marvel deserving of a spot in the Guinness Book of World Records.

It was like my Mr. Benson gave up at this point, he didn't say anything else. So, I tried to voice my concerns again, and Moe argued. Judge Mazle Dina went on talking about anger management classes and scheduling unsupervised overnights.

It was chaos.

Judge Mazle Dina then got upset with Moe because I was not the only one he was arguing with and said, "Look, you make it very difficult for me to work with you. I'll just tell you that right now because you're argumentative and you have a great deal of denial going on and it's really difficult for me right now because it sounds to me like Ms. Malvado has tried communicating and the communication is terrible. So, I'm going to order you both enroll in Talking Parents. That's how you're going to communicate from now on so it's in writing and I can look at it. Because if you're acting like you don't remember when the visits are and then you blame her for it, I can't have that either."

Despite our sound argument, Judge Mazle Dina ordered Moe to complete drug tests every two weeks, twelve to sixteen weeks of anger management, and unsupervised overnight visits with the girls from Saturday 10 a.m. to Sunday 6 p.m. on the first, third, and fifth weekends, video calls Tuesday and Thursday, along with a holiday schedule. The court wanted to then follow up in twelve weeks.

I'll be thirty-six weeks pregnant but no matter. The orders read as follows:

January 31, 2018 Court Orders

1. Sole legal custody of the children shall be
   with Mother.

2. The Father to provide a drug test to the court. The results shall be released to the Mother, the court, and FCS. Father must give results to mother. Every fourteen days at Father's expense subject to reallocation.

3. Provided Father tests negative for all substances other than marijuana, he shall have the children as follows:

   a. On the first, third, and fifth weekends from Saturday 10am until Sunday at 6pm, commencing February 2, 2018. (The first weekend of the month is the first weekend with a Saturday.)

   b. Any additional time with Father shall be arranged by mutual agreement of the parents.

   c. The Mother shall have the children at all times not designated as Father's time.

4. Neither parent shall schedule activities for the children during the other parent's scheduled parenting time without the other parent's prior agreement.

5. The receiving parent shall have a thirty-minute grace period. After thirty minutes, that parent shall be deemed to have waived his/her custodial time unless otherwise agreed by the parent.

6. Exchanges of the children on Friday shall be at In-N-Out Burger, 1065 Harriman Place, San Bernardino at 6pm. Exchanges on Sunday shall be at Cold Stone Creamery, 5244 University Parkway, San Bernardino.

7. The following holiday schedule shall commence April 2018 and shall take precedence over the regular parenting schedule which shall resume after the holiday is over:

   a. Easter: With the parent regularly scheduled to have the day until 2pm. With the other parent from 2pm until 6pm.

   b. Mother's day: with Mother

   c. Father's day: with Father

   d. Fourth of July: From 2:30pm until 10pm; even numbered years with Mother, odd numbered years with Father.

   e. Halloween: From 5:30pm until 7:30pm, even numbered years with Mother, odd numbered years with Father.

   f. Thanksgiving: From 10am until 7pm, even numbered years with Father, odd numbered years with Mother.

   g. Christmas: From 12pm Christmas Eve until 12pm Christmas day, even numbered years with Father, odd numbered years with Mother. From 12pm Christmas Day until 12pm December 26; even numbered years with Mother, odd numbered years with Father.

   h. New Year's Eve/Day: From 12pm New Year's Eve until 6pm New Year's Day; even numbered years with Mother, odd numbered years with Father.

   i. Mother's Birthday: with Mother

   j. Father's Birthday: with Father

   k. Children's birthdays: with the parent regularly scheduled to have the day.

8. When either parent plans to travel outside of the State of California for overnight or longer during their parenting time, a contact phone number and destination shall be provided to the other parent.

9. Father shall have scheduled phone/video contact with the children every Tuesday and Thursday at 7pm for 10 minutes each child, commencing February 1, 2018. If the children are not available, then the custodial parent shall have the children return the call within 24 hours or less.

10. Neither parent shall make any negative or disparaging comments about the other parent in the presence or hearing of the children nor allow any other person or family members to do so.

11. Neither parent shall question the children about the other parent.

12. The parent shall not discuss the business of the court case with the children or allow the children to read any court documents.

13. The parents shall communicate directly with one another and shall not use the children as messengers.

14. Each parent shall keep the other informed of his/her current address and telephone numbers and shall notify the other parent in writing within twenty-four hours of any changes.

15. The parents shall keep one another informed of the address and telephone number of any care providers.

16. The children shall at all times be transported by persons who possess a valid driver's license and current insurance.

17. Neither parent shall permit the children to be exposed to second-hand smoke while being transported in a motor vehicle or in any other enclosed area.

18. The Father shall submit to random drug tests as requested by the other parent. The requesting parent shall pay for the test. If the test is positive for any illegal substances, the requesting parent shall be reimbursed.

19. The Father shall not use any illegal substances twenty-four hours prior to and during all periods of time with the children.

20. The Father shall enroll in and successfully complete an anger management program of at least twelve to sixteen weeks duration and provide proof of completion to the other parent and the court.

As we exited the courtroom, Moe hurried up behind me and tried to exit out the door first, but I was one step from crossing through it.

He slipped right by me through the door, inches away but not touching, if I had not paused, we would have collided.

He turned around now blocking the courtroom exit and said, "You are a piece of s***! I hope you know where Riverside is because you're going to be there a lot!"

The bailiff saw and heard the commotion and moved toward us.

Tony moved in front of me.

Moe looked at Tony. "You and Seraphine are pieces of s***."

Moe's parents were right behind me pressing to exit. Judge Mazle Dina ignored the mayhem, and the bailiff called for a deputy to walk Tony and I out. I took a step back and let Moe's parents go out into the hallway. They coddled him and threw daggers at me with their eyes as the deputy approached.

The deputy walked Tony and I out. Moe and his parents gathered in the hallway in front of the stairs glaring at us as we passed.

Moe pointed at me and started laughing. "Look at her! She has to be escorted out by a pig!"

The deputy ignored him.

"The pig is walking out with the pig." Moe was laughing so hard he could barely stand up. His parents were silent while still throwing daggers.

The deputy said nothing.

17

SMOKEY SPRING FLOWERS

APRIL 4, 2018

It was like a switch had flipped after our last court date; Moe's behavior intensified. He refused to give me his drug results, but Judge Mazle Dina did not write any consequences. If I let the girls go with him and his drug test was positive, then I was putting the girls in danger, and it would also appear that I was willfully putting them at risk. But if I didn't, then Moe could claim I was withholding them from him. Mr. Benson said there was little for me to do about it, just to follow whatever the order stated. We told her this would happen, and Judge Mazle Dina verbally told him he needed to provide me with the drug results, and it was my duty to protect them so he could claim whatever he wanted.

Moe was also misusing the video calls twice a week to harass me. During the calls, he made little jabs and constantly scrutinized me, or the angle of the phone, or if the TV was on in the background, or that the girls were not answering his questions properly, or if the girls were not sitting perfectly still.

Moe frequently asked Cecilia who was in the background, "You getting this on video?"

"Yeah," she answered.

Moe said, "These face times are crap. We got it all on video."

Moe and Cecilia made jokes about who my baby's father was.

"Could be anyone," Moe said.

Cecilia laughed and repeated, "Yeah, could be anyone."

"They're tired," Moe said to Cecilia.

He asked the girls, "You haven't even had a nap today have you?" Moe yelled while laughing, "No naps!"

"You can tell they haven't had a nap," he said to Cecilia.

Moe turned back to the girls. "You look tired."

Then again Moe said to Cecilia, "She didn't take a nap. She's tired."

"Kay," Moe yelled.

"What?" said Kay.

"Are you tired?" Moe asked.

"No."

"You look tired," he told her. Kay didn't say anything as Moe continued to tell her that she was tired.

Most of the calls were Moe and Cecilia making jokes about me, my house, or my parenting all while he sucked on a large vape devise during the video calls. At other times, Moe would scream my name.

If Kay said she didn't feel like talking, Moe told her, "That's not nice, you have to. I don't know who's telling you to say that!" His questions were obsessive and repetitive.

If I couldn't pick up his call, he called back-to-back-to-back.

I tried to call the police and explain I had an active restraining order, and that Moe would call twenty-six times in less than sixty seconds and harass me on the calls.

They explained that unfortunately due to the court's order he was allowed to call me despite the restraining order.

It was what they called a grey area.

There was seemingly nothing I could do about it.

The exchanges were also long and drawn out. When he picked them up, he was usually late. Legally, I had to wait up to thirty minutes, and routinely, he would appear twenty-five minutes late.

The return exchanges were worse. On top of being late, he would withhold the girls until I satisfied his questions.

My response was viewed as a necessary payment in order to get the girls back. All of Moe's drug tests came back positive for marijuana. His results were so high, it was difficult to quantify. Put it this way, he was higher than Japan's national debt.

One thing that was for sure, to have THC levels that high, he would experience significantly altered perceptions, impaired coordination, euphoria, and more than likely, a whole host of negative side effects.

Moe Maldavo's Drug Test Results

2/9/18   Urine drug screen: +marijuana 26,083 ng/ml

2/ 26/18   Hair drug screen: +marijuana

3/1/18   Urine drug screen: +marijuana 5,176 ng/ml

3/8/18   Urine drug screen: +marijuana 6,052 ng/ml

3/13/18   Urine drug screen: +marijuana 5,843 ng/ml

3/19/18   Urine drug screen: +marijuana 7,643 ng/ml

3/28/18   Urine drug screen: +marijuana 19,950 ng/ml

Back in court again at thirty-six weeks pregnant was not where I wanted to be. It was difficult to walk up to the third floor.

I guess I could have used the elevator, but they were so old and small, even looking at them made me claustrophobic. I imagined stepping inside with the elevator operator then Moe jumped in just as the doors closed.

Nope. I'm good.

I took the stairs.

Tony and I were early, so we sat on the long wooden bench that stretched the length of the hallway, with a mirrored bench on the other side of the hallway.

Moe and his parents arrived. I tried not to look in their direction. I could feel them all staring at me, so I buried my face in my phone.

Moe walked back and forth in front of us just in case we hadn't noticed him.

A woman in an awful plaid fuzzy suit walked up to Moe and his family. He had hired a lawyer.

Finally, we saw Mr. Benson, and we moved down the hall to talk. The woman in the terrible suit walked over to us and introduced herself as Ms. Basket.

She shuffled through papers, and she told us all of Moe's absurd requests.

Before Mr. Benson could even answer the questions, we were being called in.

Please sit. Now stand. They swore us in, now please sit again. You're being called up; please walk to the front.

Do they know how much effort it takes to stand up and down with this belly and these ridiculous hard small wooden seats? I was already exhausted and we hadn't even started.

My Attorney Joseph Benson reiterated again to Judge Mazle Dina. "Your Honor, if we can remind the Court, there's currently a domestic violence restraining order that's in place. The 3444 presumption is in place as well. My client would reiterate her request for supervised visitation. Your Honor, if you looked at the drug tests provided by petitioner, they indicate all are positive for marijuana. Now, that is not an illegal substance. But if, Your Honor, if you look down at the bottom of the tests, the THC levels we see that the range here—the therapeutic range is fifteen nanograms per milliliter. Specifically, in regard to February 19th and the February 13th date, it's 26,000. If we look at some of these other results, now, remember that the therapeutic level is fifteen. He's got 5,000, 19,000, 6,000, 5,800. I mean, these levels are sky high. Now, the reason that's concerning is because he says, *'I have PTSD.'* He told the mediator back on January 31st he said two different things. He said, *'I got a medical marijuana card. I broke my femur a couple years ago. I need this marijuana for pain.'* Okay. But then down a little bit farther on the page, he says, *'Well, I have PTSD, and that medical marijuana helps to calm me.'* Now, those things may be true, but if he has PTSD and he's being treated by the VA, the VA does not prescribe a federally illegal substance for him to smoke marijuana. And these levels are so high during the urinalysis, that he had to smoke right before he took these tests and has to be constant usage."

Ms. Basket spoke like she was on a TV show. "Objection. Lack of foundation."

Judge Mazle Dina jumped in, apparently to give Moe an out. "He might be using edibles."

Ms. Basket promptly replied, "He is, Your Honor."

Mr. Benson then argued, "Edibles don't have the THC that alter the mind, and they tested for THC."

What are they talking about? That is not true at all, you can buy edibles with THC, but okay.

I said nothing.

Judge Mazle Dina said, "But he knows he's not allowed to be under the influence of marijuana or use marijuana prior to his parenting time."

Mr. Benson said, "I would agree with you. With these high levels, he's using it constantly if he sees the kids or not seeing the kids. Your Honor, if you look at February 1, the level—the therapeutic level is fifteen. His level is 26,000. I can't even believe how he got that high. So, Your Honor, you ordered at the last hearing—you did not honor the request for supervised visits."

"Right," said Judge Mazle Dina.

Mr. Benson continued. "And you did modify his time from 10:00 a.m. on Saturday until Sunday at 6:00 p.m. on the first, third, and fifth weekends. Now, right immediately prior to your order you said,

'Provided that the Father test negative on all substances other than marijuana, he shall have the children at those times.' Well, the problem is, and I think you saw it from the last time we were here, Your Honor, he wasn't giving Mom the drug tests. I received these drug tests from Ms. Basket three days ago, all of them. She got them on March 26th. Now, when she did receive them, the first weekend that she had them after was Easter weekend she let the kids go. She has no problem complying with the court order, but she had no way of knowing what he was testing positive for because he did not give her the tests."

Like we told you last time, this issue to Moe withholding drug test results would happen. January 31, I stated that I would pay for drug tests and then he went around and snuck and paid for it so I couldn't get results.

Judge Mazle Dina said, "That's not going to work."

Then Moe said, "It's not about having got results right here. They go straight to the judge."

Do we suddenly not remember this whole conversation? This was a foreseen issue, yet, you dismissed it as a non-issue. But here we are. Great, I'm having arguments in my head now.

Judge Mazle Dina said, "Okay. Let's move on to what the request is today."

Okay? Let's move on? No, let's deal with this. I was mad. I was feeling more aggravated than usual, but what thirty-six-weeks pregnant woman dealing with this level of nonsense wouldn't be?

Ms. Basket continued on like she was really trying to get the lead role.

I can't. I tuned out.

Judge Mazle Dina then said in a loud voice, "You know, your tests are a concern for the Court because you're maintaining a level that kind of makes me believe that you're a zombie most of the time. Those levels are way too high." She continued. "Mother has a right to have an alert functioning parent watching the children and taking care of them."

Finally.

But then Judge Mazle Dina said, "He's proven that he's using marijuana sufficiently. And I don't think his levels would get any higher, so he doesn't have to drug test anymore."

Wait... what? How does that make sense? I was confused. First, third, and fifth weekend. Next, I hear the slam of her gavel. The orders read as follows:

April 4, 2018 Court Orders

1. Father is to have visitation as follows: on the First, third, and fifth weekend of every month from 5:30pm on Friday until 6pm on Sunday.

2. Custody exchanges shall temporarily be curbside at mother's residence and will re-addressed at the next hearing.

3. Father no longer needs to drug test

4. Moe Malvado shall not consume any alcoholic beverage, narcotics, or controlled substances within twenty-four hours prior to or during visitation with minor children

5. All other orders not modified shall remain in full force and effect

My head felt like it was spinning. When we were out in the hallway, I asked Mr. Benson, "How does that make sense? All his results were through the roof so now he doesn't have to drug test anymore and his visitation gets extended?"

Mr. Benson snapped and yelled at me; I assume because he was frustrated with her judgment, too.

In shock, I mumbled, "It just doesn't make any sense. Did you get any information about transferring to a different judge?"

Mr. Benson was still upset. "It's impossible Seraphine! Don't ask."

Why was he yelling at me when it was his idea? He was so upset about everything I just walked away.

My brain was still trying to apply some semblance of logic to all of this. I felt like I was in the Twilight Zone. Maybe there was something I didn't know like last time. How does she rationalize "Moe is a zombie all the time" then infer that he doesn't have to drug test anymore? And how does she measure if he cut back a bit if all drug tests are now discontinued?

When all the check engine lights are on in your car, doesn't that mean you shouldn't make an extended road trip into nowhere? So why did she irresponsibly sending two children off for extended unsupervised stays? How does this protect the children? Maybe I missed something.

Does legal literature prove a person with impaired abilities promotes their ability to supervise? Does it endorse a decrease in the risk for potential abuse of the child? I mean, I'm sure it's written somewhere. I'll look it up. How does any of this make logical sense? Make it make sense. My brain tried to jump through hoops to make it make sense. I needed the transcript.

My mom liked to play this fun game I called devil's advocate with everything I said, it's so much fun. Now it seemed I was playing it alone in my head.

Well, technically she put "he shall not consume any alcoholic beverage, narcotics or controlled substances within twenty-four hours prior to or during visitation with minor children."

So is marijuana a controlled substance?

The devil's advocate voice took a sudden turn to some pretentious 1930s' anti-reefer commercial, "It's actually classified as a schedule I controlled substance on the same level as heroin."

OMG, marijuana is not the same as heroin. Okay, I don't have time to try and unpack all of that historical nonsense. Back to the point, do I think Moe understands marijuana is still classified as a controlled substance, and it's illegal to use while supervising the girls?

I laughed at the stupidity of the question. No, definitely not, Moe said, "It's legal now."

Great. So, the judge was basically acting like that s*** bartender that gives the keys back to the local drunk with a couple DUI's but then he says, "hey don't drink and drive" to self soothe their own moral centers only so they can shift blame later by saying well I told them not to drive, all the while knowing they were incapable of doing the thing they told them not to do.

Three days later, April 7, Anna came home with red eyes and blue circles around them from possible smoke exposure. She just got out of PICU a month ago with respiratory distress symptoms; a slurry of cuss words skated through my mind. I wanted to scream into a pillow.

Did Judge Mazle Dina even comprehend his results? Could I blame her? Well, yes for being absolutely careless but understanding the results could be difficult because no one had really published what the results meant. Mr. Benson tried to explain but she wasn't listening. With alcohol, it is quite easy to comprehend how intoxicated an individual is. A blood alcohol content (BAC) level over 0.08 percent is the legal level to warrant a DUI and a BAC level between 0.31–0.45 could be life threatening. Easy. However, they legalized marijuana before making a widely available chart of what THC levels meant.

A THC level of 18ng/ml in urine could equate light or occasional use possibly in the last 24-72 hours; 50ng/ml might mean several joints per month or a recent consumption in the last 48-72 hours; 150ng/ml could mean regular use maybe one to several times a week or within the last 48 hours; 300 ng/ml may be considered very high with either daily usage or recent use in the last 24 hours; and a level of 600 ng/ml may reveal very frequent usage at least several times per day or very recent consumption episode in the last six to eighteen hours.

So, a level of 26,083 ng/ml is like coming into an ER with a BAC of 1.5 percent. A jaded seasoned ER nurse might do a slow clap and say, wow that's just impressive, well done. The other nurses might question how the hell do you even get that drunk?

I feel like this needs to be stated. This isn't a war against marijuana, and I'm not here to argue if there is or isn't proven medical benefits. I couldn't care less if a person smokes or digests or absorbs it. That is not my issue at all. My issue is a parent that uses marijuana and becomes incapacitated to the point their judgment is impaired, should not be allowed to risk the safety of their child. Children have no choice with where they live, or what they eat, what they wear, and it's up to their parents to make the right decisions, but if they are too high, then where does that leave the child?

There is also a lack of understanding of what marijuana is today. With the legalization of marijuana has come the artistically crafted marijuana strains and the variant concentrations of THC. If you are of the mindset that marijuana is still like smoking a joint, then you have no clue. Now you can purchase highly concentrated THC in the form of wax, heat it with a blowtorch and smoke the vapor like crack. This process is known as dabbing. Like with almost everything, there is going to be a few that abuse and take advantage of anything they can, marijuana is no exception. Dabbing claims to have been around since the 1960s when it was said soldiers in Vietnam extracted the THC into a liquid concentrate. However, now through the legalization of marijuana, it has been commercialized, which makes dabbing more prevalent due to it being readily available to purchase.

"Cannabis dabbing refers to the recreational inhalation of extremely concentrated tetrahydrocannabinol, the main psychotropic cannabinoid derived from the marijuana plant. The practice carries significant health and legal risk."[1] Butane hash oil (BHO) is the main extract used in 'dabbing.' The process of making wax concentrates involves using a butane solvent under heat and pressure to extract the oils from cannabis... basically making a pipe bomb. The result, a yellow waxy concentrate, is then heated with a blowtorch and is described as freebasing weed. Dabbing BHO can have a THC concentration of 80 percent whereas in comparison to smoking a joint only has a concentration of about 10 to 15 percent THC. There is simply no comparison between dabbing and smoking a joint.

To put it into a more relatable context: A beer has an average alcohol content of 5 percent, vodka has an average of 40 percent, whereas Everclear can have an alcohol content of 75.5 to 95 percent. Comparing a joint to dabbing would be like comparing a six-pack of beer to six shots of 95 percent Everclear. The person who drank a six-pack of beer may be fine; however, the person who drank six shots of 95 percent Everclear is undeniably f****. Even though 190 proof Everclear can be argued is "just alcohol," it's toxic and can quickly cause alcohol poisoning thus making it illegal to buy in many states in the United States. There are no studies that I am aware of that have studied the effects and/or long-term consequences of frequent habitual dabbing. However, "Dabbing is linked with a number of dangerous side effect like rapid heartbeat, blackouts, crawling sensations on the skin, loss of consciousness, and psychotic symptoms such as paranoia and hallucinations."[2]

The study "Toxicant Formation in Dabbing: The Terpene Story," conducted by Atrash, Lou, and Strongin published in September 22, 2017 found dabbing "may in fact deliver significant amounts of toxic degradation products."[3]

Also, cannabis withdrawal is stated to be rare yet what percentage of people who dab experience cannabis withdrawal? "Common symptoms observed during cannabis withdrawal include anger, aggression, irritability, anxiety and nervousness, decreased appetite or weight loss, restlessness, and sleep difficulties with strange dreams."[4] Thus, this completely changes everything we presume to know about marijuana because studies are now linking addiction and withdrawal symptoms to marijuana which previously was known not to be addictive or harmful. Researching all this was my way of calm reflection.

Yet my calm dissipated when an intrusive thought wiggled in of Judge Mazle Dina saying, "I could not suspend visitation for a positive marijuana." Then like a squawking parrot, "it's just marijuana."

18

ROLL WITH THE PUNCHES

APRIL 14, 2018

"My OB said that I may be having this baby any time in the next two weeks. I am politely asking if you would pause FaceTiming just for the next couple weeks, so I may focus on delivery."

Moe said, "Seraphine, respectfully, I do not feel that it is too difficult on your pregnancy to answer the phone and let me speak with our daughters."

He offered to take the girls while I delivered.

How does a seemingly simple offer glean so much evil intent. I felt defeated. I lay on my bed and cried not being aware of the time, I missed Moe's call.

My mom and Tony started to call because Moe was blowing up their phones, again.

I had repeatedly asked him to stop, but he said, "If you would just pick up your phone, I won't be forced to call them."

I gave birth to Diana a day later, two weeks early. Due to stress, I was completely unable to breastfeed her.

Punch after punch they rolled in.

Despite Anna having what the doctors thought might be asthma, Moe continued to smoke in the car with them. He told the girls Daddy's smoke won't hurt them because he's "only" vaping.

The girls told me Daddy was a dragon.

No matter what I said or how sick Anna got, he didn't seem to care. If no one would believe me, then I guess I would just have to prove it.

I hired a private investigator. My hormones were out of control, and my maternal instincts to protect were in overdrive.

On May 4, the private investigator followed Moe after he picked up the girls and Cecelia's daughter, Mallory. Moe drove erratically on the freeway at speeds of 80 mph in heavy traffic.

Moe stopped by his friend's house. The investigator uncovered he had been convicted and charged for rape of a minor in Michigan.

The investigator reported that he witnessed the father smoking and allowing friends to smoke cigarettes in direct proximity to our girls and Mallory, during visitation. The investigator couldn't get a clear read on the cans they were drinking. However, he believed Moe was drinking alcohol as well because another girl on the porch stumbled around seemingly intoxicated, and Moe was drinking from the same can.

When Moe returned the girls on May 6, Anna was lethargic, coughing, wheezing, and barely able to hold an oxygen saturation of 90 percent, so I ran her to urgent care. They prescribed albuterol every four hours and told me to come back if her symptoms worsen.

She did not improve over the next few days. When she developed a fever, I took her back in on May 11, and they prescribed steroids for five days.

One afternoon of partying cost Anna ten days. I sent everything to Mr. Benson, but he claimed if we go back to court, we would only annoy Judge Mazle Dina and warned me that we don't want to get on her bad side.

PUNCH

Blow after blow, the punches kept rolling in. Sometimes the only thing you can do is take the punch and endure.

I don't remember going to court on May 17, 2018, but the orders read as follows:

> Party receiving physical custody shall be responsible for the children's transportation on the custody exchanges. Mother pick up shall be at the Father's city local Police Station and Father's pickup shall be at the Mother's city local sheriff's station.
>
> If either party is more than 15 minutes late without prior notice to the other party, the visit is cancelled. The grace period for each party, with notice, shall be a maximum of 45 minutes.
>
> All other orders not modified shall remain in full force and effect.

So, I was less than three weeks postpartum, and the court wanted me to be in a car for two hours? In a country that offers no national paid parental leave am I surprised? Perhaps I was being too pessimistic, it's not like pregnant women or women forty-two days after pregnancy in the US have the highest death rate when compared to other wealthy and developed countries. My phone rang… it was the girls' preschool. Moe drove straight from court over to the girls' preschool and asked the school staff if he could pick up the girls. It was Thursday, his visitation starts on Friday at 5:30 p.m, he shouldn't be there. The staff knew that he was not supposed to be there, so they called me then the police. When the police arrived, Moe acted smug and denied he was there to actually pick up the girls but rather he was only asking if he could. Police left and nothing happened. Tony helped with the pickups and drop-offs while I took care of Diana.

POKE

On May 20, 2018, Moe quit his warehouse job exactly six months to the day of being hired and attempted to file for medical disability. Moronically, Moe submitted paperwork to the court that showed he had been misappropriating benefits from the VA by claiming we were still married.

Our divorce was finalized years ago. He filed to reduce child support to zero immediately after quitting, using the excuse he didn't have a job. The court didn't seem to even read his paperwork, and when I brought it up, the court stated that if what I claimed were true, then I'd receive less in child support. I don't understand. He can steal money from the VA but the ones the courts want to punish are our children? They also saw nothing wrong with him collecting benefits from the VA for both girls but trying also to terminate paying child support altogether. Approximately six separate times he filed through the court for zero child support while I was on maternity leave.

The matter of child support was continued in June, then continued again on July 18, then to Sept 13. In September, Judge Dina Mazle granted Moe's request for zero child support because we were a "no show" due to a clerical error. The hearing was calendared for 1:30 p.m. but was changed and set for 8:30 a.m. in error. My attorney at the time had to prove the court made an error and was able to fix it to have the matter re-heard with us present. His child support was a mere $688 per month. However, by December 28, 2018, the court deviated again from the guideline recommendation of $827 a month and granted $375 per month. Although, it didn't really matter what the courts ordered. Moe withheld paying child support while I was on maternity leave because I assumed he felt my financial status would be at its most vulnerable. Later in 2020, Moe would get even that amount reduced again to $206 a month for both girls. Moe was never required to obtain or even look for a job by the courts, and to my knowledge, over the next five years Moe remained unemployed.

BACK FIST

Moe's current fixation was to force the girls to watch the movie *Coraline.* The villain in the movie is the mother. The girls would have night terrors and wake up crying asking if they could sleep with me because they didn't want the spider to take out their eyes and sew in buttons.

"I don't want buttons eyes," they cried.

I tried to talk to Moe about it. I said I did not think it was age-appropriate, Anna was three years old and Kay was four, and that it gave the girls night terrors.

He made them watch it even more, claiming it was their favorite movie. He obsessed over that movie so much that later he would make them dress as Coraline for Halloween and used it as the theme of their birthday parties.

This went on for several years. The more I brought it up, the more he forced them to watch it.

He didn't care that it gave them night terrors for the majority of those years. The girls eventually grew out of the night terrors caused by the film.

THROAT STRIKE

Attorney Joseph Benson switched me over to another attorney who worked in his office. She kept calling me and asking me to go over the same questions she had asked me the week before.

With my pregnancy hormones still coursing through me, I couldn't stop myself when I emotionally answered her questions.

On June 6, we went back to court for child support. The new lady my attorney pawned me off on walked out of the private chambers with Ms. Basket laughing. You know that feeling you get when you just know you're about to be cheated? Yeah, I was feeling that.

My "new attorney" was still smiling when we walked into the courtroom.

In front of the judge, both lawyers tried to be super technical by strictly only using form numbers, claiming such and such number form wasn't filed thus we have to ask for a continuance, *Your Honor.*

The judge went over the paperwork then peered up at them holding eye contact with both of them then struck the gavel down continuance granted.

Now, if you lived with gear heads, motor mechanic guys, you know this trick well. When they are vetting a new guy and want to see what they actually know, they also only talk in numbers. For example, they might say something wrong with confidence "the 823 factory heads are the best when building a LM7." If the new guy just agrees quickly and doesn't banter, then it's likely he doesn't know what they are talking about and doesn't know much about motors.

She charged me thousands of dollars for court preparation fees and presentation fees, to then ask for a continuance because she claimed the paperwork had not been filed? This was the legalized version of an auto mechanic up charging their labor for fake parts or services; it was like charging $55 for blinker fluid. We call these types of auto mechanics crooks; it was the same here, she was a crook. No such continuance was needed because the paperwork they claimed wasn't filed was in fact already filed, but now they could each charge us again for the next court hearing... those slippery snakes.

PALM STRIKE

When I called Attorney Joseph Benson's office to voice what she had done and that I shouldn't have to pay the $4000 she charged me in a week, he began yelling at me.

I guess claiming one of his office associates was attempting to pull one over on me was personal to him, and without being capable of explaining the exact technical details because I didn't have the knowledge of a lawyer, he had me at a disadvantage in the argument.

Joseph Benson ended by telling me he would only be willing to take off $1000 from the total bill, but this "discount" was only good if I came in the next day with the remainder of the balance in cash. He added if I didn't pay, he would take me to court and have my wages garnished. It wasn't much of a choice... for whatever reason at the time, I thought I had to pay it, so I pulled out all of my savings, which was five thousand dollars and took it to his office the next day. It still wasn't enough to cover the remaining balance that was six thousand plus dollars, but I thought maybe it would be just enough, like my dad would say when I was younger sometimes you just have to put the money on the table. Maybe then I could sever ties.

His office claimed he was out, and they had no knowledge of any "deals" I claimed he had made. They said they would, however, take my money and put it toward my balance.

When I asked if they could call and find out if the amount I was offering would satisfy the balance, they said they claimed they could not reach him.

"He must be golfing."

I could see what was happening. He wasn't going to honor any deals he made over the phone. It was all lies. So, I didn't hand them any of my money. Now I needed it in writing.

I called the next three days, and he was nowhere to be found. The next week I finally asked his office for a substitution of attorney form.

He called me that same day and yelled at me again claiming that I owed him the full amount now because I refused his offer. Furious, he said he was going to file an arbitration if I did not pay him in full.

When I asked for my file, Mr. Benson intentionally or mistakenly did not return the most recent court documents of my file that I would need for the next court hearing.

On June 14, 2018, Moe, his girlfriend Cecilia, and his mom Edith showed up to the girls' preschool graduation unannounced.

Restraining order was still in effect, but it didn't matter, Moe and his family thought they were entitled to be there. The ceremony had already started. I didn't want to make a scene.

However afterward, they refused to leave until they had one-on-one time with the girls. I asked them politely to go. Moe refused. All three of them followed me when I walked Kay back to her class. I stopped at the door and asked them again to please leave. They swarmed around me, pushed me, and tried to open the door behind me.

I ran into Anna's class with Kay. I must have been white in the face because Anna's teacher said I looked like I was going to faint.

Just as she said that Edith pushed the door open and pushed me aside to give Anna a balloon.

I called the police. When the police officer arrived, he asked me if Moe had pushed me with one hand or two. The officer then explained that if he had pushed me with two hands then he could have done something but because he only "touched" me with one hand that there probably wasn't that much exertion, therefore, Moe didn't really do anything. I told him I had a restraining order against him, but it didn't make a difference. The officer gave me an incident number and left.

June 19, Anna drew a picture where everyone was bleeding, and her teacher was concerned.

Moe still called militantly twice a week for his ten-minute conversations, if I did not answer on the first ring, he would call until I answered. The video calls became weirder and weirder. Sometimes if the girls wandered away from the call, Moe would literally just sing to my couch. Other times, he would put his whole beard inside his mouth and stare at the camera.

On June 21, Kay told Moe she didn't feel like talking.

Moe said, "Kay, that doesn't sound like something you would say. Did your mommy tell you to say that? What else does your mommy tell you to say?"

Kay became more withdrawn and began saying she didn't have feelings, only secrets. When she was at my house, she started to stare off while biting her fingernails down past the skin.

Kay would come home from visitation saying she was nervous and scared.

He would interrogate her about *my* personal life. Kay would suck in her lip and roll it around in her teeth.

There was nothing I could do because it was all hearsay evidence. From the moment Kay could talk, Moe used her as a spy to get information. Kay was a chatty four-year-old; Anna was three and quieter, so Kay was used for questioning.

This continued, every week, every visit, every month.

We had our restraining order renewal hearing in July. "Are you ready?" the court asked. I responded, "Yes." I then tried to tell the court everything that he had been doing. Ms. Basket cut me off telling the court that I didn't put that into writing, therefore I couldn't speak on any event that had happened. I didn't know I had to submit a written letter ten days prior to that hearing outlining all the new things he had done.

I just thought I was supposed to go into court and tell the judge.

Moe's lawyer, Ms. Basket, made sure to note that was not in accordance with the law, so I had no right to speak on anything if it wasn't previously submitted in writing. I was so frustrated I started crying. Ms. Basket reminded the court that I stated that I was ready earlier. Every time I tried to speak, Ms. Basket shut me down.

Ms. Basket then tried to do the same thing she was accusing me of, and the court noted it and reprimanded her.

Mrs. Basket accused me of "shopping around" because I filed the restraining order from the county where I lived and not the county where our family court hearing was normally heard.

She then said the only reason I filed for a restraining order in the first place was because of family code 3044 subsection (1). *What's 3044 subsection (1)?* Ms. Basket continued that her client deserved custody and that I was just trying to prevent him from filing for custody and alienate him from our daughters. Since I didn't write a statement ahead of time, my evidence was silenced. With no new evidence to offer that he had done anything wrong, or that he had violated the restraining order, the judge removed the restraining order. I felt like my voice had been gagged.

I felt so small.

I felt hopeless.

I felt like I didn't matter.

That our daughter's suffering did not matter. All because I didn't know about the ten-day rule. I cried for days after.

No one had explained the rules to me. It was almost impossible to navigate through court without having a degree in law.

I had to hire a new attorney again.

SIDE KICK

On July 18, 2018, Moe's attorney, Ms. Basket, tried to still claim deficient documents were filed… what Ms. Basket didn't know was that I obtained the transcript from the last hearing and gave it to my new temporary attorney. She said, "There's no deficiency. There's an RFO on calendar with the proper declarations. It's a 319 as in the pleading attached to a 158, and it has all the documents."

Judge Male Dina replied, "Okay. So, looking at her respondent's request for the order March 27th, 2018, she attached documents, a ledger of all payments received, and exhibits. So, I don't know, what deficiency you are claiming?" The judge threw her under the bus. She was caught.

Ms. Basket scrambled and started grasping at straws. "They're mandatory judicial counsel forms."

Judge Mazle Dina asked, "Do you have the numbers for those forms?"

Ms. Basket said, "I had them before." She was frantically pushing papers around pretending to look for them.

My attorney said, "I think what Attorney Basket is alleging is 319, 158, and 157. Mr. Benson's 319 was done in the—it's 319 is the attorney's declaration. The 319 Mr. Benson did not use the actual form, but the form was very clear. You can use the 319 or you can do a declaration that provides the same information as a 319. Mr. Benson filed on March 27th along with his RFO. The 158, which is attached for the justification is also attached to his declaration. 157, everything is there."

A momentary win, but there was still the arbitration battle with Attorney Joseph Benson.

SUCKER PUNCH

I assumed during arbitration that the arbitrator was going to mediate the conversation and ask us questions, but when I went, Mr. Benson just unleashed.

I had walked into a Russian chess tournament thinking we were playing checkers.

No, it was more like I went to an MMA heavy weight championship fight having never been in a fight before.

I got my ass handed to me. At the end, I asked the mediator if I did okay and if all arbitrations go like this. The mediator didn't even say anything. He looked at me with pity.

I imagined I must have appeared as Tyler Durden after his encounter with Lou in the basement in the movie *Fight Club*.

I don't know why I even asked him. I was ordered to pay him everything.

So, I did. What could I do?

He'd come after me with a lawsuit and garnish my wages if I didn't, he already threatened it. Besides, he won. I tried. I just needed to let it go. I had no control. It was a brutal onslaught from all directions, but something unexpected happened. Internally, things began to shift and realign.

Slowly, I was changing… the punches kept coming.

On October 16, 2018, Moe overdosed Anna, who was three-year-old, with Benadryl.

Moe accused me, saying it was my fault that he had to medicate her because I let her play in the grass. Then he shifted the blame onto Anna and accused her of medicating herself. There was no reversal agent for Benadryl, you just had to allow it to go through the body. Anna passed white stool for four days after visitation. I filed an emergency court hearing.

October 16, 2018 Court Orders

1. No medication given to minors in Father's care without Mother's permission.

2. Father not permitted to go to children's school without notice of events occurring.

3. Father to pay Mother $352.42 in payments at the rate of $50.00 per month commencing November 1, 2018, until paid in full.

4. Petitioner Moe Malvado to pay $2000.00 in attorney fees directly to respondent Seraphine J. Soyla at rate of $100.00 per month commencing January 5, 2019.

— OVERHAND —

Moe then again bombarded me with Talking Parents messages almost every hour during his visitations suggesting the girls were seemingly sick during every one of his visitations scheduled on the first, third, and fifth weekends.

He began calling my cell phone at 2 a.m. until I answered and would yell for twenty minutes. I had developed gastritis, and my stomach ached all the time.

Moe would tell me, "I have to have permission from you to give them anything. This is what you wanted!" If I tried to avoid his calls, Moe would just call Tony and my mom.

We repeatedly asked him to stop, but he didn't.

Between my stomach and my nerves, I lost it a little on November 17, 2018, on Talking Parents I sent, "I have just been notified that you have been calling and texting Tony and my mom, however, I do not have a single missed call or text from you. Please do not yell at them on the phone and do not interrogate Tony as to why he's not living with me. The girls were not sick at all yesterday, so if you want me to come and pick them up, you let me know. Thanks."

To which he replied, "So, straight up you're a jerk, not to me but our daughters. Kay has been running a fever since I picked them up, they both have been coughing nonstop. You didn't say a word at ALL DURING PICK UP. They are both sick as hell. Either tell me what to give them or drive up here and give it to them yourself. Since me and my bachelor's degree can't medicate them. You're a piece of work. No, it's my visitation, either give me permission to medicate them or come up and medicate them. They had stuffy noses and red cheeks and were coughing when they got into my car from your car, and Kay has a fever. So, you can medicate them here or give me permission to medicate them, it's your choice."

But Moe claimed they were both sick nearly every time he picked them up. They weren't, yet somehow, this tactic was, I guess, going to somehow prove to the court what that I didn't share what? His delusions? His lack of boundaries? His compulsions?

On the occasions they were actually sick, and I did have to allow Moe to give them medication, I found out he would medicate them around the clock.

I asked him one day, "How many doses/times did you give Anna Mucinex?"

Moe said, "The bottle states every four hours. So did the bottle I bought, you can keep yours, 8 p.m. Friday night, 2 a.m. Saturday morning. She woke up coughing a lot 8 a.m. Saturday morning, noon Saturday—noon. Should I continue? Every four hours like the bottle states. I did not give her Tylenol because I was not authorized to give it to her. Even when I told you she had a fever, you did not give me permission to do so. I am limited to what I can do for her unless *YOU SAY* otherwise. So, I medicated her with exactly what you have been giving her."

There was no regard for the recommended max dose in a specific timeframe, and if I asked what their temperature was, I usually never got a straight answer. It was typically a long rant or "they felt hot." If they truly had a fever, I don't know, but they were at greater risk for another drug overdose because he had no concept of medication limits.

FIST PUNCH

On November 19, 2018, Moe withheld the girls, called the police, because he wanted to know what my relationship status was. Tony had done most of the exchanges while I was at home with baby Diana. Typically, they went smoother with Tony but not today.

Today, Moe demanded to know what his relationship status was with me and refused to exchange the girls. The police called me at work, upset about the situation. Moe had made the girls sit in the cold for over an hour waiting for the police, then after one hour talking to the police, he then agreed to let Tony leave with the girls.

CROSS HOOK

On December 14, 2018, during the exchange at my local sheriff's station, Moe took the girls to his vehicle. However, Moe's girlfriend, Cecilia, stood behind my van refusing to let me leave until I answered her questions. Moe was hanging outside the window screaming and yelling with the girls inside his vehicle. I asked her to move, so I could leave. Instead, she crossed her arms and said, "Not until you answer my questions."

"I'm not playing this game with you, move." I got in my van, turned it on, Cecilia still refused to move from behind it. Part of me wanted to just run her over, but I knew I'd be the one going to jail, so I threw it back into park. It was after business hours, and the station was closed, and I had forgotten my cell phone at home.

I got back out and asked her again to move. She refused. Fine, have it your way... let's chat. Arms crossed, she yammered on and on about what I can't remember, but then she said, "You're just mad cause he left you, and you still want him!"

I started laughing. "Is that what he told you? Guess you'll believe anything huh?"

She grumbled something. Moe, at this point, was hanging his head out the window of his SUV screaming that I could go f*** myself.

I was able to stay calm. "You know, I really do pity you."

Genuinely shocked, Cecilia responded, "What?"

"I feel bad for whatever you must have gone through in your last relationship to think that this," I pointed at Moe, "is an upgrade."

She was not prepared for that statement, and with that, she left. Moe told me later that I was forbidden to ever speak to her again.

Two days later during another exchange, Cecilia yelled out the widow as they drove away, "Congrats on baby daddy number three!"

My mistake, these two were the perfect pair. I don't think Cecilia even owned a driver's license; she was completely dependent on Moe. He got Cecilia kicked out of her welfare housing. I'm assuming because she did not report him living with her. She had to move, and they ended up renting a house. They had to have her sister and boyfriend move in to help cover the rent, which I think was twelve hundred dollars a month, split four ways, that's three hundred a month each.

A few days later, Moe and Cecilia drove down to the girls' school to attend their Christmas recital despite court orders. Moe acted like it was a football game and was yelling from the back at the girls. Moe created such a disruption he had to be asked to leave by school staff.

ELBOW STRIKE

On December 24, 2018, Moe followed me back home after the exchange with the girls in his vehicle and called police because he claimed I did not provide Anna's inhaler. I told him it was in the middle of being refilled by the pharmacy.

He said on Talking Parents, "I was simply asking about her inhaler. I waited in my vehicle, windows up, and off your property until the sheriff came out. I did what I was instructed to do by the sheriff. If you do not want police involvement when it comes to things like this, then communicate with me, so I am not backed into a corner. Merry Christmas, Seraphine Malvado."

This was not normal behavior, yet, it was so frequent that it had become normal. Due to health reasons, my new temporary attorney had to quit, so once again, I was pro per.

SIDE PUNCH

Starting off the New Year January 3, 2020, the girls started saying things like, "Daddy said you and Tony are liars." By the end of the month, January 29, Moe yelled during the court ordered phone calls, "If someone would f****** co-parent! Your lack of coparenting is really pissing me off!" By this point, if he began cussing or yelling, I would just end the call. Moe claimed he still had however many minutes left and would call over and over demanding his phone time. I just ignored him. Moe then began asking repeatedly about my new baby, Diana. I asked him not to inquire about a child that is of no relation to him.

Moe refused and said he was only asking out of his deep concern for her.

Moe continued to attempt to talk to and about Diana during the court ordered phone calls scheduled every Tuesday and Thursday and said he felt uncomfortable not responding to Diana when he perceived her to be talking to him, and that it was not his fault that babies just loved his voice. I would also end the call when he did this as well. Moe said if I disapproved of him talking to my baby, then I should lock Diana in another room.

Cecilia would also jump on the calls and yell at the girls, "Girls, you need to turn off that TV right now and talk to your dad!" The calls became shorter and shorter.

KNEE STRIKE

On February 1, 2019, after his knee surgery, Moe Malvado said on Talking Parents, "As far as the court orders state, I am not allowed to be under the influence of any ILLEGAL SUBSTANCES." Implying that it was okay to be under the influence of prescription medications, because they are prescribed, and marijuana, because it is now legal, while he had the girls.

On February 4, 2019, on Talking Parents, Moe said, "As far as inquiring about Diana, you are right, she is not my child. However, Ms. Malvado, she is our daughter's sister, therefore, I care about her safety and well-being as well as Kay's and Anna's.

"Can you please answer my question regarding the Hatchimals (a children's toy with small parts you have to break out an egg)? And as for Tony, I have never said he wasn't a real dad. I said he isn't their dad, and you know what, Seraphine? He IS NOT THEIR DAD! I am. Only me! So, there is nothing wrong with me correcting them when they call YOUR EX-fiancé dad. He is Diana's dad and that's all."

On February 6, 2019, on Talking Parents, Moe said, "Seraphine, if you don't want Diana talking to me, then clear her out of the room and turn the TV's off. But your nine-month-old comes up and starts babbling to me on the phone. I'm gonna talk to her, I'm gonna call her sweetie because I'm not a jerk. If you don't want Diana on the phone, then simply supervise her unless you're not into that sort of thing. I do really like how you to get on here and make accusations that are generalizers. Like, Moe, you were cussing at me on the drop-off. Well, Seraphine, I wasn't, but if you can't tell me what I supposedly said. I pretty much laugh off your feeble accusations. You have a sweetie for a daughter, what can I say. She loves my voice. Have a good one, Seraphine."

I replied, "I am trying to work with you. However, I will not tolerate you talking negatively to or about me during your calls. This is not the intended purpose of the calls. I have also asked you not to talk to or about Diana, a baby, that is of no relation to you. Thank you."

Moe was clear he had no intention of stopping. "I will not ignore a child who is interacting with me. I'm not a jerk nor will I be just to please you. Also, introduce your new boyfriend to me."

Moe would then steer the conversation into left field. "I appreciate the call back. I just wish you could read and understand the court order about rescheduling. Oh well, maybe we should translate it to a different language! Or maybe you could use the court interpreter tomorrow. How funny would it be if we both used an interpreter. Seeing as though you have my Hispanic last name of Malvado."

The thing about that was English is his first and only language. An interpreter's role was to help communicate when two people speak different languages not because their surname was of Hispanic origin. He didn't speak Spanish, and I'm as white as they get. I speak more Spanish than his entire immediate family combined, and that's not saying a lot. What was he even talking about?

Moe continued to talk to and about baby Diana despite me asking him repeatedly to stop; he became so inappropriate that I had to terminate the court ordered Tuesday and Thursday phone calls entirely.

Moe messaged me after I stopped the calls. "Seraphine, I called at 7pm, three times to be exact. That is uno, dose, tres, in Spanish just in case you need it in translated. We've all watched Dora I'm sure, lol. Please look over the orders. It does not state you can stop the calls for any reason. I expect both my calls next week and ten minutes per child. Thank you!"

VERTICAL STOMP

Moe was getting weirder and weirder, and I started to feel unsafe, so I asked a male friend to drive with me to the exchange.

Moe got out of his SUV and came up to my friend, staring him up and down and asked him what his name was.

My friend was not intimidated and did not answer him.

Moe was not satisfied and questioned the girls to get information he wanted. How do I know this? Because immediately after his visitation, the girls asked, "What is your boyfriend's first and last name?"

If the girls did not tell him what he wanted to hear, they got in trouble. Later, I would find out Moe would hit the girls if they did not appease him, and he would yell and cuss at them if he thought they were giving him the wrong answer.

Moe would lie to the girls and tell them that Mommy's new boyfriend was bad and punched Daddy in the eye and would encourage them to hit any man in my life and destroy my cell phone. Anna broke our cat's leg. If I dated someone, it would make things worse for Kay and Anna. If I didn't date, there would be less information for Moe to interrogate Kay about thus making it easier for her. At work we called this risk verse benefit. Continuing to date anyone would put Kay and Anna at risk. Is the benefit of being in a relationship greater than the potential emotional harm Kay was being put through? No. Tony and I mutually ended things.

HAYMAKER

On February 16, 2019, I told Moe that Anna was sick and suggested she not go.

Moe said on Talking Parents, "I am her Father whether she is sick or not."

Not more than fifteen minutes after Moe picked up the girls, Anna threw up in his car. Moe then returned Anna and asked to have next weekend when she was not sick. I declined.

Moe said if he could not have Anna next week then he wanted to keep Kay longer. I declined.

Moe then sent me a picture of Kay to show me he cut her hair. Kay's bangs were butchered.

Moe had never cut their hair before, and he did not give any notice before he did it. Just a picture after the fact to upset me.

Moe smugly denied any wrongdoing. On February 17, 2019, on Talking Parents, he said, "Cecilia did nothing more but try and fix it a bit." He continued. "By the way, are you pregnant again? You bring so many men around the girls it is causing a disruption and isn't healthy, Seraphine. Also, introduce your new boyfriend to me since he'll be in the picture and is clearly around our girl's full time. Maybe we can all spend time together as a family, do things.

"Have a great evening Ms. Malvado."

He then ranted on and on for several pages wanting me to engage with him.

EYE STRIKE

On March 3, 2019, Moe was mad that it took me twenty-two minutes to get back to him while I was at work, so he had Cecilia call Tony telling him there was an emergency leading him to believe Kay was seriously injured.

I said, "I was notified that your girlfriend called Tony on Saturday and told him to notify me immediately because there was an emergency with Kay but refused to say what the emergency was. If you're going to call Tony, then it would also be helpful to explain what the 'emergency' is instead of saying it's none of your business. It is unacceptable to lead him to believe Kay was seriously injured when she only had a cough and cold."

Moe's response. "Again my girlfriend has a name, it's Cecilia. I messaged you on Talking Parents, called you and sent you text via phone. You did not respond to anything. So, Cecilia called Tony because he always answers her calls or calls her. Now, she did state that it was an emergency but told him she wasn't hurt but she was sick. She just did not go into detail about her fever or anything like that. She told him to have you call me, and he said okay. It was an emergency, our daughter was running a high temp, she was crying because she was so miserable. She barely ate anything; she was coughing so much she was threw up. If you don't want me or Cecilia to have to call Tony or anyone else then please respond to my text, phone calls, or Talking Parents' messages. If you can do that then there will be no need for a third party. Oh, and again send Anna's spacer next time. Have a good evening."

I replied, "I did in fact responded back to you in twenty-two minutes on Talking Parents."

Moe snapped back. "Because we called Tony. Thanks for proving the fact we had to call Tony. In the past you have not responded in a timely manner for anything, even when I have the girls, so when something is actually important like our daughter's health, you give me no choice but to use a third party. Tony is pretty active in their lives still, so Cecilia called him. I don't see the issue in this."

Tony had to eventually block both Moe and Cecilia's numbers because they would not stop, and I had to get a new number because he would call from different numbers.

It seemed like he was only escalating.

19

BLAME THE DOG OR THE CHILD, BUT DON'T BLAME HIM

"I walked into the room six inches. A big black dog bite me," Kay said in a robotic voice. To any and all questions asked her, Kay's only response was, "I don't know."

Kay showed the doctor the bite mark on her tiny waist right above her jeans. The physician stated the bite mark was "perfectly circular and only superficial. Wound is approx. 3.5 cm x 3.5 cm no deep puncture wounds, no irregularity as seen with most dog bites."

"This doesn't look like any dog bite I've ever seen. It looks like a human bite to me." The doctor swiveled around to his computer and typed something. "I'm recommending she takes a week of antibiotics for this bite because it could lead to a serious infection."

The room was quiet. Kay curled into my side. "Daddy told me if I tell you what happened he is going to go to jail. I don't want Daddy to go to jail." The doctor then looked me directly in the eyes and informed me that he was mandated to report this finding to CPS because he was worried about possible physical abuse. It had been only two hours since I picked them up, and Moe's lies were swirling in my head. My mind reviewed the conversation I just had with Moe prior to coming to the hospital.

He told me minutes before dropping them off, "Seraphine, Kay got nipped on her stomach this weekend by our dog. It isn't bad at all, and not nearly as bad as it was when Kingsley bit Anna. If you have any concerns or questions, feel free to ask."

I didn't even know he owned a dog or was capable of taking care of one for that matter. "What kind of dog do you own? How exactly did that happen?"

Moe snapped back. "You already know of one dog, Bixby, a black lab mixed with a coonhound. Mary Jane is a very nice dog. However, when it comes to my girlfriend's sister's bedroom; her sister gets slightly territorial, it's been like that during her pregnancy. The girls, including Mallory know this. The girls were all playing outside with her when Mary Jane came inside to go into her kennel. I guess Kay thought it was okay to follow her into the bedroom. Kay cried for a few seconds and was fine after that. She was more scared than anything. You can see it was more of a pinch than a nip. I cleaned it up and made sure she was more than okay."

I knew he was lying the minute he said she cried for a few seconds because Kay is naturally dramatic. Like drop a handkerchief, throw the back of her hand over her forehead as she slowly slumps onto a fainting couch in her fine Victorian dress; dramatic.

Kay would cry all day if she dropped her ice-cream cone. I know she didn't cry for "a few seconds" over this. Combined with not telling me until minutes before handoff, downplaying the injury saying "more a pinch than a nip," and mentioning irrelevant details like Bixby.

Bixby was my Hungarian Vizsla I bought when we were married that ate a grain free non-artificial additive diet. Moe took him because "you got the kids it's only fair I get the dog." However, he pawned Bixby off onto his parents who fed him dogfood they bought at dollar mart. Why is he bringing up extra random facts that are not relevant. I messaged Moe while I was parked at the exchange location waiting for the girls to get in.

"I thought Bixby lived with your parents," I said.

Moe was immediately defensive and tried to veer off onto a different topic. "I never said Bixby lives here, did I? You asked what dog I owned. I answered you. But what would it matter if Bixby did live with us?"

Okay, this isn't going anywhere, I thought, so I circled back to the bite. "Just because you told the girls that the dog is territorial does not mean it is the children's responsibility to ensure their own safety around the dog. It's yours. So, what are you going to do about this dog that bit Kay?"

Moe replied, "She is safe around the dog, both girls are. What did you do with Kingsley after he bit both my nieces and then bit Anna twice on the eye and head? What would you like me to do?"

Kingsley never bit either niece, his mom claimed he growled at them while we were on our honeymoon, that's how long ago this was, and he thought this was somehow relevant now. Everything he was bringing up was an attempt to mislead the conversation, so I stayed on course. "Obviously, they're not safe if the dog just bit Kay. I got rid of Kingsley, but you already knew that because that happened when we were married."

Moe exploded. "This is literally the only incident that has happened while they have been in MY care. You realize that right? I watch them like a hawk. Because their safety is a huge concern to me. How many times has Anna been bit? Burned? How many bruises are always on her? How about the huge scratch on Kay's arm. Maybe you should be more concerned about their safety when they are in your care. You didn't get rid of Kingsley right away. Which is why he was able to bite not one but three kids. And he bit Anna after you gave him to your parents, twice. And we were not married when he bit Anna, twice. Your parents watch our girls, so they are obviously around Kingsley still. She was snapped at once. MJ is not vicious and is actually really good with the kids. She doesn't have a habit of snapping or biting anyone. My girlfriend's sister can make sure MJ is in her kennel while in the room when the girls are here and have her door locked at all times while the girls are here. Why must you always do something to cause a problem? Why is it that you always point out the bad when they are with me but fail to ever own up to what happens when they are in your care? I understand that you hate me but do not sit here and act like I am not a good father to our daughters. Does that solution meet your approval?"

Moe liked to use what I called the shotgun approach. He fired so many scattered questions, accusations, and misinformation at once to increase the odds his buckshot would hit. Yet, the more damaging reaction was trying to explain any of this to anyone else especially if they inquired what he was referring to because then I have to explain this long backstory, his manipulation of events, how the information was inaccurate, and by the time the story ends, the other person doesn't believe you. It's difficult to dodge his extreme responses because they were intended to hit, snare, and trap me into an argument.

My mind was trying to untangle the trap. This was not the *only* incident. Next, he placed high importance on himself "*MY* care." "I watch them like a hawk." "Huge concern to me." He was already teeing up the notion "unlike you." I watch them like a hawk, "unlike you." Because their safety is a huge concern to me, "unlike you."

Then the spiral, flinging blame everywhere and lobbing exaggerations or lies about events like grenades. He vilified Kingsley to then contrast praise to MJ who "is actually really good with the kids." He sprinkled in a distracting dash of false safety as a decorative flare. "My girlfriend's sister can make sure MJ is in her kennel while in the room when the girls are here and have her door locked at all times while the girls are here," trying to make me feel safe. Yet, the nanosecond he thought I felt safe, he turned and said, "Why must you always do something to cause a problem?"

Ah, yes, because I am to blame and must hold myself accountable for my actions here. The cherry on top, "I understand that you hate me" because let's not forget who the victim was here. The ironic thing was Moe even handed you the serving plate everything rests on. I didn't have to say anything disparaging because he still constantly said it internally to himself, do not sit here and act like I am not a good father to our daughters. I never said anything about his parenting or him, the subconscious reel in his head ran on a loop, "I'm a bad father, I'm a bad father, I'm a bad father." At the very end he asked, "Does that solution meet your approval?"

No. No, it didn't. None of this crap worked on me. My pregnancy hormones had dissipated, and all of this was clickbait. None of it was about Kay. The girls were in my van, and now I was examining the bite.

"When did Kay get bit?" I asked.

Moe said, "Seraphine, please first answer this. Why is it that you can voice your concerns, ask numerous questions, and yet you dismiss anything and everything I say? Why is it that you refuse to answer questions I have asked you?"

He was trying so hard. Moe waited two minutes before firing off another round. "Also, you have stated numerous times that Talking Parents is OUR ONLY platform for communication. If that is the case, don't address me with questions outside of Talking Parents. That's your rule, not mine. I am more than willing to talk on here, in person, or any other way. But if you're going to make rules, you need to abide by them as well."

I was driving back down the hill. I was not biting, none of that answered my question.

Twenty-two minutes went by. "Seraphine, you know what. I am not going to stoop to your way of co-parenting." He continued. "She was bitten this weekend. Yesterday to be exact. Had it been worse I would have immediately notified you. But it wasn't bad, and I took care of it."

I said, "Just informing you that I will be taking Kay to the doctor today to get this bite examined."

Moe said, "When will you be going, so I can accompany our daughter to the doctor's office since that is part of our court orders, I will bring the vaccination record down with me to the doctors. When should I meet you there?"

Why? When he claimed the bite was so insignificant and he took care of it. So now he wanted to interject himself into the doctor's office? You know, Ted Bundy actively sought to insert himself into the investigation of his own crimes. Seems pretty sus.

Also, why was he trying to gaslight me? It's not part of our court orders that he attended all doctor visits?

I was already at the urgent care front window.

I replied, "There is no such court order."

Triggered, Moe said, "Did you take Anna to the doctors to be examined when she was bit by Kingsley? Her bite is not infected, it's not bad and it barely broke the skin. This is just you trying to make it seem like it's bigger than what it is because it happened while she was with me. But the girls can constantly get hurt, have access to scissors, get their Hatchimals taken from them because your third child chocked on them. Maybe I should bring that up more often, or maybe I should voice my concerns about their safety to someone more qualified to assess those situations. Let me know when to meet you at her doctors. You cannot tell me no because I am in fact allowed to go."

If I was just trying to make it seem like it's bigger than what it was, then this was Moe trying to control the narrative and divert the attention off himself. You might be asking yourself what's his deal with the Hatchimals (tiny toys found inside eggs you have to crack open to get)? When Diana began crawling, I asked Kay and Anna to pick up all their tiny toys and put them in a shoebox to ensure baby Diana didn't get a hold of them and choke. From the words Hatchimal, Diana, and choke, Moe transformed this into an action-packed adventure where baby Diana almost died and was heroically saved by first responders. Why? So he could claim the girls were not safe in my care.

Moe's threats were covertly subdued. "Maybe I should voice my concerns about their safety to someone more qualified to assess those situations."

Who might that be? CPS? So, what he was saying was if he didn't get to go to the doctors, he's going to call CPS? That was literally the dumbest threat ever. Their first question would be about the bite.

I replayed his last line in my head, "You cannot tell me no." He was throwing so many red flags. It was hard to ignore the parade of warning signs.

Moe continued to rant on desperately trying to get me to engage with him.

I can say no.

I can say no to *a-l-l* of this.

I exited out of our communication log.

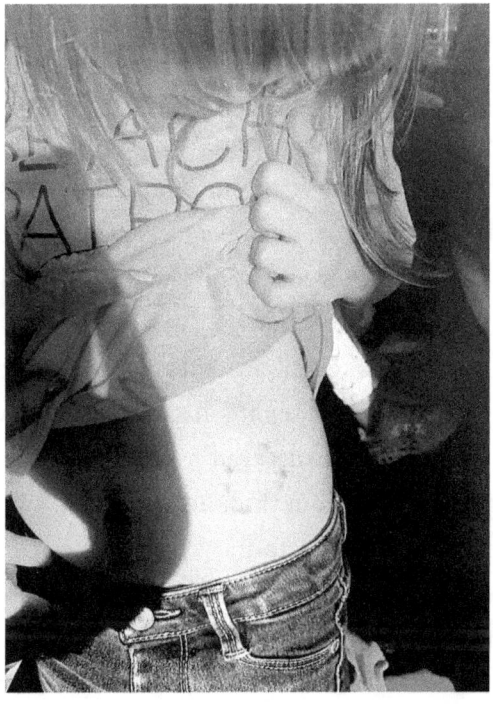

20

TIME TO FORGET
STUDID MISTAKES

MARCH 21, 2019

Thursday afternoon a deputy and social worker from CPS came to my house. The social worker had dark hair and spoke with compassion. As they made their way into my house, the girls swarmed the deputy. He was white, average height, and answered their many questions that mainly revolved around the things on his belt.

"Is that a real gun?"

The social worker looked all around my house. She asked to see the girls' room, she asked to see if I had diapers, she wanted to see inside my refrigerator, and she even asked to see the water heater which I thought was a random thing to ask.

After the probative house tour, we sat in the living room. She asked me question after question. When the question popped up as to whether Moe or I had ever been investigated by CPS, I had to tell them about 2016. When I told them what the deputy in

Moe's hometown told me, the deputy became visibly upset and threw his pen.

He said, "They told you what?"

"They asked me if the minor had access to a computer and that because he was fifteen years old, that he would probably look up pictures like that anyway. Basically, no harm, no foul," I said.

The deputy was now trying to hold back his anger and mumbled some comments about the other deputies back then. I continued. "They arrested him for possible drug charges with the minor, but everything was dropped. I don't think they ever got a hold of the minor." The social worker switched topics and asked when Moe had the girls next and what my plans were.

"Not this weekend but next weekend, and I'm filing an ex parte," I said. She said, "Good," then asked to talk to the girls. I walked down the hall and asked the girls to come out of their room. "The lady in the living room wants to talk with you girls while I talk with Grandma, okay?"

They were already running down the hallway excited to see the police officer with a gun again.

A little time later, the deputy and the social worker thanked me for my time.

When they left, the deputy pointed to a statue of Michael the archangel. "I like your statue. Is someone in your family in law enforcement?"

Confused, I said, "No, I got that in Italy. I just like him."

He said, "He's the patron saint of police officers."

"Oh, I didn't know."

He was in my driveway talking with the social worker when I closed the door.

I woke up to a message from the social worker notifying me that she had set up a physical exam for both girls.

Inside the hospital was a door with an ambiguous sign with the letters C.A.N. above it. This is where the forensic exam was to be conducted. We walked into a tiny waiting room with a few chairs and kids' toys in the middle of the floor.

The girls ran for the toys while I checked in.

We waited a bit before they called us back. I was not allowed to go with them, so I waited on a small couch.

An office assistant came to the side door to tell me they were going to cut some of the girls' hair to do a hair follicle drug test because of Moe's drug history.

Minutes felt like hours while I waited.

While I was sitting on that small sofa waiting for the girls, Moe was at the courthouse filing for 50 percent custody.

Cecilia filled out the paperwork. On a FL-300 form she hand-wrote, "Both Kay and Anna are at the age where equal time with both parents will be beneficial to their wellbeing. And being able to have a more secure, lasting relationship with both parents is something both girls need." She included a new schedule for the courts to adopt.

She also requested Tony Malta be removed. "I no longer want Tony Malta to be involved in any of the drop off or pick-ups."

Moe included an attached declaration MC-031 form that he also filled out by hand stating, "Over the course of four of co-parenting with Ms. Malvado has been difficult, and the last sixteen months things have only gotten much worse. I have tried relentlessly to effectively co-parent with Ms. Malvado, and every time, I am ignored and dismissed. I believe things have gotten worse over the last sixteen months because of what the mediator said in her report after our Jan 22, 2018, appointment. Clancy Billbottom stated, 'As the parents have not demonstrated they can co-parent effectively, recommended Ms. Malvado retain sole legal custody for the present.' I feel as though Ms. Malvado took that and ran with it and made it next to impossible to co-parent with her. I do not wish for things to be like this anymore nor did I ever, I just want the chance to be a father to our daughters and to be in their lives more. I have attached a parenting plan and schedule that I would like to be set in place as well as a change in custody. I have added character reference letters as well."

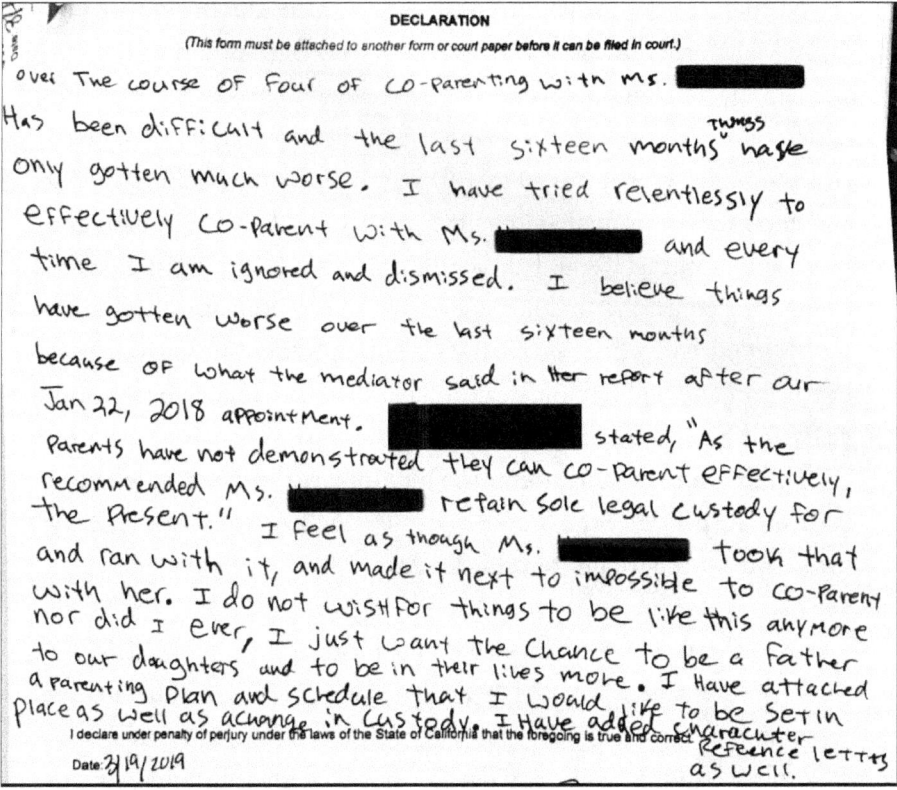

DECLARATION

(This form must be attached to another form or court paper before it can be filed in court.)

Over The course of four of co-parenting with Ms. ████ Has been difficult and the last sixteen months things have only gotten much worse. I have tried relentlessly to effectively co-parent with Ms. ████ and every time I am ignored and dismissed. I believe things have gotten worse over the last sixteen months because of what the mediator said in Her report after our Jan 22, 2018 appointment. ████ stated, "As the Parents have not demonstrated they can co-parent effectively, recommended Ms. ████ retain sole legal custody for the Present." I feel as though Ms. ████ took that and ran with it, and made it next to impossible to Co-Parent with her. I do not wish for things to be like this anymore nor did I ever, I just want the Chance to be a father to our daughters and to be in their lives more. I Have attached a parenting Plan and schedule that I would like to be Set in place as well as a change in Custody. I Have added character reference letters as well.

I declare under penalty of perjury under the laws of the State of California that the foregoing is true and correct.

Date: 2/19/2019

Attached were nine reference letters by his parents, sisters, girlfriend, and a friend that Moe quoted he met in rehab.

He also attached six pages ranting how "she is trying to alienate me from our daughters."

Moe attempted to justify how he yells during the court ordered calls. "I find myself having to yell out to them just to get their attention. If she'd just eliminate the distraction, they'd be more focused."

He also attempted to justify his communication with and about Diana. "But when a child who isn't mine talks to me more than my own children do, that creates a problem. And then I get in trouble by Seraphine if I respond to Diana in any way. I do not feel comfortable ignoring a child, even if that child is in no relation to me."

He also included at length everyone I had dated and how he perceived them to be his new friends. However, he currently distained Tony Malta and how he was the victim of false accusations. Then he said, "Four years ago, I made studid, reckless mistakes that cost me custody of my daughters. I made the choice to relapse after being clean for eight years prior to that. It was at that time Seraphine went and filed for an immediate change of custody. I was in rehab, and there was nothing I could do at the time to change what she was doing. The courts granted her sole legal and physical custody because I admitted I had a drug problem and willingly went to rehab. I have been clean and will remain clean, I have also drug tested the last four years and have always tested clean."

If your gonna lie and attempt to manipulate the court, at least run it through spell-check… studid… really? He had truly unburdened himself from the weight of knowledge.

Over the next few days, more and more things bubbled to the surface. Kay said Moe told her, "It's six o'clock. It's time to not remember."

At first, I didn't really get what she meant, then as I thought about it, the meaning clicked.

I picked them up at 6 p.m. every other Sunday. When they got in the car, I always asked, "How was your weekend?"

They would usually always respond with "I don't know," "I forgot," or "I can't remember."

I wouldn't think anything of it and just figured they were tired and moved on. Yet, now I knew Moe was telling the girls not to remember anything about his weekends.

Who would say that to a kid? What was happening during his visitations that he felt he needed them to not remember any of it? The girls would continue and tell me how they would get disciplined by Moe if they ever called him by his first name instead of Daddy. Why would he discipline them for innocently calling him Moe? They thought me having a different name other than Mommy that adults used was funny. But if they didn't call him Daddy, then he hit them until they did? They said sometimes they got hit so hard it would hurt to sit down. Tears ran down my face when they were telling me this, and I held them close to my chest, so they couldn't see me crying.

I just listened. My heart felt like it was shattering into a thousand pieces.

21

IT WASN'T PROBABLE, IT WAS INEVITABLE

The day of the ex parte arrived. I attempted to gather myself after what the girls had told me, and I wrote:

I am requesting no visitation at this time pending the findings from the open/current CPS investigation and/or Moe can provide a clean drug test and undergo counseling. Moe openly admits to using marijuana and all his drug tests within the last year have come back positive for THC at astronomical levels. It is unclear whether it is Moe's mental health issues or use of marijuana that are currently clouding his parental judgment and our girls' safety, however, there are now signs of child abuse and neglect. Moe receives disability from the VA because he has been determined to be 70% disabled due to a diagnosis of PTSD. Moe also has a history of substance abuse which includes, but is not limited to, using methamphetamine, Norco, Percocet, oxycontin, trammodol, mushrooms, marijuana, and alcohol.

Moe claimed his roommate's "territorial black lab mixed with a coonhound" bit our five-year-old daughter, Kay. I was informed minutes before the pick-up exchange on Sunday, March 17, 2019, however, the incident was claimed to have happened sometime on Saturday, March 16, 2019. Moe neglected to seek any medical attention for Kay and also failed to notify me when the incident happened. Moe then blamed Kay for getting bit and immediately downplayed the injury and told me that "Kay got nipped on her stomach," "It isn't bad at all," "you can see it was more of a pinch than a nip" and that "she is safe around the dog. Both girls are."

When I assessed the bite, it was a perfectly round symmetrical bite that did not seem consistent with the mark of a dog bite and looked more like a human bite mark. Kay's story of the incident seemed coached and rehearsed because it contained details that are out of her scope of knowledge: "I walked into the room 6 inches." Her story quickly unraveled and did not make sense. She also told me that "Daddy told me if I tell you what happened, he is going to go to jail."

The physician that saw Kay noted that the bite was "Perfectly circular and only superficial. Wound is approximately 3.5 cm x 3.5 cm no deep puncture wounds, no irregularities as seen with more dog bites."

Based off his exam, the physician called CPS and reported the bite mark as possible physical abuse. He also prescribed a week of oral antibiotics. Moe's behavior has consistently been inconsistent, argumentative, hostile, and has only been escalated over the last year since. Since our last hearing in October 2018, there have been issues every single weekend. I am very concerned for our daughters, and it is currently unknown the extent of the abuse. I believe the girls are being coached to say they do not remember every time he has visitation, which is extremely disconcerting. I am also requesting that the court ordered calls twice a week be terminated at this juncture because he is using them as a form of harassment and is incapable of stopping his inappropriate remarks nor does intend to stop as he's stated to me on Talking Parents. I included our Talking Parents messages and pictures of human bite mark on Kay.

Looking back, perhaps I could have typed it better and been more concise, but I got the facts across.

Judge Mazle Dina noted she saw an upcoming pending custody hearing that Moe filed and threw it out with no other comments or concerns. Moe attempted to whine and plead, but her judgment came swift and hard:

March 28, 2019 Court Orders

1. Sole physical and legal custody of the minor children shall be awarded to Seraphine Malvado.

2. No visitation is ordered for Moe Malvado until further order of the court.

3. Petitioner visits and phone calls with the minor children are suspended pending further hearing.

4. Petitioner may write letters to the minor children.

I felt like I could finally breathe. The girls were safe now. That afternoon, I made the girls dinner, they watched cartoons, bathed, and got ready for bed. Normality had returned to their lives.

But putting the girls to bed wasn't normal.

They were reaching for me and crying, "Don't leave us!"

I gathered them in my arms. "I would never leave you girls. I love you both very much."

They asked if they could sleep in my bed.

As we crawled into my high queen-sized bed, Kay's hair got snagged in the struggle up, and she started wailing.

I tried to console Kay, and my eyes met Anna.

Standing on the bed over Kay, her face was pale.

She started sobbing uncontrollably. "Is Kay going to die?"

"No one is going to die. It's gonna be okay, baby. Come here."

I held both of my sobbing girls in my lap. They clung to me, and I rocked them until they calmed down and fell asleep.

What was going on? Kay had cried many times before this night, but it had never triggered Anna to cry like this. In that moment, I realized that whatever happened at Moe's house caused Anna to think Kay was going to die.

Moe claimed Kay only cried a second, but Anna's reaction to Kay crying was so intense, and from her question, it seemed that Anna really wasn't sure if Kay was going to live or die.

That must mean Kay was screaming so loud it caused Anna to fear for Kay's life.

The residual damage had been devastating. The girls were not the same. Kay now talked about killing herself, often refused to eat, and Anna cried and hid under furniture.

When Kay got upset now, she bit herself. I would hold her and tell her how much I love her. She was only five years old and already she wanted to leave this world.

My heart hurt. What happened that day? Everything out of Moe's mouth was a lie. And then, I remembered what Kay said, "Daddy told me if I tell you what happened, he is going to go to jail. I don't want Daddy to go to jail."

How dare he! How dare he try to place that weight of guilt onto our child for something he was responsible for. I could imagine Moe crying and telling Kay, "You don't want Daddy to go to jail do you?" That's how far he'd go to avoid accountability... he shifted the burden of responsibility onto our five-year-old. He put it in her head that she would be to blame if he went to jail.

I scrolled through my phone to find a therapist to hopefully help Kay talk about her feelings she couldn't seem to tell me.

The social worker called to update me on the case.

She told she had met with Moe. "It was the most bizarre experience I've ever had."

She saw the worst of society, and she was telling me her interaction with Moe was the strangest? That's unsettling.

I mean, as a nurse, we all see crazy things and to hear another nurse say, "I saw the craziest thing," typically meant something graphically horrific or so disgustingly gross that it could make normal people grab for something to throw up in.

So, when a social worker that deals with the most unpleasant scenarios says her interview was the most bizarre, I was concerned. Because you must be circumspect around CPS, I am going to tell you a little space odyssey adventure about a land where toxic yellow gas could befuddle the mind and spacecraft damage required certain Empire-mandated regulations to be followed:

This tale begins on a voyage to a wild and barren region. The investigative arm of The Empire deployed one member on a mission to contact Corporal M on the outskirts of Balsperia near Mt. Victimhile. The star agent landed their commanding fleet airship and walked up to the front gate. The star agent was dressed in full regalia of the Empire of all white adorned with royal blue embroidery and golden buttons. Two figures emerged from the front door. The star agent announced their arrival to Corporal M, "I am Lieutenant General on behalf of the Empire Spaceship's Regulations Department. Is Corporal M present at this post?" One of the two figures wave their hand attempting to deploy a Jedi mind trick stating, "Corporal M doesn't reside here." The Lieutenant General pulled out from their pocket the exact coordinates of where they were supposed to land and asked if they landed in the wrong location. "No, no, those coordinates are the ones you seek. However, the person you seek is not here," again waving their hands over their face walking backward back inside. They slammed the front door, and the Lieutenant

General walked back into the airship. From the front of the aircraft, the Lieutenant General watched as a person walked out of the bunker and entered a space rover parked nearby. The person slowly cruised by the Lieutenant General's airship suspiciously eyeing every facet only to quickly return inside the bunker. With no time to dillydally with absurd behavior, the Lieutenant General then radioed for the Imperial Security Bureau to send a security droid to the location. When the security droid finally arrived, the Lieutenant General returned to the front gate. The same two figures came back out, and seeing the security droid, they welcomed them in. When the Lieutenant General questioned why they were not first welcoming, they claimed, "We thought you could have been an assassin sent to kill us." Lieutenant General said, "I announced my arrival and stated my name. Plus, you can clearly see the Empire's insignia alongside my airship." Corporal M responded, "Well, we heard you say you were looking for Corporal W...." The Lieutenant General said, "You verified the coordinates of Corporal M were correct and stated he wasn't here, yet here you are." Corporal M responded, "Again, we thought you could have been an assassin. You never can be too careful. Our sincerest apologies, my lord, right this way." As they opened the bunker door, a thick noxious yellow gas meant to illicit illusions billowed out. The Lieutenant General noted the gas immediately as the automatic safety air filter device activated inside their helmet. Protected from the effects of the toxic yellow gas, they entered. The chamber was dark, and it was hard to see with all the gas lingering in the air like a thick fog. The Lieutenant General proclaimed they were sent to get intel on this bunker, as there were reports their spaceship had suffered damage that was suspicious. Corporal M became wild with rage and proclaimed he had the best spaceships and how dare one say otherwise, as he slammed his fists on the table. He ranted on and on then demanded to know who sent the Lieutenant General. "It's that damn station commander across the way isn't it?" Corporal M unleashed his disdain of that commander. Corporal M's private also began yelling in his defense. "How dare you say an ill word of Master Corporal M. He is the best spaceship pilot in the whole galaxy!" The private lurched forward, and the security droid had to deploy laser beams to protect the Lieutenant General. Switching topics, Lieutenant General asked, "Corporal M, do you use any enhancing substances when commanding your spaceships?"

"I only siphon the tiniest amount of yellow gas and ONLY yellow gas! It's all legal! I need it to maintain the safety of this bunker," Corporal M replied.

"It is not legal to have in or around your spaceships though…" Lieutenant General looked at the report awhile longer then up at Corporal M and continued. "My report here states yellow gas was found inside your spaceship, combined with the damage report of the spaceship, we, The Empire, have concerns of misuse."

Corporal M began screaming, "I only use the yellow gas once a week to maintain the safety of this bunker, and it was the spaceship's fault! The spaceship hit that parked commuter shuttle, not me!"

"The spaceship, sir?"

"Yes! It was the spaceship's fault! I mean, it may have been the wind. I programmed the auto navigation system to steer clear of any commuter shuttles, and what does the spaceship do, it doesn't follow any of my programmed instructions. The wind pushed me straight into that parked commuter shuttle! How am I to blame if the emergency stop apparatus isn't on? It was really windy, and the wind caused the commuter shuttle to smash into my spaceship! My spaceship! It caused the damages to me! They are to blame!"

Lieutenant General stated, "It was windy in space, sir?"

"Uhhh…"

"It was reported that the incident happened in space. There is no wind in space, sir."

The private yelled, "Well, it must have happened just as Master Corporal M said! He's the best spaceship pilot in the whole galaxy! How dare you question his abilities!"

Lieutenant General turned to the private. "The report also stated your spaceship is primarily in Corporal M's care. Was your spaceship present when the damage occurred to Corporal M's spaceship? May I see your spaceship to inspect its integrity?"

The private pointed out the window at a ship parked far away. "As you can see it from here, it is perfectly up to code, boarding it is not necessary. I keep my spaceship in mint condition." The private refused to let the Lieutenant General go near the private's personal spaceship. As Lieutenant General walked around the bunker, they noticed yellow gas spilling out from under the floor down the adjacent corridor. The private quickly hit the automatic door lock and declared, "There was nothing to see down there... in fact, you saw nothing" as they both waved their hands across their faces again. The Lieutenant General's eyes rolled, and said annoyed, "You two don't have Jedi mind powers. Care to explain why I see open toxic yellow gas leaking out of that door?"

Corporal M stated, "Um, well, we recently had a meteor hit the bunker that caused a small leak in only one of my collection tanks just yesterday, but I assure you it is normally always contained, and we have the best air quality filters money can buy. However, the meteor also damaged that, too, and I had to siphon some of the yellow gas manually out of the bunker before you came. I do apologize for not notifying you sooner when you came in that I am not myself. I had to for the protection of my bunker."

The private ran to Corporal M who was now theatrically fainting to the floor. The private glared at the Lieutenant General. "This is your fault! You hurt master!" The Lieutenant General departed. They had seen and heard enough.

A few days later, Corporal M called the Lieutenant General and admitted that he has to routinely siphon the yellow gas at least four times a week due to the dangerous area in which they lived, and it is up to him to keep the bunker safe. Corporal M then asked why the Lieutenant General didn't inquire about any possible illegal enhancing substances that may be in the other containers. The Lieutenant General reminded Corporal M that he claimed to have only possessed yellow gas in his containers.

"Oh, yeah, I forgot. Yes, that is correct. There is only yellow gas here. Only mellow yellow daffodils here. Go ahead ask me what my favorite color is? Ha, it's yellow. Yellow rubber ducky!" he laughs. Corporal M apologized for the hostile and agitated state he was in before and admitted sometimes he suffers from spells… along with occasional racing thoughts from hyperspace jumps, mild mind spasms, dizziness, blurred vision, syncope, irregular heartbeats, heartburn, nausea, indigestion, and occasional uncontrolled verbal outbursts. "It's all under control, though. I take prescription medications."

A couple days later, the private called the Lieutenant General wanting to obtain information. "The information about Corporal M or his spaceship is classified." Upset no information was provided, the private began screaming, "You know you asked for Corporal W how dare you try and make Master Corporal M look foolish! You're a liar! And my spaceship is always in mint condition! Mint! You're a liar! A liar!"

The Lieutenant General reported there could be reason to be concerned for the integrity of the private's spaceship due to numerous issues found within Corporal M's bunker where the spaceship primarily was docked; along with the inconsistencies when cross-examined with the documented incidents. The Lieutenant General recommended the private's spaceship is assessed by their local jurisdiction. However, the local general didn't want to be bothered and claimed the spaceship was probably fine.

The Lieutenant General concluded that there were major safety issues that could lead to potentially more dangerous and serious problems if not addressed. The Lieutenant General noted Corporal M made several excuses that were not grounded in facts and found it disturbing that he would blame his spaceship for the damages from the parked commuter shuttle while the spaceship was under his command. The Lieutenant General reported Corporal M was not of sound mind during the crash based on his own admission later he had siphoned yellow gas. It was also reported to The Empire that, due to his confession of having various mind spells and his self-admission to frequently siphoning yellow gas while commanding his spaceships, the Lieutenant General concluded that it was not probable that the crash happened, but rather, inevitable. The Lieutenant General did not believe Corporal M was safe to navigate his spaceships in accordance with any Imperial standards and stated he was a high galactic space threat who may cause further damages or worse.

22

I'M GONNA THROW UP

The police called and told me to meet them at a place designed to talk to children.

The colorful designs in the lobby were off-putting to me because I knew the reason why we were here. The colors were supposed to make the children feel safer, but they made me feel nauseous.

They took Kay into a back room. "It's gonna be okay, I love you." Minutes again felt like hours, and my thoughts raced. Between the cheery safe colors and my jumbled thoughts, the room felt like it was spinning. A lump formed in my throat. I felt sick, and I couldn't breathe.

I ran to a door and pushed the metal horizontal bar with both hands. The sun blinded me for a second, my lungs hurt, and everything turned white. I thought I was going to pass out. One of the deputies on Kay's case came outside. "You okay?"

"Yeah, fine."

I had so many questions.

If both girls were in the house, why did only Kay come back positive? Did Moe purposefully get Kay high? Why was the bite on her lower abdomen? Why did he claim a dog did it? A dog would likely bite a child's face, hands, or limbs. It doesn't take a Sherlock Holmes investigator to know Moe likely bit Kay but why? If I bite myself, I might leave a small indentation of my teeth for a few minutes, but it wouldn't even bruise. How hard would someone have to bite to break skin all the way around in a circle? A bite like that would be complete loss of control. What could trigger someone to lose control like that? Could he have been that high? Pondering on it some more, I remembered that he just had surgery on his leg a few months ago; pain could make someone lose control. I imagined Kay accidentally hitting his fresh stitches. A sudden jolt of searing pain mixed with being high... but how did the bite end up on her lower abdomen? I don't think Cecilia witnessed it. Moe must have told her what happened. He fed her a lie. Their whole relationship was based on lies. What's one more?

I talked to the deputy about the case.

At some point, I asked if they could match the bite to one of the five people who were in the house at the time of the bite, Moe, Cecilia, Cecilia's pregnant sister, her boyfriend, or Mallory.

"This isn't CSI. We don't do that."

He told me that without Kay's confession, it was likely Moe was going to get away with it.

Get away with it?

I couldn't contain my thoughts, and everything spilled out at once. "But Moe confessed this happened at his house. You all know it's a human bite mark, you know Kay was coached... along with what he said and how Moe acted afterward. How can he just get away with it?"

He sighed. "Look, if you walked up to someone, shot them in the head, and no one else sees it, well you would probably get away with it. That's all I'm saying."

Bewildered, I just stared at him. Was that a joke? This didn't seem like the time or place to say such a thing.

Kay was inside getting questioned about a human bite she sustained, and this man, this officer, was telling me a person can get away with murder as long as there are no witnesses?

Everything around me faded into white.

We're in court. It's May 30, 2019, and Moe had hired a lawyer, Mr. Bladderwort. "My client needs to have time with his children, she is just alienating the children away from their father." The sound of the gavel hitting the wood echoed through the courtroom, hurting my ears.

May 30, 2019 Court Orders

1. After the minor children's interview with law enforcement and CAC, Father is to have 10 hours per week of professionally supervised visitation with the minor children at his expense.

2. Mother is to notify Father once the interviews have taken place.

The messages began to pour in on Talking Parents like a kid in the backseat asking are we there yet, are we there yet, are we there yet?

However, Moe wasn't even in California. He was in Tennessee and Illinois with his friends shooting RPKs, AR-15s, AK-47s, pistols, and various other guns from June 3 to June 27.

He took pictures holding the guns and made one his social media profile. Moe was standing with crazed eyes, mouth open, holding an assault rifle. He was wearing black American flag shorts with marijuana leaves as stars. Behind him hung the flag of Amsterdam in a small wooden room.

"The risk of femicide by an intimate partner increase by 500 percent when the abusive partner has access to a firearm."[1] I was entering into a situation where there was a high likelihood I might be killed.

By the first week of July, Moe already had chosen a supervised visitation provider and instructed me to contact him. At the bottom of the message, he wrote, "Thank you for your cooperation."

Moe frequently reminded me he got ten hours, and that his schedule was wide open. Yeah, wide open because Moe hadn't had a job since he quit the warehouse job last year so he could try and file a fake disability claim.

Moe told me he wanted this day and that day, at this time and that time, at this location then that location. He wanted to pick them up here, then drop them off over there. He said he's going to bring his parents, Cecelia, and Mallory. Moe liked to remind me that I "need to comply with the court orders and respond back to me within 24 hours" and my "cooperation is not only necessary, it's court ordered.'

He messaged me nearly every day multiple times. The day before my birthday, he said he was going to notify his lawyer about my noncompliance of not replying to all of his many messages, and he instructed me to "tell Kay and Anna that Daddy loves them. Thank you. Happy early birthday."

I felt sick.

On July 25, 2019, we had another court hearing. Mr. Bladderwort approached me in the court hallway. I had my paperwork laid out on a table.

He stared at the ground when he told me what Moe was requesting; that he have unsupervised visitation reinstated every first, third, and fifth weekend. He also was requesting makeup time for the no contact time.

Mr. Bladderwort stated I should agree to this, or things were going to get drawn out, and it's likely his request was going to be granted anyways. It felt like an or else threat but extremely passive aggressive.

Why would I ever agree to that request? It's absurd.

Had this man even read the CPS report? He couldn't even look at me in the eyes. I told him that I did not agree to his client's requests. During the court hearing, I poured out the findings of the CPS investigation, but it seemed all my comments fell on deaf ears.

Maybe Judge Mazle Dina is acting reserved because this information is for the trial. Cecilia and Moe's parents sat in the back scowling at me. This was probably the only court hearing where Moe came in business attire; he always wore the exact same blue flannel, jeans, and chucks. Today, he was wearing an ill-fitting suit, and a tie adorned in the center with his Purple Heart pin.

Moe wrote in his declaration, "I have a bachelor's degree in respiratory therapy and also while in the army as an artillery soldier, I was medically trained as a 'combat lifesaver' secondary to my combat position."

Whether that was true or not, that was fourteen to eighteen years ago. And why was he now masquerading as a medical professional... ask him how many days he worked as a respiratory therapist. Zero. Even his basic CPR card was probably four plus years expired, but yes, do tell.

Moe continued, "From that experience, I did not believe a doctor's visit was required."

Interesting, because the *actual* doctor said medical attention was required. Mr. Bladderwort maintained Moe's story "the dog did it."

Judge Mazle Dina looked at the picture of the bite and rolled her eyes. She stated she didn't believe Moe was being truthful about the bite because anyone with a pair of eyes balls could see this was not a dog bite. She asked if he had any other excuse to offer on how Kay sustained the bite. Moe doubled down.

Judge Mazle Dina didn't make any other comments on the subject and moved on.

I brought up my concern that Moe might have an assault rifle and wanted to meet up in a park alone.

She seemed angry that I even mentioned the word *gun,* and she said, "Well, you're not going to go to that park are you?"

Ah, yes, avoid public parks, that would save me. The problem was not the park, it was Moe. About the crazed picture he publicly posted, "He went back and added a comment boasting that it has more than fifty, less than a hundred rounds. Which again, is disconcerting to me that he would change the thing and..."

Judge Mazle Dina interrupted and yelled, "Is it really? Is the gun around the kids is he pointing at them with the gun? Is he threatening the kids with the gun? It's okay for him to own a weapon. You can own one too."

Great, let's all get guns! How would I know if he was threatening the girls with a gun when I didn't even know he had been telling them to forget everything that happened during his visitation time, and even if he did ever threaten the girls with a gun, she'd never believe me anyway. It would all be hearsay. There would have to be a bullet hole though one of the girls before she'd believe me.

Mr. Bladderwort seized the moment and accused me of possibly exposing Kay to marijuana because he had no information regarding my possible drug use.

This was his defense? If his client were to put a bullet in my head, his defense would probably be, "Well, I have no information proving it wasn't a ghost that shot Ms. Malvado. Even though my client was found with the same gun that matched the bullet, and there was DNA evidence to link him to the scene, you can't blame my client for shooting her because I never personally physically saw my client shoot her. It's a fact that ghosts have not been proven not to exist, therefore we cannot exclude that as a possibility. That information just can't be proven here today so case closed I think."

Mr. Bladderwort requested that the court restore the former visitation because now he accused me of manipulating CPS and police with no other intent but to deprive his client from visitation and alienate him from his daughters.

Was this guy serious?

Cue the tears; Moe started crying. Suddenly, he couldn't afford to pay both child support and pay for supervised visits, of which there had only been three.

Judge Mazle Dina changed the bulk of the supervised visits to be supervised by his parents to soothe his tears. I couldn't believe this performance was working on the judge. Moe switched again from crying to yelling and accused me of not responding to his messages. So, the judge ordered me to respond to his messages within ten hours of receipt. I know it might not seem like I tried, but I did. The court still seemed upset about the gun thing, like I was personally trampling on her Second Amendment rights. The air in American politics right now was extremely polarized. You are either A or B, and I must have struck a nerve. There was no steering that train around. I just wanted our girls to be safe.

July 25, 2019 Court Orders

1. Father visitation with the minor children shall be every Monday from 3pm until 6pm; every Wednesday from 3pm to 6pm, and every Saturday from 8am until 12pm.

2. The Monday and Wednesday visits are to be supervised by the paternal grandparents, and the Saturday visit shall be supervised by a professional monitor.

3. If the Father is more than 15 minutes late for a visit, the visit is canceled.

4. Custody exchanges are to be at McDonalds.

5. The parties are to respond to messages on Talking Parents within 10 hours of receipt if a response is necessary.

I walked out of the courtroom. The gun thing bothered me. If I was a mentally unhealthy individual, this could have easily translated "you can own one, too" to mean you should get a gun, too. Judge Mazle Dina didn't even address Moe's substance abuse issues or mental health before increasing his supervised visitation time. She still hadn't ordered him to take a drug test knowing Kay was positive. I didn't understand how increasing the frequency of exchanges to three times a week, every week was going to decrease conflict when we had issues at every exchange when they were ordered three times a month, on the first, third, and fifth weekends. Judge Mazle Dina knew this. That's now fourteen exchanges a month. Judge Mazle Dina then ordered his parents to supervise the bulk of them? The same people that came to every single court hearing and scowled at me and allowed their son to scream and cuss at me? If I was a mentally unhealthy individual and I perceived the courts were not going to protect our children, that the judge told me I should get a gun because it was up to me to protect our children… would a gun help the situation? Does research show that by owning a gun in a high conflict/abusive situation deescalates or resolves the situation?

"As an indication of the politicization of firearms, conservative legislators have occasionally attempted to increase abuse survivors' access to firearms, contrary to research findings that such measures would increase lethality to the abused individual, the survivor's children, and the broader community."[2]

- 30% of child firearm deaths under age 13 are connected to domestic violence (NIH)

- 50% of firearm deaths among women and girls are connected to domestic violence (Everytown/CDC)

- "Domestic dispute calls make up 41% of fatal calls for police" Department of Justice 2015–2016

"The risk of femicide by an intimate partner increase by 500 percent when the abusive partner has access to a firearm."[3]

I felt like I was entering into a situation where there's a high likelihood the girls or myself might be seriously harmed.

This felt like a set up.

23

PANDORA'S BOX

July 29, 2019

M oe started messaging me on Talking Parents every ten hours. "Seraphine I just want to remind you that you are well past the ten-hour mark to respond on Talking Parents. Your cooperation is necessary. This is not acceptable co-parenting. Thank you."

The very moment Judge Mazle Dina changed the professional supervisor over to his parents, chaos ensued. Pandora's box had been opened.

Moe immediately made the visitations supervised by his parents a family affair. He would bring at least four to seven other people with him.

What I couldn't understand was Cecilia and Moe's parents had heard from five separate sources a dog did not bite Kay. Yet, it didn't seem to matter who informed them it was a human bite or what proof was offered. They were all faithful to Moe's tale that the dog did it.

His parents allowed him to do the exchanges himself. He gave a small bag of candy or cheap ninety-nine cent toy to the girls after each supervised visit.

Moe shouted at me as his family and Cecilia circled around me and the girls with their phones out recording my every move. They'd move in closer and closer attempting to catch me reacting, so they can reverse it in court... look see what she did.

My level of anxiety was through the roof. I told Moe on Talking Parents that his family doesn't have my consent to record me, and they were making me extremely uncomfortable.

Moe answered that they were not breaking any laws, that "your comfortability isn't my concern," "I don't think you feel uncomfortable," and that he was instructed by his lawyer to film me for his protection.

How many different angles were needed for his protection? I thought that the supervised visitation exchanges of the girls were to be as peaceful and unprovoked as possible, yet, they were anything but. This wasn't right.

I scoured every court website link, every search engine to try to find something, anything with information about supervised visitations.

Either that information was restricted from public access, or it just simply did not exist. The only information provided on supervised visitation was the qualifications of the supervisor.

By August 1, 2019, Kay had started peeing herself during the supervised visits. Moe informed me of her accidents and said, "I always have panties just in case. She is wearing a pair of panties that I will need back on Saturday."

When I picked up the girls, Cecilia and his parents moved closer toward me, so I put my hand up politely signaling them to stop.

They didn't. Instead, they started waving their cell phones in my face.

Once safely in my van, I messaged Moe, "This behavior is unwanted and uninvited and is creating a hostile environment. Please stop."

They disagreed, the same behavior continued and only got worse.

Moe approached my vehicle. "I was hoping you would have brought the panties like you said you would. Thank you very much and have a blessed day. God be with you."

I asked him to please not approach my vehicle during the exchange and again asked him to stop recording me.

Moe said, "My parents and I do not need your consent. This is public property. If you feel any law has been broken, by all means, bring the police next time. I advise you not to, as we are doing nothing wrong. But by all means. Dial away. If you have concerns, contact my lawyer. I look forward to your cooperation. We will still record. End of discussion."

Moe started pulling his vehicle directly alongside mine. I moved parking spaces. He followed. Today, before Moe handed the girls back, he yanked them back and kissed them on the mouth while he stared at me. All cameras on me the entire time.

After the exchange on August 5, 2019, Anna blurted out, "We talk a lot about you, Mommy."

I don't know why I even brought it up because Moe's response was, "If you have concerns, contact my lawyer."

Moe's parents still let Moe do the exchanges on his own. He continued to yank the girls and kiss them on the mouth while maintaining eye contact on me, so I asked, "Next Monday, please have either of your parents handle the exchange."

He noted, "My mother has recordings of these exchanges, would you like to view them, or should I submit them to court, so Judge Mazle Dina can see that you are causing problems. We have recordings for the last two years, care to view them?"

Moe's mother Edith was so preoccupied recording me that she couldn't even hold the girls' hands when they ran across the busy parking lot. A car nearly struck Anna.

I was trying to juggle my work schedule around this chaotic supervised visitation schedule. Moe asked if he could have extra time with the girls later that week. "We should be willing to co-parent, work together, and be willing to compromise with each other. It shouldn't be one sided. It is my birthday, Seraphine. I'd love to spend more time with the girls on Saturday. Please be willing to do this, not just for me but for them.'

That same day he sent me that message, August 15, 2019, Tony Malta had to conduct the exchange. Moe refused to allow the girls to leave with him claiming he was uncomfortable.

Moe called the police and told them no third parties were allowed to pick up the girls. Moe threatened to take the girls back to his house before he realized that he didn't have any car seats, so he just made them sit in his trunk for two hours until the police arrived.

In reality, law enforcement does not seem to want to be involved in any domestic affairs, and nine out of ten times they are going to tell you "this is a civil matter" and walk away. I have heard that so many times I've lost count. Then when I would go to civil court, they would tell me that it's a criminal matter, and the police would deal with it.

It was like a never-ending game of ping pong. Neither side was going to do anything. They're just going to toss the ball into the other court.

After that, Cecilia tried to provoke me by moving closer and closer to me with her cell phone at the exchanges.

Less than a week later, on August 21, Moe called the police to do a wellness check at my house because he wanted to know if I owned a cat. Anna had gotten a scratch on her arm at her preschool from playing outside. However, Moe claimed he received conflicting stories.

I assumed Moe was trying to collaborate his dog bite story by somehow creating a cat scratch story.

"I did not give you two conflicting stories. I told you Anna came home today from school, and I saw the scratches. I also noticed she was itchy and was scratching, so I put both Anna and Kay in the bathtub. You claimed it to be a lie, made up a different story, and then called the police, again."

Moe added, "Cat scratch fever is serious."

He also claimed they were both "dirty" and "filthy."

Their hair was still wet from their bath. It was like whatever I did he claimed the opposite. He claimed Anna had told him it was really a cat and asked if I was going to take her to the doctors.

Moe wrote, "So, I ask again for the truth before I make any calls." Implying the threat that he was going to turn CPS on me.

Moe then wrote that he had taken pictures of Anna and sent them to his lawyer. "I am waiting on a response as to what step to take next, so before we take any steps, I am asking you as their mother, my coparent, what happened to our daughter." I didn't respond.

He told me if I had just answered him, he wouldn't have had to call the police. Moe said, "I did not call cps, I called the Sheriffs to do a wellness check."

Moe wrote pages and pages about the scratch that he was now calling a "gash" and stated the cop informed him of a man down my street with a dog. "What about the friend that lives down the street, the man with the dog?"

I truly had no idea what he was ranting about, but one thing he said seemed especially concerning, "and none of them looked clean. You said you gave them a bath, but both our daughters were completely filthy, I gave them basically a complete wipe down with baby wipes."

What? So, during his three-hour supervised visit, he gave her a bath in McDonalds?

August 28, 2019

I filed another ex parte to seek help and bring a stop to this chaos. Moe was back to his casual attire, no suit, or Purple Heart pin today. His whole family showed up as usual to glare at me.

I sat alone in the hall with my face buried in my paperwork. Moe did his little peacock strut back and forth in front of me just to make sure I knew he's here. Ugh.

We got inside the courtroom, and I communicated all the things that had happened since July to Judge Mazle Dina.

She immediately dismissed and minimized the issues. "I didn't see really anything new."

So, all of this was normal? This wasn't normal. This was chaos!

Judge Mazle Dina continued. "I've already structured this. That protects the minors."

Judge Mazle Dina only commented on the issue of him bathing the girls during the supervised visitation. "You are not allowed to take their clothes off and wipe them with baby wipes all over the place. I'm just telling you, let's talk logic. You don't take your little girls' clothes off at a McDonald's and wipe them down with baby wipes."

Judge Mazle Dina then said, "He needs to have frequent ongoing contact."

I kinda snapped, "He doesn't even utilize the professional supervisor visit on Saturdays." He wasn't paying child support or paying the professional supervisor. "With the professional supervisor, he behaves, and nothing happens during that time. When the parents are doing the exchanges, they have no control over the exchange at all. They try to provoke incidents," I said.

Judge Mazle Dina snapped back at me, "You are being vague and unreasonable right now."

I shut down. I was just seeking peaceful exchanges. I tried to move on because it seemed she had no issues with how his parents conducted the exchanges.

"Can we ask that they not video record me at every exchange and put cameras in my face?"

Judge Mazle Dina denied my request. "They are allowed to video record everything. And so are you."

With her final words, she offered Moe some advice. "And remember, if you are not getting a professional, it is going to be very difficult for me to change visitation without it." Attorney Bladderwort interrupted, but Judge Mazle Dina continued. "Because that was the rule, so I can have some feedback."

I just walked out feeling defeated and unheard. *I guess she needed more proof,* I thought. I began recording them recording me, so I could bring Judge Mazle Dina more proof with the hope she would put this chaos to an end.

August 28, 2019 Court Orders

Third parties can handle exchanges of minors with notice to the other parent

Father to have visitation as follows: Monday and Wednesday from 4pm to 7pm supervised by paternal grandfather

Saturday visitation is to be supervised by a professional monitor from 8am to 12pm

"Seraphine, is that you?" I was so lost in thought I didn't even notice him. "Jacques?" He had on grey slacks, a white button-down shirt with a sweater vest overtop while wearing a grey Moto jacket. A scarf covered his neck. "I haven't seen you in years. How have you been?" I've known Jacques ever since I can remember.

"I've been good," he replied.

I asked, "What are you doing here?" He had these pensive eyes that felt like they could penetrate through your soul. He looked like he could be a French male model.

"I am conducting some research on some legal matters. What are you doing here?"

I sighed. "That's a long story."

Jacques said, "I was actually heading out to get a bite to eat. Join me?"

Moe stood down the hall, staring. Jacques asked, "Is that your ex?"

I responded, "Ya." Jacques' mouth didn't open as a low tonal mmm came from his throat. He stared back showing no emotion as he did a quick head to toe. Jacques then said, "Come, let's get out of here, fill me in on everything." We walked down to a local diner. I told him everything.

"So, she dismissed everything you had to say," he replied.

"Maybe I just didn't have enough evidence."

After a long stare, he said, "Well, we'll give her so much evidence she can choke on it, but first things first, you need to prepare for that trial."

"Okay."

As we departed ways, Jacques said, "Please call me and inform me on what happens."

Nothing changed over the next month before the trial, and the girls were deteriorating under the stress. I had to watch as they lost a little bit of their light. They laughed less. They talked less. I felt like I was watching their souls be ripped apart from their bodies. This felt worse than the months after the initial bite. I can't protect them, and every supervised visit after felt like we were sinking deeper into a hole.

If anything, Moe was becoming bolder, and so was his family.

When we had professional supervised visits, Moe would wait inside McDonalds as the guy did the exchange. He was completely different when his parents did the exchanges.

Moe began utilizing the paid visits a little bit more due to what the judge had said. Yet, when his parents supervised, it was still chaos.

Jacques called me to check-in. "How's everything going?"

"Same. Worse. Cecilia came the other day as the supervisor."

"What?"

"She shouted at me. Everybody knows minute orders are not real court orders Sera-phine!"

"Are you serious? How dumb is this girl?" Jacques said.

I said, "Very, but are you really surprised? I didn't have the energy to explain, so I just said that she was incorrect and that she could not be the substitute-acting supervisor for the day.

"She then told me 'I have more than a legal right to be here these are going to be my stepchildren I am very much allowed to be here.'"

"I'm sorry, what? The audacity of that girl!" His voice trailed off as he mumbled to himself before he got silent then blurted, "So wait, what did you say?"

"I just left, and no visit happened."

Jacques said, "As you should, this is crazy, the minute orders are still enforceable court orders, and they must abide by them. I don't understand how they think they can just do whatever they want and disregard the court orders. Does he do this often?"

"Yes, unfortunately. I tried to ask Moe ahead of time if the court ordered supervisor, his father, was going to be present at the exchange to conduct the visit. He just said that it is my responsibility to show up with the girls regardless. Or he just lies or simply refuses to answer."

"This is just a game to him," Jacques said.

"It feels like he's just ramping up, too. It's all just escalating," I said.

"I'm sorry you and the girls are going through this. Document everything, and I'll touch base with you later, chin-up, you got this. You are going to be okay, okay?"

"Okay, thank you. Talk to you soon." I hung up.

Between managing the exchanges three times a week, working three twelve-hour shifts a week, and preparing for the trial, I was exhausted.

Jacques and I made a list of questions to ask during the trial. The option of getting a lawyer was just too expensive for me at that time. I looked. In one of the consultations, the lawyer stopped me and said, "Look, I don't think you need me, if you explain to the court the way you did right now, I don't see any problem. You are well spoken and seemingly well informed." The going bid to hire a lawyer for the trial was ten thousand dollars.

Moe still gave the girls small bags of candy or a tiny toy when the exchanges occurred. Moe then started accusing me of improperly dressing the girls and would have to re-dress them in what he thought was proper clothes. September 21, 2019, Moe messaged me, "Good morning, Seraphine. I put a pair of shorts on Kay this morning. Could you please return them Monday along with the undies I put on Anna two weeks ago? Thank you and have a good day. Also, could you dress Kay in pants/shorts, she trips on the long dresses, and I don't want her getting hurt."

Moe would inspect their bodies for bruises or scrapes and would photograph them. He would send me some of the pictures that he had taken over time.

On October 14, 2019, Moe messaged me that Kay got slime on her shorts and that her panties smelled like mildew, so he had to change them. He then asked, "Please bring the shorts and panties to the next visitation."

The day before the trial when I went to get the girls, Moe was kneeling down on the ground crying at the exchange. He had a tight grip on their wrists holding them in front of him. The girls were crying… I didn't know what was going on. He gave them each another ninety-nine-cent toy and some candy before releasing them.

By the time Anna got into my vehicle, she was sobbing. As we were driving home, Anna said, "God has to kill me, so I can be a part of Daddy's family. God needs to kill me to get the bad seeds out. I need to die to be a part of Daddy's family. When I'm dead, I'm gonna miss you. I'm going to miss you, Mommy."

When we got home, I just sat and held Anna. "You're not going to die. There are no bad seeds in you. I love you so much, baby."

The girls fell asleep in my bed. I couldn't sleep.

It's the night before the trial, Jacques texts me, "Remember it's just a matter of perspective. You are an experienced ICU RN. What I mean is you are capable of not only sustaining the life of your patients, anticipate the needs of the doctors, advocate for your families but also you are an active voice in rounds. Just picture the courtroom like rounds with the team of doctors. They both have their quality measures and protocols to cover. Wait for your time to speak. That's when you deliver. If you are able to have multiple attending physicians hear and respect you, then the judge will, too."

I was still trying to process everything, so I just said, "Thank you."

24

REMEMBER THE RULE

The big day arrived. Today was the day of our trial concerning the human bite mark and marijuana found in Kay. I still had Anna's words swirling in my head. I wore a full black suit and with my hair up in a bun. I sat in the audience behind the lawyers waiting to be called up. Moe strolled in wearing his usual uniform of a blue flannel long-sleeve shirt, jeans, and chucks.

When our trial began, Attorney Bladderwort handed new evidence to Judge Mazle Dina but did not provide me a copy.

I said, "I haven't received a copy."

Judge Mazle Dina watched but made no comment while Mr. Bladderwort shuffled around some paper pretending to look for another copy.

"Well, one came to the court I'm sure because the..." His voice trailed off.

Judge Mazle Dina jumped in. "Is there an extra copy?"

She continued. "The findings and order after hearing documents the orders that were previously made for the supervised visitation. Monday, Wednesday, and Saturdays. It appears to conform with the court orders that are current."

Attorney Bladderwort replied, "May I address that, Your Honor?"

"Sure."

He never handed me copy, and they continued on as if that just wasn't important anymore. He had a way of speaking that made you feel like you're drowning in his speech. It's an endless wave of words told just above a dry whisper in complete monotone. Each sentence lapped against my ears like waves in an ocean that bring only a sense of seasickness.

He went on and on talking about the schedule and the visitations. It was difficult for me to fully concentrate because I was so in my own head with Anna's words still sharply floating in my head. I had all my questions written out. I had prepared for trial for weeks, but it was hard to focus. I practiced what I was going to say, how I was going to say it, and my paperwork was filed perfect. I felt sick.

Of course, this would happen the day of the trial.

"Ms. Maldavo, you understand that he is asking a 730 evaluation for a psychiatrist to do an analysis of the family along with psychological testing?"

Attorney Bladderwort had just made a comment questioning my motives, "Mother alleges Father has mental health issues. We believe that there are serious questions regarding the motivations in the approach the mother is taking to this case that are detrimental to the child."

This miscreant was using a ploy to shift the blame off his client but how was he going to explain how he was literally being paid by the VA to stand here and spew this nonsense? Where did you think your client got his money when he doesn't have a job? He got $1,800 a month because he's 70 percent disabled with PTSD, so I'm not alleging anything.

But that's his job. Discredit the advocate, a.k.a. the accuser, and then introduce a new suspect to take the blame for his client's misdeeds, me.

Take the high road, Seraphine.

"I have no history of any mental illness," I said.

Judge Mazle Dina explained it's an evaluation for both of us, that it's for the girls, and that teachers, therapist, and social workers are going to be asking questions for an overall evaluation of the family, and that I would be required to pay half.

Knowing that these evaluations could cost anywhere from $5,000 to $10,000, I reminded the court of the continued financial strain because Moe was refusing to pay any child support.

Judge Mazle Dina asked, "Is that true you don't pay child support?"

Moe whined. "Your Honor, I had to choose between seeing my girls with a professional supervisor in the last two months of supervised child support."

The truth was he rarely utilizes the paid supervised visits because he was using the money that was supposed to go to our girls to pay his lawyer.

Judge Mazle Dina rolled her eyes. "I have a feeling that this is a historical problem. So, she can't right now, she's not getting any child support."

She threw in a jab at me, "which I wouldn't use to pay for a 730 because the child support is to support the children. So, I mean…"

I wanted to roll my eyes so bad because why did she fall for his sub-pair dramatic performance on July 25 if it was such a "historical problem?" She didn't have any questions or concerns then.

The Court allowed me to speak, so I began diving in the issues at hand: the human bite, marijuana found in Kay's hair follicle test, and the professional reports.

Mr. Bladderwort then interjected, minimized the marijuana found in Kay's system. "It is of such a tiny amount that someone could have blown smoke in her hair and that's how it came to pass."

In attempts to defend Kay, I said, "She is five years old. She shouldn't have tested positive for marijuana at all."

Judge Mazle Dina yelled at me, "And you are interrupting because?" Drawing out the word b-e-c-a-u-s-e.

She let Mr. Bladderwort continue. "And Mr. Malvado did smoke. And I think a number of people who have PTSD or aches and pains do that as a successful way of avoiding opiates. I think it's reasonable to believe that either Mom or Dad was around at a place where there was some smoke, and the child's hair was exposed to the smoke. There is no adjusting. That's clearly off the table. But for the sins that brought this to the court, to have Mr. Malvado restricted so much, I think are resolved."

Judge Mazle Dina nodded in approval then moved onto a different topic.

Whenever I attempted to bring up anything pertaining to the CPS report and the human bite mark found on Kay, Judge Mazle Dina completely shut down the conversation or refused to respond.

I informed Judge Mazle Dina. "It should be noted that Anna was exposed to drugs in an unhealthy environment. This was based by the father's own admission that he was under the influence of prescription medications and marijuana while providing care and supervision his children." Crickets.

I continued and said that CPS was "worried that the father will fail to provide adequate supervision to the children, which could result in them being injured or worse. The forensic medical examiner said that because of the mental health illnesses and substance abuse, that this was not a probable event that this was inevitable. And if we are not correcting either of those, then that means that this abuse will continue to happen to these two girls."

Judge Mazle Dina's only response was "okay."

I kinda thought she'd have more to say than "okay." I continue. "If that is not possible, then it has to be a supervised visitation with a professional because the parents do not... they have no control over him."

I told Judge Mazle Dina, "In the CPS report, it repeatedly said, I'm the only protective parent. That I was cooperating with them. And that there was nothing on my side that would have caused issues. However, there were numerous issues in the father's household from the initial visit. Him slamming the door in CPS's face and saying that the person doesn't live there. And doing all these weird erratic things even with a professional. He acts like this with police and CPS. So, it's not just me that he is acting very aggressive and erratic toward."

There was no response from Judge Mazle Dina.

Is she smiling? Why is she smiling? Did I say something funny.

When the subject of his mental health was brought up, I said, "I don't know what psychiatric issues are going on. I know he is diagnosed with PTSD."

Judge Mazle Dina said, "But aren't you speculating about his mental health just as it would be unfair for him to speculate about your mental health."

"It is not speculation. He was diagnosed."

But she already knew that because Moe yelled in open court on January 31, 2018, "I have PTSD!" Not to mention Mr. Bladderwort just supported that his client was diagnosed with PTSD to excuse his drug use not more than fifteen minutes ago, "I think a number of people who have PTSD or aches, and pains do that as a successful way of avoiding opiates." Suddenly, she had amnesia and was just ignoring those details? Was she really going to sitting up there accusing me of being "unfair" and "speculating?" In addition, the CPS reported Moe admitted to multiple other mental health issues. So, again… wtf? If these issues weren't arising from mental health issues or substance abuse issues, then was Judge Mazle Dina suggesting Moe's behavior was normal?

Judge Mazle Dina never questioned Moe about the human bite mark, nor did she allow me the time to question him either. She just made a statement, "I mean, the bite thing still bothers me, don't get me wrong, because I don't think there has been honesty with that," then moved on.

I thought this was a trial on the CPS and law enforcement findings, but instead, the bulk of the "trial" Judge Mazle Dina diverted to talk about the issues I had filed in the ex parte back in August that she originally minimized and dismissed. I'm confused, but I've never been in a trail before maybe this was how they go. I don't know.

Judge Mazle Dina went on to list all the problems that I had brought up on August 28, 2019, validating them one by one.

To the issue of Moe withholding the girls, Judge Mazle Dina said, "It shouldn't have been any big deal for him (Tony) to go pick up the kids. But, instead, Mr. Malvado, you withhold the kids and insist that mother come and get them because he is one or two boyfriends ago. I mean, that's incredibly rude." She noted the issues with all of the additional family members at the exchanges and the cameras being held in my face. "How come he brings all these people with him to his visits? It's causing chaos and it makes the children feel that father doesn't care about them when he has all these other distractions."

Judge Mazle Dina stared at the evidence. "Who is the person that is holding the camera in your pictures during the exchanges? Why is this person holding a camera up on every picture? Let's not gloss over it because how uncomfortable is this for the kids to have somebody that is supposed to be a person that they respect and obey and a parent figure to hold up a camera on their mom or even on the dad questioning their ability to parent. So why are we making all this so much more stressful. It's almost like, go ahead and do something wrong. I have you on film."

Exactly what I was saying a month ago, and it hasn't stopped.

Judge Mazle Dina sighed. "I'm just letting you know what I think because right now, based on the reports, I can't un-supervise your visits. Because of the behavior, and all the people, and the chaos. And you should put your foot down on all of this." *Wait, what did she just say? She wants Moe to govern his own actions? Hasn't he proved he can't?*

Moe replied confused, "Foot down on what, Your Honor?" He didn't see anything wrong with any of his actions. *He doesn't see anything wrong with his actions, and she wants him to self-regulate?*

Judge Mazle Dina said, "On all the people. All the behavior. The screaming. And now the stories that they are telling when they get to their mom's." If no interventions were provided and Moe didn't recognize any of his behaviors were wrong or couldn't even grasp the fact any of his behavior was detrimental to the girls, how was anything expected to change?

Maybe she needed a reminder that these issues were continuing to happen during the paternal parents supervised visitations yet there were no issues if and when the professional monitor conducted the supervised visitations which was why I requested him solely last time.

So, I said, "During the visitations, there are still numerous issues. I will drive down to Colton. But he will not have adequate supervision. I would then be met by the girlfriend that tells me, "she is soon to be their stepmom. And so, she has more than a legal right to be there.'"

Again, noting the parents had no control, allowed, and even contributed to the chaos during the exchanges. Our daughters and myself had the right to neutral exchanges during supervised visits, and I suggested a professional monitor other than his parents be utilized.

"Well, there's a lot of animosity between the families, I'm certain," Judge Mazle Dina said. She remained steadfast to her prior decision and refused to change the supervised visit supervisor to a neutral third party, yet, she also knew his parents could not be impartial.

My head was spinning, didn't she just scold them? Didn't she just note how uncomfortable that made me feel? Didn't she also note how rude it was for them to withhold the girls? Shouldn't he get in trouble for withholding the girls during a supervised visit? It was all so confusing.

Judge Mazle Dina then announced, "Honestly, I don't have any issue with your client's parents. There is nothing documented here that indicates they are interfering with the parent's ability to co-parent."

It was like a bomb exploded in my head. There was nothing documented. She just pointed out a whole list of issues. Our ability to co-parent? That's not even relevant right now.

Why was she insisting on pushing the narrative of co-parenting when Moe was currently on supervised visitation and even that wasn't going well.

Judge Mazle Dina then acted perplexed by the whole case. "I don't even know if the supervised visits are helping. I mean, I've never been under the circumstance where supervised time with the offending parent hasn't restored the relationship."

What was she talking about? So, what's the plan? Do nothing? Didn't she realize the girls were withering away? Their smiles were slowly fading, and that spark of life that used to shine was flickering.

Panic set in and the words of Anna ran through my head, and I started to cry. I told the court when I picked the girls up yesterday, Anna told me, "God has to kill me, so I can be a part of Daddy's family. I have to die, so I can be part of his family. God has to kill me to take the bad seeds out of me. And I've been I'm going to miss you, Mommy, when I'm gone."

Judge Mazle Dina seemed annoyed. "Did they go to church and there was some kind of weird sermon or something?"

"No," I cried. *What was she taking about?*

Mr. Bladderwort interjected. "I'm going to object as hearsay, Your Honor."

Judge Mazle Dina yelled down at me, "Ma'am, did you do any of those things that are called 'co-parenting?'"

She continued. "And the kids are probably questioned after the visit. And your daughter saying something to you yesterday that means there is one thing for her to have a safe place to express her views about dad or why she's afraid of death or this conversation you had. Ultimately, you can probably turn it around to a healthy conversation instead of a scary one. But that should be shared with dad. You know, the question should be asked." She suggested that I should have said to Moe, "She brought up death tonight after your visit. Do you know what happened? Did somebody mention that an animal died or something? And get to the bottom of it so you can have a healthy conversation instead of you being upset and then claiming he need a mental health evaluation."

Ignoring the fact Judge Mazle Dina was making assumptions and accusing me of questioning the girls, I replied, "It's not just one thing, it's just repeated things that our kids say. And you're correct, Your Honor, I need to work on communicating these questions and stuff, but it seems like every single time I ask something I will tell him something and he says, 'No, you are lying. This isn't true.' Like he asked about the scratch on her arm, and I said, 'She got it at school.' And then he ended up calling the police and doing a wellness check at my home because he said that he had conflicting stories. Yet, I only said one thing, and then he makes up this entire fantasy story of something else. So, it is challenging for me to try to communicate. And when every single time it is difficult, or it's met with aggression."

Dismissing the topic, Judge Mazle Dina said, "Okay. Well, you both need to take a parenting class."

Parenting class? A parenting class isn't going to fix this! These are not normal problems. The words seemed to blurt out of my mouth, "He is still removing and changing their clothes. He also took her panties off and said they smelled like mildew."

Mr. Bladderwort yelled, "Your Honor, this is really…"

Judge Mazle Dina cut off Mr. Bladderwort. "Isn't this the couple where I told you that you're not allowed to undress the minors at the visit? I already admonished you regarding taking the girls' clothes off and wiping them down with baby wipes. I already talked to you about it of how inappropriate that was. They don't need to take their clothes off in the bathrooms, especially in public bathrooms. So, I've mentioned these things."

Mr. Bladderwort started fumbling around trying to explain and then stated his client's parents will pay for the 730 evaluation subject to reallocation before veering off on a different topic.

Mr. Bladderwort ranted on trying to dig his client out of the hole, and I can't help but to emotionally respond; it's now just a total shit show.

My eyes started to lose focus, my hands were shaking. "The girls are coming back, and they are saying these crazy things. Moe says that 'Mommy and Tony are liars.' And that 'Tony is not a real daddy.' He told them that one of my friends had punched him in the eye so they will start being physically aggressive if I'm dating somebody. He told them, 'It's six o'clock. It's time to forget.' He told them to lie to me about the bite."

Judge Mazle Dina put her hand up gesturing me to stop. "At this point, you are just telling me things that the kids have said to you, which is hearsay." She looked at Mr. Bladderwort. "Mr. Bladderwort, quite frankly I think the visitations need to continue as supervised because I don't know where this stuff comes from."

Mr. Bladderwort replied, "I don't think it's true. I would have to believe that mother makes this up out of the air."

Judge Mazle Dina agreed.

I snapped back. "I'm not making this up because it's written in the CPS report."

She smiled as I continued on. "Also that he is telling the children to lie to me. And he lied to the CPS worker about drug usage. He lied to the CPS worker that he had no prior history of substance abuse."

Mr. Bladderwort put his arms up and smugly said, "At the end of the day, if we spend all day trying this case, the court will know that CPS has closed all of the investigation. They are all closed. All of the CPS investigations are closed. The other problem is just this horrible inability to work with each other to and not affect the children. I believe it is seriously affecting the children. I think the only way to get to the bottom of that is the 730 evaluation."

Judge Mazle Dina replied, "I can tell you reading the reports that there are problems with the kids. I don't need a 730 evaluation to tell me that."

Her voice got louder. "I mean, they are screaming during the visits and there is problem with the exchange."

She was yelling at us now, "I've told you guys this before, the kids are going to end up in foster care and they are going to end up being removed from both of you if you can't co-parent!"

She noted how the girls are screaming in the reports and went on to say that if she was in the McDonalds, "I would have gone to a manager and asked them to be removed." *She would have what?*

Mr. Bladderwort saw his opportunity to save the judge and blamed me by noting it was my fault the children behaved this way with his client. "Does that fall on dad's side? I think it's a child who, if raised 90% of the time in moms' home, needs to have some more built-in control."

Judge Mazle Dina nodded. "And it's the same admonition to her. You are allowing your kids to run amuck at McDonald's, that means you are doing it at home."

Mr. Bladderwort tried to push his luck and attempted to minimize the girls' behavior during Moe's supervised visitation time. "But as I read the report, the only issue seems to be that this child sometimes goes out of control."

Judge Mazle Dina responded, "Oh, that's not the only issue, Mr. Bladderwort. We have an unexplained bite mark, we have marijuana use by the petitioner, we have marijuana discovered in hair follicle of the minor, we have CPS reports, now I'm hearing about dirty smelly underwear and changing their clothes during the visits."

Judge Mazle Dina scolded me. "And, ma'am please put yourself in check in the sense of making allegations, throwing out allegations, without having evidence. Right now, I have no evidence that he needs a mental health evaluation. There is nothing before me that says that any of these things are preventing him from becoming a good parent."

But then Judge Mazle Dina ordered the 730 evaluation. I just stood there. Everything I said after this point was immediately shot down by the court.

Judge Mazle Dina shifted in her seat. "So I want to, I'm going to close this out and talk to him about expanding his parenting time until you come back. Because I would like to re-instate your overnights, you know? I would like to do that but you're also not paying child support, which is weird. And I don't know why."

No parenting class was ordered, and the only question the court asked Moe was "Is the dog still at your house?" Yet, she didn't believe it was a dog bite nor did the forensic examiner report say it was a probable dog bite. In fact, he stated the opposite and so did she... so why would she ask that?

Did she even read the report? Did she even care about our girls? Again, I felt like I was living in some version of the Twilight Zone. Her words echoed in my head, how was I to blame for how our daughters behaved during his supervised visitation time? She said she would have gone to the McDonald's manager and asked the girls to be removed from the McDonalds? Was she blaming the girls? The children she is supposed to be protecting. She's a judge, it's her duty to protect their safety, welfare, and health.

Crack! She slammed her gavel down. I stood there, stunned. Judge Mazle Dina grabbed her papers and walked back to her private chambers. Moe and Mr. Bladderwort shuffled out behind me.

October 15, 2019 Trial

The request for EC 730 evaluation is granted. Each party is ordered to cooperate. Petitioner to advance the cost, subject to reallocation. Parties are to provide each other with three names of potential evaluators.

Father visitation with the minor children shall
be every Monday from 4pm to 7pm supervised by a
professional.

Every Wednesday from 4pm to 7pm supervised by
one of the parental grandparents.

Every Saturday from 8am to 12pm supervised by
one of the paternal grandparents.

Alternating Sundays from 8am to 12pm supervised
by one of the paternal grandparents, commencing
October 20, 2019.

Visitations are to take place in a public setting such as a park, library, or restaurant for
example.

Cecilia is not to be present at the visitation
exchanges.

I don't remember walking out of the courthouse. I was just suddenly outside walking in the direction of my van. I could only hear
the clicking of my heels. The sun cast shadows of the trees along the
sidewalk. I called Jacques. As soon as he answered, I said, "I don't
know what happened."

"Tell me," Jacques said.

"I thought you were supposed to ask questions during a trial. I
thought you were supposed to go over the evidence."

"Well, didn't you?" Jacques asked.

"I tried to go over the CPS reports, but the court didn't make
any comments on them. When she did comment, it was extremely
dismissive."

Jacques said, "So, she was stonewalling you?"

"No, the court just withheld any comments on it to hear me
out, I guess."

With the tone he used, I could just imagine Jacques rolling his eyes thinking ya, so she was stonewalling you… instead he said, "Okay, what else happened?"

"Well, then she validated all the issues I brought up at the ex parte a month ago."

"Good, she finally held him accountable then," Jacques said.

"Well, no, not exactly. The court suggested he regulate his own actions, basically the court doesn't think he has any mental health issues that she sees as problematic and that I was making everything up."

Jacques said, "So, the court simply ignored the CPS report where he admitted to having mental health issues, and the fact he is 70 percent disabled with PTSD? I suppose the court also expects him to adhere to her unreasonable expectations of self-control. It's not like he's been displaying obsessive and compulsive behaviors."

"She then criticized me for not co-parenting," I added.

"Your ability to co-parent? You two are so far from a co-parenting arrangement. He's on supervised visitations! A co-parenting parenting arrangement 'requires two parents who are able to maintain a civil and child-focused relationship post-separation. Ideally, there should be mutual trust and respect that promotes good communication between parents.'[1]

"In fact, 'Co-parenting is contra-indicated by high conflict and/ or incidents of family violence, before, during or after the separation, or lack of a foundation of any relationship between the parents. These contra-indications are usually demonstrated by a clear history of poor communication, coercive interactions, inability to problem-solve, and a lack of child-centered focus by one or both parents. A serious mental health problem or substance abuse suffered by one or both parents would also contra-indicate a co-parenting arrangement.'[2]" Jacques was on a roll, he continued.

"She sounds like she doesn't know anything about parenting arrangements because even parallel parenting would be contraindicated because 'Parallel parenting assumes that each parent has a positive contribution to make in his or her time with the children, but any direct parent-parent contact may be harmful to the children due to ongoing acrimony. This acrimony may be based on mutual mistrust, personality conflict, or inability of one or both parents to move past the separation and focus on the future. Any clinical or legal finding that one parent poses a physical, sexual, or emotional threat to the children, or that there are concerns of violence towards the other parent, would contra-indicate a parallel parenting arrangement.'[3] Yet, she is recommending you two co-parents while *he* is on supervised visits?" He scoffed, "What a joke."

"She said our girls are going to end up in foster care, and they are going to end up being removed from both of us if we can't co-parent!"

Jacques responded, "She said what? So, she threatened you because that comment holds as much water as a colander."

"The court stated that there was nothing before her that is preventing him from becoming a good parent, and she increased his visitation time and decreased the professional supervised monitors time," I said.

Jacques said, "Nothing? Really? So, this is all just 'normal' behavior? Now I felt like I am going crazy. Didn't she just validate that there are extensive issues happening during Moe's supervised visitations including withholding, bring excessive people to the visitation, harassment, intimidation, excessive use of cameras, removing the minor children's clothes and inappropriately giving them 'baths' in a public space. Not to mention she just implied the issues are so grave the girls are going to end up in foster care! I don't understand, she says things that demonstrates she is aware of abuse however is simultaneously also denying it. And why would the court decrease the professional supervised monitor, he is providing the reports she claimed she needed because that's 'the rule.' She knew that Moe rarely utilized the professional supervisor, and she reduced the paid professional supervisor visitation time thus diminishing the professional reports that she stated were a requirement to expanding his visitation time.

With less reports, less things will be reported, though."

Jacques paused. "I don't have a good feeling about this, Seraphine. She increased his visitations despite all the issues?"

"Yes, she expanded his visitation time from six hours to eleven hours and increased the visits from three to four times a week. That's now eight possible exchanges a week, with the alternating Sunday... that's now thirty exchanges a month."

Jacques replied, "You and the girls are being exploited by them for their own gains... the court is erroneously portraying themselves to have altruistic motives, but I think she is just trying to break you like you're a wild horse. I, uh, have to go... I have to... I need to do a little research. I'll call you back later."

He hung up before I could respond.

25

I DON'T CONSIDER THAT A PROBLEM

Later, people would tell me it probably went so badly because I didn't have an attorney, but honestly, I don't think it would have mattered. The next day, Wednesday, we had a supervised visitation scheduled.

Nothing changed. His parents continued to record me, still allowed him to conduct the exchanges, and Moe continued to yell at me during exchanges. Cecilia still continued to be present at the visitations, and additionally, he wanted every exchange to be at separate locations that he chose.

I had learned that if there was any way for Moe to manipulate the court orders, he would. Moe claimed Cecilia wasn't "exchanging the girls," therefore, she wasn't "at the exchange."

Moe wrote on Talking Parents, "She is not to be a part of the exchanges, she was about fifty yards away. Which is following the court orders." He was exaggerating her distance.

I said, "That's not true. She was right there."

Again, I searched on Google, looked on court websites, everywhere that might have information. The information was mostly about the supervisor and even that was minimal… basically they must have a driver's license and not be a convict. I did find a power point on ncjfcj.org, one slide was on supervised visitation. To summarize, it stated that the children need to benefit from contact, the behavior needs to be monitored by appropriate staff, the court should specify time/place, and the rules of conduct must be followed. Okay, but what *are* the *rules of conduct* for him exactly?

No visitation would then be appropriate if: no willingness to change is displayed by the abusive parent, abusive parent fails to abide by court orders or standards of conduct, and no meaningful parent-child contact seems possible.

Well, Moe didn't follow any of the court orders, his behavior had not changed just intensified, and having the girls sob after supervised visits wasn't demonstrating meaningful parent-child… it was traumatizing them.

None of this was right. I felt like I was going insane. I started having immense ear pain, any sound was agonizing. Maybe I should get noise canceling headphones to block the sounds. Sometimes, movies helped my mind to zone out.

My mom came over and wanted to ask me questions, but just the sound of her voice made me want to cut my ears off.

I dreamed about getting a depravation tank to block it all out. Floating in warm, dark nothingness. It cost ten thousand to thirty thousand dollars to buy my own… ugh. A standard bathtub held forty-two gallons, and they recommended six pounds of salt per gallon. Did the grocery store even have two hundred and fifty-two pounds of salt? My tub could maybe allow a four-foot person to float unobstructed but not my five-foot eight inches self. I'll just sit here, watch another movie, and dream about floating.

On November 9, 2019, Moe started sending me messages about the color of Kay's urine.

Moe stated on Talking Parents, "This is the second visitation that her urine is was very dark."

Why was he telling me about their pee?

I replied, "Her urine is dark?"

He said, "Ya, she went pee, and it looks like she is dehydrated. Same on Wednesday. She was in the stall herself, when she finished, she came out without flushing the toilet. So, I walked into the stall and flushed it."

What?

I had so many other questions, like why was he telling me this?

Why was he in the female bathroom? Why was he looking at her urine? Did he *really* go in the female bathroom?

Then it came out that Moe was taking them into the male bathroom alone, changing them into different clothes, then changing them back into the clothes I dressed them in. Didn't the court just admonish him for a second time just a couple weeks ago for this *same issue,* and he's still doing it? Why was he taking them into a male bathroom alone? Why didn't his mom or girlfriend take them into the bathroom? Who was supervising the girls? Wasn't this discussed thoroughly in court, *twice.*

He said on Talking Parents, "I took her into a stall (IN AN EMPTY BATHROOM and made sure no one came in) and let her dress herself. My only recourse is to do the best I can when I have them. If that means taking them into a male bathroom, because I can't go into a female bathroom because I'm a MAN. I make sure the bathroom is clear of anybody else. I take them into a stall, and make sure NOBODY ELSE COMES IN. If it eases your mind I will call you and you can meet us and change them. Even when we at church in Hesperia or whatever local place we are at. I'm a single father, that means I have to do certain things, like have them change into more appropriate clothing for outing."

Moe had both of his parents "supervising" the visitation plus Cecelia was present, yet, he felt compelled to take the girls alone into a public male restroom? His parents and Cecilia were all present during not only the trial but the ex parte as well. They heard Judge Mazle Dina explicitly say not to take off their clothes during the supervised visitations, and they allowed it to happen multiple times during this four-hour Saturday visit.

Moe then told me that Kay had hurt her vagina on a teeter-totter ride because he rocked back too hard, so he took her into the park's public male bathroom, took her into a stall, pulled her shorts and underwear down to examine her.

Kay came back from the Saturday supervised visitation crying inconsolably the entire car ride home. When we got home, she told me she hurt her vagina. Her story matched his all the way up to the end. Kay told me Moe spread her vagina apart with his fingers making a pinching motion with her fingers, and Moe said he never touched her.

Kay was screaming saying her vagina still really, really hurt. I didn't know what to do.

I took her to urgent care. The only thing I kept thinking was this should never have happened. I told Moe I was taking her to urgent care, he said, "You realize the more this happens the more likely our daughters will be taken away from both of us. Judge Mazle Dina spoke on that, you were there! And you just won't stop."

He denied he touched her, but Kay told me he did. I believed her. This entire incident should not have happened. Where were his parents that were supposed to be supervising the visitation? Why were they allowing him to continue to undress them during the supervised visits when the judge had stated directly not to? What's the point of them all coming to every hearing if none of them listened to a word of the court? Why didn't he ask either his mom or Cecelia to take her into a female bathroom? Why was he taking her into a male bathroom alone?

Kay was still crying and telling me her vagina hurt a lot. At urgent care, the nurse that triaged us also frequently worked on my unit. I told her what happened.

She was aware that Moe and I were in court all the time, and she said without even thinking, "That sick bastard probably molested her. "

I just started crying. I couldn't hold it together anymore. She said she was going to have to transfer us to the ER.

When we got to the ER. I told the new nurse what Moe told me, and she acted like yeah so what's wrong with a father taking his daughter into the bathroom.

"He's on supervised visitation. He's not supposed to be in a bathroom alone with them." She didn't get it. A social worker came over at a distance. The nurse walked over to her and would look at us then look at her. The social worker then left. The doctor came out and looked annoyed to even be there.

He had me and the nurse pull her pants down and looked from three feet away, "looks fine," and left.

The social worker came back and told me someone would get in contact with me, and we left. This should never have happened.

I felt embarrassed and guilty for even bringing Kay. This should never have happened. I filed an ex parte. During the ex parte on November 14, 2019, Judge Mazle Dina had Mr. Bladderwort go back into her chambers where they privately discussed what happened.

Judge Mazle Dina came out and told me that she didn't like the way I questioned Moe. Judge Mazle Dina kept the visitation the same. She added that the children should go to therapy on his Mondays if appointments were available, and she ordered, "Father is admonished that he is not to be alone with the minor children."

She refused to replace his parents, who could not be impartial, with a professional supervisor. I don't understand why she was so obstinate about replacing his parents with a professional supervisor when things were clearly not okay.

November 14, 2019 Court Orders

Mother is to have the minor children on the 2nd weekend of every month.

All custody exchanges shall be at the McDonalds in Colton.

Father is to bring the minor children to therapy on his Monday visits if the appointments are available.

Father is admonished that he is not to be alone with the minor children.

A CPS worker some days later called me and asked to meet me at my house at noon. He didn't show. It's almost three o'clock, and I left to go pick up the girls from school. He called and announced he's at my house.

I said, "I'll be right back," then explained that I had to pick the girls up from school. I also noted that I had to drive the girls to the court-ordered supervised visitation at 4 p.m., and it would probably be better if we rescheduled. He said he'd just meet me at my house when I returned. I said, "Um, okay," before he hung up.

I pulled into my driveway, where he was waiting for me in his car. It's already fifteen past three. As I unbuckled the girls out of their car seats, he walked up. I said again it would be better if we rescheduled.

I don't remember if he said anything. The girls ran for the door. I unlocked the door, and he was standing right behind us, so I invited him in. He walked about ten-fifteen feet into my house. I put my keys up, the girls' backpacks away, and tried to push their shoes they immediately threw off aside. He was standing in the open area between my front living room and dining area just watching me. I looked at him. He said his name and explained to me what his job was. I briefly tried to tell him what happened, but it was nearly impossible. I was selective with every word because the girls were running all around us. I looked at my watch... I had to go if I was going to make it there on time. "Can we reschedule?" He just watched me as I put the girls' shoes back on. I asked him, "If I stay and speak with you... would that supersede the court orders?" He didn't have an answer. I told him that I had to leave. He smiled at me and took a few steps for the door as I opened it and asked the girls to get in the van. Moe would take me to court for missing a single visitation, and the judge the way she had been would likely side with him and throw me in jail.

We maybe spoke for ten to fifteen minutes. He didn't check anything in my house like the other lady, so I figured he would just reschedule because today was unproductive. He handed me a paper. "Here, sign this." I assumed he was going to come back, but he never did.

Sometime later, my head hurt so bad it felt like my eye was going to burst. It felt like something was behind my eye pushing it out. The pain was excruciating. I almost would have rather been in labor. Nothing I did at home was helping touch the pain, so I went to urgent care. The doctor ordered a CAT scan to rule out a brain aneurysm because my blood pressure and pain were so high.

The doctor came in. "Not an aneurysm. Thank God. I guess possibly a severe migraine." They ordered a cocktail of IV medications. The side effects made me feel like my skin was crawling. I didn't know which was worse, the migraine or the side effects. I went back home and went to bed.

The next day, the string of chaos continued.

December 1, Moe called me a "stuck up b****" because I didn't answer his questions during exchange.

December 4, Moe canceled visitation (he rarely utilized the professional supervisor visits canceling most of them).

December 9, Moe, and Cecelia got married and moved into his parent's house.

December 18, Moe told the girls, "I'm sorry you have to go back your mommy. Your other mommy loves you and your sister misses you."

December 21, Moe requested that I pick up the children early because Anna was sick. He wanted me to take her to urgent care. When I went to pick up the girls, Moe and his parents refused to hand over Anna until I answered their questions. "Send me your questions on Talking Parents. I'm not doing this with you. You called me. Do you want me to take her to urgent care or do you want to make her stand in the parking lot another hour?"

Anna ended up testing positive for strep throat.

December 28, Moe canceled visitation.

December 29, Moe canceled visitation.

December 30, the supervised visitation was arranged with a professional monitor from 4 p.m. to 6 p.m. with *no issue*.

~ New Year's 2020 ~

January 4, 2020, Moe canceled visitation.

January 5 the supervised visitation was arranged with a professional monitor from 3:30 p.m. to 5:30 p.m. with *no issue*.

26

AM I THE ONLY ONE?

JANUARY 10, 2020

By our next court hearing on January 10, 2020, Moe only utilized two professional supervised visits. Decreasing the number of professional reports that the court would receive, if she even cared about any of them. His parents made the exchanges horrid after the park incident. At one exchange, Edith followed me almost to the door of my van. I asked her to please stop. She smiled as she stepped closer holding her phone out. I could tell she was enjoying making me feel uncomfortable. It was clear where her son got it from. Apple—tree. I attached her smiling picture to my paperwork.

Back inside court, I reiterated to Judge Mazle Dina again, there were no issues with the exchanges when the professional mediator conducted the exchanges. However, when his parents conducted the exchange, they had no control and aided in the hostility.

Judge Mazle Dina responded, "Why don't you pick someone else to do the exchange for you because you guys have been in here so many times. I'm kind of over it. I mean, I hate to say it that way, but every time you guys have a court appearance it is always something about the exchange or the people supervising. And so perhaps you should remove yourself from the exchange, so you don't have an issue with it anymore."

I'm sorry, what? Perhaps I should remove myself, so I didn't have an issue with it anymore? It being... Moe berating me in front of the girls, or his parents' inability to be impartial, or having them withhold the girls, or multiple people filming me, or Moe constantly undressing the girls on his supervised visits, *or* is she referring to the girls each inconsolably crying after one or more supervised visitations?

You know, I am really getting mixed signals because the judge previously stated at the trial these were issues, yet now, she was implying she didn't have an issue with any of this. It was just me? *I* should remove myself, so *I* don't have an issue with it anymore because she's *over it.* Maybe if she didn't keep handing the keys over to the drunkard at the bar, there'd be less DUI accidents.

I was so sick of this.

Judge Mazle Dina rejected everything I said about what was going on at the exchanges that was causing our girl's undue stress, and instead, she asked whether they're in counseling.

The children's best interest? What an absolute joke! Yeah, why don't we just put them on antidepressants now because you're so obstructive to the truth. Next, you're probably going to suggest doubling the dose. That's not a solution. Maybe she didn't understand root cause analysis. A problem-solving method used to identify the underlying causes of a problem or issue. Once the root causes had been identified, appropriate actions could be taken to address and resolve the problem, and steps could be taken to prevent the problem from occurring again in the future.

Instead of saying all that, I said, "I think we are losing sight of the primary focus which is to protect the kids."

This rattled Judge Mazle Dina. Fumbling with her words, she replied, "There's nothing—hold on. There is not an issue in the report and historically on *'protecting the children.'* There have been problems, yes. And those problems, the father has been counseled. But with the supervision that's in place, the children are protected. They are not getting bit. They are not having people smoke marijuana around them. They are not. He knows about the merry-go-round and the injury and going into the bathroom. And he knows about washing them. He has been admonished."

Was she kidding me right now?

How many times did he need to be "counseled" on the same things? I recounted how many times his parents had withheld the girls during exchanges, how many times did she have to admonish him not to take off the girls' clothes, how many times I had been cussed at in front of the girls, which I said was *unnecessary and harmful.* And yet all of the problems continued to persist.

Judge Mazle Dina said, "So, let's point to the problem then instead of just throwing everything out there against the law. If you are asking me for him to have somebody else help with exchanges, I will do that."

In the end, she put Cecelia, who was now Moe's wife, back in the exchange. Mind you, she was kicked out of exchanges less than three months ago. We were just going in circles. This was madness.

The court then insinuated that all the girls' issues that occur during the exchanges were because I must have anxiety, and I was letting that anxiety rub off onto the girls. She said, "And the kids have already reacted during their interviews with the mediator that they are already having anxiety. And if you're letting that anxiety rub off on the kids, the situation is going to get worse and not better. I mean, you know this. Sometimes I think that it's almost, you know, Ms. Maldavo you have these two children, you have to accommodate and work on co-parenting. And I'm probably going to appoint your 730 evaluator today."

Did she hear herself?

So, what was she saying? That I needed to make more space to allow Moe to take the girls into male bathrooms and undress them or give them baths in public places? Or should I be more accommodating with his *need* to act hostile and erratic. So, I should just adapt when Moe calls me a *stuck-up b*****. I should just be more understanding when his parents withheld the girls and demanded their questions be answered. Because this all had to do with *my* ability to co-parent.

None of these things were in my control, and this arbitrary statement made by the court was rooted in nonsensical bias and was promoting further abuse. Perhaps, just maybe, the girls were having anxiety because their father was yelling, their grandparents were yelling, there's numerous people at every exchange, two to four people were still always recording me, they were being withheld, they were being undressed in public spaces, they were being bathed in McDonalds, they were being taken into male public restrooms alone.

Judge Mazle Dina states, "The children are engaged in counseling. So, I'm not so concerned because mother has sought medical treatment for them." Why do they even need 'medical treatment' in the first place? Perhaps it's the constant chaos that the court has fostered and allowed to continue.

She continued. "But on the issues of exchanges, if parental grandparents can't be so called 'nice to you' during an exchange or if they are causing conflict, which I think is what you are saying?"

No, that was not what I was saying at all, why was she minimizing the issues with the girls. Seeking medical treatment for them didn't resolve the root problem. I circled back. The following conversation ensued:

Judge Mazle Dina: So, when the kids are with you and anybody says anything bad about the mother, what do you do?

Moe: No one—I correct anybody that says anything. And—

Judge Male Dina: Why would people even be around your kids that would talk poorly about the mother?

Moe: No one does that. Two years ago, there was a conversation—the girls were out of earshot—I literally stopped my mom and said, we can have conversations any other time. And that's what we do. We don't talk about Seraphine in front of the girls. The pickups and drop-offs are not as she says. They are just not.

Judge Male Dina: All right. Well, there's a picture that was attached—that I'm thinking it would be your dad, I see here—that he looks pretty angry in this photograph with his finger pointing. And I would imagine the kids were there.

Moe: Well, Your Honor, she records everything. She will not file a recording, what she does is that a recording and pick out the worse picture of my dad's face or my mom's face and report that to the court. What was going on was she didn't do the girls hair at all. She didn't get them ready at all. And when Anna was dropped off.

Judge Male Dina: So, your father then engaged in an argument about the children's hair?

Moe: This is not what happened.

Mr. Bladderwort: I wish the court had more time. I know the court doesn't have time.

Reminding the Judge Mazle Dina of her statement earlier: "I have a trial starting so I don't have a lot of time to go back and forth with the two of you."

Judge Mazle Dina then said, "Well, I'm not at this time ordering that the children have no contact with the grandparents, but at least for now, for the next six months, if it's causing problems with the exchanges in which the girls are uncomfortable in any way because the mother is being mistreated in some way, then they can't be there. Your wife will have to help you."

So, the girls must endure an additional six months of this chaos? I said, "the only time they (the exchanges) are peaceful is with the professional supervisor. And the handout that the mediation said that there should be no contact between us. Yet, every single time he asserts himself to be the person that is exchanging."

I continued, "What's the point of having the (parental) supervisors when he is doing the exchanges every single time for the last six months?"

Judge Male Dina replied, "So let's stop fighting about it then."

She continued, "Okay I'm proposing this. I will do what you're asking and make it the first, third and fifth weekends if they are overnights for him on weekends."

I replied, "But that is not addressing the safety of the kids when we have an open CPS case?"

Judge Mazle Dina said, "Yes, it is when the parental grandparents are supervising."

I pushed again, "but they also let him go into the bathroom alone and touch her private area."

Judge Mazle Dina said, "he has been admonished about that. So, I don't understand—again, you have to co-parent."

You kept using that word. I do not think it means what you think it means. I was not asking for no contact with his parents, I was asking that the professional monitor be in charge of the exchanges because his parents had no control over their son and also aided in hostile exchanges of the girls. The court then embroiled the whole situation and discontinued the professional supervisor altogether and solely made the parental grandparents the primary supervisors. Basically, proposed that if for another additional six months, the girls were uncomfortable witnessing me being mistreated or if they were grossly physically abused resulting in a permanent physical injury or that his action proceeds from pure malice then—maybe, she might, do something. So, the court rewarded Moe's behavior by expanding his visitation time, made total sense, if we lived in 1867. How was this in the best interest of the children?

Judge Mazle Dina expanded Moe's visitation time from 8 a.m. to noon to 9 a.m. to 6 p.m. every weekend except the second weekend, and when Moe asked, "Am I allowed to take them home with my parents as a supervisor so I can have better one-on-one time with them?"

Judge Mazle Dina said, "I've never restricted your locations for visitation. You can go wherever."

I felt sick. So, Judge Mazle Dina was acutely aware, and had been aware, of the girls' trauma, that they were showing signs of anxiety and stress. She was aware that Moe yelled at me. She stated she was certain his parents had animosity toward me but never seemed to question their ability to be impartial. She was aware that they yelled at me, they withheld the girls, and recorded my every move. She was aware of all the issues with undressing the girls, yet, her solution was to simply place the girls in therapy, add back Cecilia, discontinue the professional mediator altogether, and expand his visitation time?

At this point, it didn't appear that anything I said mattered, and that Judge Mazle Dina would continue to advance his time regardless of the facts.

And I was the crazy one? Guess she didn't need those reports to expand his visitation time after all. It seemed that Moe's parental right to have access to the girls superseded their rights to ensure their health, safety, and welfare. It seemed the girls' health, safety, and welfare were *not* a priority of the court at this time. Law F.DEM. 11.94.19 was the only law Judge Mazle Dina followed.

Judge Mazle Dina was seemingly not ensuring her duty to a "child's right to be safe and free from abuse."

Instead, it seemed she wanted to continue to expose the girls to an unhealthy environment, and her seemingly lack of action, lack of ability to recognize abuse was perpetuating possible further abuse, and what was worse, she didn't seem to care. What was even the point?

January 10, 2020 Court Orders

1. The Father shall have supervised visits with the minor children as follows: on all but the 2nd Saturday of each month from 9am to 6pm, supervised by the paternal grandparents and on alternating Sundays, except for the 2nd Sunday of each month from 9am to 6pm, supervised by the paternal grandparents.

2. The Mother shall have the children at all times not designated as father's time.

3. The parents shall enroll in and successfully complete a co-parenting class and provide proof of completion to the other parent and the court. (See attached resources.)

4. The children shall participate in counseling with a licensed therapist or agency for a minimum of 8 sessions or until released by the counselor regarding mental and/or emotional health concerns that may be related to the parents' separation and custody issues. The parents shall cooperate and participate in the children's therapy at the discretion of the therapist.

5. All other orders shall remain in full force and effect.

6. Cecelia Maldavo can assist with exchanges.

7. Seraphine Maldavo can designate a third party to assist exchanges.

8. Visitation can occur at any location.

9. Parties not to leave their vehicles during exchanges.

On January 13, 2020, I notified Moe I had scheduled two future therapy appointments for Kay on January 18, at 4:30 p.m. and February 1, at 4:30 p.m. prior to court. I asked if he would like to take them because they now fell under his visitation time. Moe declined and requested that I reschedule the therapy appointments during my time because he said it cut into his time.

On January 14, 2020, I asked Moe if he could help with $683.99 out-of-pocket medical/dental bills. Moe agreed to help if I sent him a copy of the bills. I sent Moe a copy of all the bills. Moe said he never agreed to pay half. Moe said he wanted 50 percent legal custody, and he wanted to put the minor children on his insurance, IEHP. He wanted me to drop them off my insurance. Moe then told me to send the bills to his lawyer with my proposal with the threat to go back to court again. Again, Moe purposefully withheld payments as a financial game using ploys and deception with malicious intent.

On January 18, 2020, Moe claimed Anna broke her leg, *it was not broken*, and that she was unable to walk. The court had ordered us to stay in our cars at the exchange, and this was a ploy to get me to break the court orders. He acted like don't you care about our daughter as he walked her over to my car and requested that I get out and come get her from his arms. He then proceeded to get within inches of my face for no legitimate purpose. I physically felt sick as his finger touched my arm. I couldn't do this anymore. I just wanted peace. I filed for a restraining order. On February 5, 2020, the court continued the matter until February 25, 2020, a domestic violence restraining order hearing was heard.

February 5, 2020 Court Orders

Court appoints Dr. Bedlam, pursuant to Evident Code 730

Dr. Bedlam's report shall be admissible without foundation, subject to cross examination if received 10 days prior to the next hearing

Each party is ordered to cooperate

Pursuant to stipulation, the hearing set for
February 21, 2020, is continued to February
25,2020 at 09:30 am

27

GENERATIONS HAUNTED BY ANGER AND SHAME

Months had gone by without a word from the CPS worker, so I called and asked what the status was with the case. The secretary asked me when the case was opened, I told her.

She said, "Oh, hun, that was a long time ago. I'm sure it's closed by now. Let me see. Oh, no, you're right. It's still open. Umm, I will write a note and hand it to him when I see him."

"Okay," I said, and we hung up.

He called me back very annoyed, *man*splaining the process of his work, how busy he was, and how I just didn't understand the complexity and process of it all.

He was so rude on the phone. I called the secretary back concerned with how irritated he seemed. There was a pause, and then she apologized. She told me she wrote on a sticky note "nothing has been done."

She realized he must have assumed that I had said, "he had done nothing" and said, "He's normally not like that." She promised she would clarify that was not what I said and that I had only called to see what the status was.

A couple days later, I got a call at work from Kay's school. The school secretary told me that CPS had gone to the school, pulled her out of class, and question her in her office.

She then told me everything he said, and how awkward Kay must have felt.

The CPS worker asked vague questions like "Do you like your daddy" but never questioned about that specific day in the park. I called Anna's preschool and asked the secretary if he had pulled her out of her class, too. The secretary was just as shook up and told me everything he did and said. I was mainly concerned that he didn't ask specifically about November 9, 2019, but also that he never called to even let me know.

I waited and called him on my lunch break. He was furious that the school called me. He told me I had no right to know anything, and that he did not have to be transparent about anything he did. I was in shock he was yelling at me. Another nurse walked in, so I got up and stood by the window and cupped my hand around my mouth. This was a mistake calling him at lunch, but I couldn't hang up now. I asked him why he didn't tell me he had taken her out of class, it had been hours he could have called after the fact. He said again that he didn't have to be transparent with me about anything he does and that he was in accordance with CPS guidelines. He just kept repeating the same thing. I quickly glanced back at the nurse sitting at the table trying to keep her eyes on the TV. I sat down in a chair right next to me and leaned down still cupping my hand around my phone and mouth. I tried to move away from that topic and told him what Kay had told me. Moe claimed he only looked at it but didn't touch it. I said, "I believe her. But if you never asked her about that day…, isn't it important that Kay feels heard and believed?" That seemed to make him madder. He claimed that his questions were sufficient, and she didn't act like the other kids he had seen before that have really been raped. "What?"

He finally yelled, "You're the one that called us claiming he raped her!"

I said, "Hold on, I didn't call you, the hospital did, and I never said that. I said Kay said he touched her, and he denied it."

He replied, "Well, how do you know he touched her sexually?"

I'm trying hard to whisper, "I don't know what his intent was, all I know is that Kay said he spread her labia apart, and she made a hand gesture with her thumb and index fingers, and that she was in a lot of pain. I said the whole thing should have never happened because the court has already admonished him twice for taking off the girls' clothes during his supervised visits."

"Oh," he replied.

The conversation quickly dissolved, and he said that he was going to close the case. "Close the case? But you never even asked her anything about November 9, 2019, the day in the park."

"I'm closing the case." My lunch break was over, and there was nothing I could do. I called his supervisor later, but that was a total waste of time. You know those sounds actors make in those 1950s films when the husband is reading a newspaper and his wife is talking to him? Then finally she asks, "Are you even listening?" It was a lot like that. I didn't fight it any further because fighting CPS was like fighting the IRS—you're never going to win, so just move on. I'm supposed to protect her, and I couldn't even get someone to hear her. He didn't even care to ask. I couldn't tell you what that felt like. I carried a lot of shame with this whole incident for a long time. I could see the bottom of that dark hole. I almost lost all hope.

My phone rang, it was the police… they wanted to question Kay. It had been months. I didn't even know the police were involved. They had me take her to the same place they investigated the bite. The investigator had on superman socks. He took Kay back and talked to her alone. They talked for a long time.

I wanted to be mad at that CPS worker for a long time, but I learned that they had almost no ratios like most nurses out of state. There were nurses expected to try to manage eight to ten medicine patients in other states. The ratios were for the patient's safety. One nurse couldn't safely take care of that many people. In California, the max was five, but mostly they assigned three or four patients to a single nurse. In the ICU, the max was two patients per one nurse. CPS workers in our county had no ratios, were frequently expected to see over *sixty-two* children a month, along with writing all the reports, driving to their locations and appearing for court case reports. *How did that make sense?*

Teachers' ratios were capped at around thirty children. So, shouldn't a CPS worker who was working with the most vulnerable group of children have a ratio less than teachers? How were they expected to do their job properly if they were all burned out? The only people losing the most were the kids they were supposed to be protecting.

How could I be mad at someone who was set up to fail? Social workers worked with some of the hardest circumstances imaginable, and were hated by many. There was nothing glamorous about their jobs.

Nursing wasn't always glamorous either, but at least, most of the public and media viewed us in a positive light. Nurses were a vocal bunch, and many were trying to join together to pass laws for safe patient-to-nurse ratios. But who was fighting for safe child-to-CPS ratios? Who was listening to them?

"Silence creates it's own violence." ~ Jeff VanderMeer

28

GIVE BEFORE YOU TAKE

FEBRUARY 25, 2020

On February 25, 2020, walking into the courtroom, I thought *Here we go again.* Chaos seemed to be the governing factor that propelled our case forever forward that made as much sense as trying to pour tea while walking down a slip-n-slide. I was stuck playing a game I never wanted to participate in and where they kept changing the rules. I was told left meant right, up was down, and north was west. This forever unpredictable courtroom produced confusion and fear which results in anxiety and frustration like a paranoid feeling when you leave on a trip, Did I leave the oven on?

No rationales were ever given, so you're just left scratching your head. How did one plus X equal sassafras? Was I hallucinating, or did these rulings seem to defy all logic leaving me to question my reality and sanity. When you came with the expectation to find law and order, but instead found a dismissive authority and backward logic, you eventually lose all faith in our "justice" system.

The seats were a row of individual wooden seats linked together with iron rods. I sat in the seat. It was cold and hard. The seat had a slight slant that did not allow you to sit straight up. I kept sliding down, so I had to constantly readjust.

The great seal of the state of California hung in the front center of the room against the decorative crown molding while red oak filled the room. Above us hung nine huge alabaster pendants, looming over the room like moons. The ceiling was painted with two mermaid fairies facing away from each other holding fruit conches above them in one hand, and in the other, they held a red flower below them. There was an umbrella with water drops at each point in between them. What they had to do with law, I don't know. Maybe Sally and Molly up there were promoting feelings of affection and empathy, all a fake ruse.

The bailiff asked us to stand and swear in. "Raise your right hand. Do you swear to tell the truth and nothing but the truth, so help you God?"

Like God had anything to do with this place.

I never really understood the point of swearing in. Why bother when lies were tossed so effortlessly around and even mentioning perjury to any lawyer would get a good belly laugh. Family court should change their oath to *The truth, the whole truth, and nothing but lies, oppression, and abuse.*

The legal secretary was seated on the right nearest the bailiff, and the court recorder seated on the left. The bailiff announced the judge, and she entered from the back right.

I noticed a young Hispanic girl sitting across from me, her mom stood a distance back. The girl folded her arms and plopped down in a chair muttering defiance.

A small angry storm cloud almost visibly hung above her head.

Her mom ignored her.

The girl got called up.

The girl's grandma had filed for a restraining order because she broke a window or something. The teenager clearly had some issues going on.

I wondered, *Can you issue a restraining order on a minor? Maybe if she was eighteen.*

The girl kept her arms folded in front of Judge Mazle Dina while her grandmother talked.

The grandmother didn't seem angry. She spoke with tenderness and desperation. Clearly, she wanted to help her granddaughter but didn't know how.

Judge Mazle Dina turned to the girl after the grandmother finished. "Do you have anything to add," she asked.

"No," she said still with a defiant attitude.

"I'm issuing a three-year restraining order. We're done here." Cold, swift, and unsympathetic. The girl was clearly a troubled youth. The girl said, "That's not fair!" The court could have offered some semblance of kindness, guidance, or counseling, but instead, she uttered, "the punishment fits the crime."

Nothing learned or gained. She was like a Nile crocodile devouring whoever she could.

The bailiff called us. Ugh, here we go…

They ran through the legal pleasantries before I spoke. "Again, we are having issues with the exchange. He is getting, like, less than six inches from my face. He is holding the kids and, like, yelling at me while holding the kids. And now that you have let the wife back in, I now have three people videotaping me at every exchange, and it's just—there's no legitimate purpose for any of this. There is no reason why he needs to get, like—why he needs to get six inches from my face. I am in my vehicle. It's just to intimidate me and harass me, and I feel extremely uncomfortable during all of these exchanges, and I don't need three cameras on me at all times."

I continued. "These, again, are supervised visitations. There is no reason why he needs to be doing the exchange. We had just gone to court over it, and you stated, 'You need to stay in your car during the exchange.' And, again, he ignores anything that the court has to say and just does whatever he wants to do."

Judge Mazle Dina stated, "Okay. And for the record, the court on—I think it was the last time that you were in here—January 10th, 2020, the court had ordered that parties not leave their vehicles during exchanges. And you, Seraphine Maldavo, could designate third parties to assist. And Cecelia Maldavo can assist to exchange. So, the court will take judicial notice of these prior orders."

I submitted into evidence a picture of Moe's large glaring eyeball. She thanked me for providing her with a large color copy. The hairs on my arm stood up. That's odd, was she just nice to me? She never thanked anyone. The court moved on.

Judge Mazle Dina stated, "Does you client object to the restraining order? She would like him to have no contact with her. I hate to say that we are at this point."

Mr. Bladderwort responded, "We strongly object to a domestic violence restraining order. The court has the authority and has made orders regarding the exchanges. I don't think that needs to be—"

Judge Mazle Dina said, "But your client has violated the orders clearly in this picture. If this was taken from her car, right?"

Mr. Bladderwort said, "Can I have a minute?"

Judge Mazle Dina continued. "I mean, they are supposed to stay in their cars."

Mr. Bladderwort said, "I'll address that, Your Honor, with the witnesses."

Judge Mazle Dina said, "There is absolutely no reason for him to approach her car."

Mr. Bladderwort then had Moe's newlywed wife come up to the stand, and his attorney asked several questions that went on and on. These questions spanned over thirteen pages on the transcript. His tactic, I thought, was to circle around and around the dead carcass of his defense until we all just died from boredom.

It almost worked.

I interjected before he persisted further and killed us all.

But Judge Mazle Dina was conjuring her own plan. She announced,

"So what I think I'm going to do is continue the restraining order for 90 days with a stay-away order."

A stay-away order is a subset of a restraining order that by definition is always temporary. A stay-away order only limits the physical presence of the two parties involved and has lesser penalties if violated than a restraining order would. Welcome to family court where they give ~~high-fives~~, ~~hand shakes~~, a slap on the wrist to abusers.

Mr. Bladderwort asked, "So the court is going to continue the temporary for 90 days and consider us in the progress."

Judge Mazle Dina said, "Well, the temporary was an issue. I can do that."

Jacques voice nagged inside my head, *They are making open deals in the middle of court.*

Mr. Bladderwort shifted and then asked if Moe could have overnight visitation.

Judge Mazle Dina said, "Also there's a request and I typically—I would not entertain this request due to the conflict between the parties, but Ms. Maldavo, have you given anymore thought to instead of this Saturday and Sunday visit exchanges, the kids just stay overnight? Typically, I would not entertain this."

Yeah right. I don't believe anything that came out of her mouth. Is it common during a restraining order hearing to request additional visitation time to the perpetrator?

I responded, "No, because in December we have gone over that he is not to be alone with the children because they are still pending a police case. My child is saying that she was touched in her private area, and he is denying that it even happened. So, we have gone to the C.A.N. thing, and she has said that to the police that yes, it did happen. And he is still denying that it ever happened. So, we have these human bite marks, we have her being tested positive of marijuana, he overdosed a three-year-old. We have all these things and there's a safety concern of the children with overnights."

Judge Mazle Dina turned to her computer sitting beside her and said, "They—I don't know if you got this or not—but they attached in the declaration of the police department with the interview of your child."

I said, "The blacked-out thing? I just received something today."

The bailiff had handed me an almost entirely blacked out police report before we were called up.

Judge Mazle Dina continued. "Mr. Bladderwort, I've reviewed the report. I don't know if she received this. I'm going to wait for the 730 evaluation to discuss the request for overnights. There is the interview here of the law enforcement officer I was able to quickly scan and it appears that the minor advised the police that he did look at her vagina and touch it."

She continued. "I wouldn't be surprised if charges were filed, quite frankly. But the 730 evaluator should review the report. And probably I would imagine there will be some additional counseling for Mr. Malvado regarding appropriate behavior around the girls."

The gavel was in hand and with a swift tap, the hearing was concluded.

What, what? She had only peered at her computer for a split moment. Not long enough to read that report. She must have read that report prior to us walking up. Why would the court request consideration to Moe having overnight visits when she already knew what the police reported and she herself stated she thought he needed "additional counseling regarding appropriate behavior around the girls" and "wouldn't be surprised if charges were filed." My head was being thrashed with questions.

I don't understand why the court would request consideration of Moe having unsupervised overnight visits when she already had the knowledge of what the police report said.

Was this normal?

And she still refused to have a professional monitor supervise the visits? How was she protecting the girls?

The words kept replaying in my head. She thought he needed additional counseling regarding appropriate behavior around the girls and wouldn't be surprised if charges were filed yet obstructed answerability and withheld access to any shield of protection.

The simplest answer, she was not. She was not even trying to protect the girls. Her tactics were intended to reduce my moral and decrease my will to advocate for the girls safety. She had steadily extended his visitation despite the evidence presented while sweeping all his misdeeds neatly under the rug. However, the mound under the rug was becoming so high, it was overtly apparent to all that enter, but she looked on with superior arrogance that no one dared comment or question her for fear of her authority. Now, she's shifting all the responsibility to the 730 evaluator?

I did a mental recap: she cast me into the fire for two hundred and sixteen days (216), then granted a temporary ninety (90) day stay-away order that didn't even cover half of the days suffered? Yet she gave that young girl a three-year restraining order because she said she deserved it?

For what… breaking a window?

We were of no consequence to her.

Now she had my full attention.

29

BOWTIES AND CAMERAS

Casting aside any chance that Judge Mazle Dina was even remotely impartial, I was putting all my faith on this 730 evaluation. I quite liked psychology. I believed Dr. Bedlam would notice Moe's behavioral pattern was abnormal. Dr. Bedlam had twenty years' experience as a lawyer in family law and had been practicing the last two years as a psychologist. I had all my documents meticulously organized, photographic evidence, and a pristine timeline of events.

To say I was prepared was an understatement.

I called Dr. Bedlam's office to coordinate an appointment, and a woman answered the phone. She was pleasant and arranged our first office interview for February 26, 2020.

They wanted both Moe and I to attend together, so they could observe how we interacted together.

I wondered if there was going to be an incident in the parking lot. Was he going to bring his parents or Cecilia and have them wait in the car? Was he going to yell at me during the interview? Was he going to try and touch me?

The thought of him touching me made me nauseous, so I stopped thinking about it. *It'll be fine.*

Dr. Bedlam's office was on the second floor of a large rectangular building with a small pond in the center of the courtyard. Walking into his office, I was greeted with a tiny waiting room that could only fit a love seat couch and coffee table.

Well, this was going to be uncomfortable if they had Moe and I wait for any length of time here.

The woman I spoke to on the phone popped her head around the doorframe near the right end of the waiting room. "Oh, hello, you must be Seraphine."

She was Dr. Bedlam's secretary as well as his wife, I found out later.

Dr. Bedlam's office was shaped like a weird clover. Opposite the small secretary room was Dr. Bedlam's office, and between their two rooms was another door that I assumed was their file room.

I heard Moe's voice when the front office door opened behind me.

Dr. Bedlam stood. "Ah, you're both here. Great."

He ushered us into his office. It was larger than the waiting room. His large desk in the middle of the room had an oversized computer screen on the left corner. He motioned us to two chairs closely placed in front of his desk. Another desk sat behind those two chairs.

Moe greeted him with a firm handshake, a joke, and confidently marched ahead of me into his office. I rolled my eyes. *The peacock was out on a full performance mode today. He must have been instructed on how to act by his lawyer.*

Wearing a suit, Dr. Bedlam was a tall, thin, white man. He wore thin rectangular glasses.

Moe plopped into a chair. He eyed my chair that was less than a foot away, and smirked. I wondered if this was done intentionally for observational purposes.

I suddenly felt sick, sat down, and leaned away from Moe.

Dr. Bedlam seemed oblivious while he frequently looked at his computer and energetically told us how he was going to conduct the 730 evaluation. His qualifications, his book, how he was going to implement non-bias, and how he liked to use an open approach.

"I like to use one question; what do I need to know?" He said by this method of only using one singular question it allowed us the freedom of opening up.

He slapped both of his knees as he concluded, stood, and picked up a camera explaining he needed a picture of the two of us for his evaluation.

I had to remind myself that I was court ordered to cooperate as I tempered my nausea. With a big smile, Dr. Bedlam held the camera in front of him and snapped the picture.

I was so happy to be done.

Dr. Bedlam scheduled all of my online personality tests to be completed in his office on March 10, 2020. When I arrived, he gestured me in to sit at the smaller desk adjacent his desk, and I waved hello to his wife. He eagerly explained the process, the methods of the individual tests, and approximately how long it would take to complete all of them. Dr. Bedlam clapped his hands together and smiled.

He walked to his desk behind me and sat down as I began.

Dr. Bedlam left the door open to his office and conferred with his wife about his schedule. As the time passed, Dr. Bedlam answered phone calls behind me talking to and about other clients. If I looked to my left, I could directly see into the file room. His son was in there going through paperwork. "Dad, where do you want these files?"

Dr. Bedlam jumped up and chatted briefly with him. As he turned to enter back into his office, he stopped in the doorway and started talking with his wife. I tried to drown out what they were talking about, but I couldn't.

They were talking about the Enneagram personality test they took at church.

I chimed in. "I took that test, too. I thought it was very interesting."

Dr. Bedlam began sharing his results with me. "I am an Achiever." He said that he admired praise and admiration, however, he viewed this desire as a negative virtue and the downfall of his personality. He continued to say that he must learn to embrace that about himself.

He looked vexed as he glanced down to the floor, so I attempted to joke. "Well, I tested as a number eight, the challenger."

I laughed. "Do you still want me to continue with these tests since now you know who I am?"

Maybe the joke didn't land because he appeared to get distracted by something else and wandered away. I refocused on the computer. It took six more hours to finish.

"I'm done."

"Great." Dr. Bedlam moved the mouse around on his computer. After a series of clicks, he said, "Do you want to see your results?"

"Sure."

"Everything appears normal on most all of your results." He explained what each thing meant.

"Oh, it looks like you tested a little high on…."

He said the word, but I couldn't remember what it was. He asked, "Do you know what it means?" I shook my head no. He didn't know what it meant either, so he gleefully said, "Let's look it up together."

He pulled a book from the bookshelf on his wall. He flipped through it until he found the word. He silently read the definition then started laughing. "It means you don't like people very much."

I just kinda shrugged but didn't say anything. If you work in any public service job, you unfortunately know there were a lot of enti-tled, insufferable people out there.

Just the other day, I was screamed at for not getting socks the moment this girl demanded them; despite the fact I physically couldn't at that moment because I was holding a needle in her grandmother's arm. Seconds later, she was screaming in the hallway, "Who do I have to talk to around here to get some damn socks! These f****** lazy nurses won't get me socks! Where's the f****** charge nurse?" Ironically not even my patient. The patient's nurse was busy hanging medications on her new admit.

The charge nurse had to call security to have her removed.

Or the twenty-eight-year-old that tried to bite me, or that patient that tried to kick me while I was eight months pregnant.

None of this even compared to the stories from ER nurses. OSHA just reported last year "over 75% of the 25,000 workplace assaults reported annually in the United States took place in hospital and other healthcare and social services setting."

I'm only surprised I didn't score higher.

With a big smile, Dr. Bedlam reassured me that my results all look "great," "uber normal," "no need to worry."

That concluded the visit.

The next visit was the interview then the bonding study. During my talking interview, Dr. Bedlam asked, "What should I know."

I thought the best way to give him all the information was to stick to the timeline I made. Yet, there was so much stuff that had happened in even the last few years it was difficult to simply summarize, and Dr. Bedlam wanted to get through all of it in one day.

I rolled through the details of all the events, then Dr. Bedlam looked at the time and asked if I could step out for a little bit because he had to use the restroom and make a phone call to another client.

I waited for over thirty minutes before finishing the rest of the interview. He claimed he needed another picture of me for the report before I left. Cheese! Click.

Next was the bonding study where I had to bring both of the girls. This time his office was empty, and he used his wife's secretary office. Her desk was right next to the door, tucked into the corner, with a small sofa against the wall.

Dr. Bedlam instructed us to play a game by ourselves, so he may sit back and silently observe us and take pictures.

Next, we were to do a group project where we were supposed to answer the question, "Where we wanted to go on vacation and what would we bring?"

Our answer was to be written on a large piece of white paper that was taped to the door. After that task was completed, he took Kay and Anna separately into his office with the door slightly cracked.

Shortly after our bonding study was done, the only thing left was the exit interview.

We each could read everything online that the other submitted to Dr. Bedlam.

Remember when I told you I had submitted a timeline of events. Moe copied my format and, in retaliation, created a timeline he called Facts of Evidence.

It was wild. It was basically twenty pages explaining how he was the true victim. No evidence to support any of it, but it didn't matter, he had to have the final word.

I laughed through the first read. Did Cecelia really fall for all of this? After the jokes fell, I pondered what I read. A chill traveled down my spine. Did he really believe what he was saying was true? Was he that far gone?

He truly believed he was the victim. Moe claimed that I cheated on him during the cruise to Alaska. That I randomly disappeared… no mention of any argument. He claimed he searched high and low for me but was unable to find me. He wasn't looking for me, he knew exactly where I was.

He claimed Anna might not be his daughter. Moe claimed I went to bars and got in fights with men and often took his truck leaving him all alone without any transportation while he tended to Kay. He also said that I was going out three out of four days a week to bars where I would stay until 4 a.m., and that as a result, he was unable to study because he had Kay and received no help from me to care for her.

Mind you, this was when I was pregnant with Anna. He was so distracted conjuring up lies he forgot I was pregnant. Or was he implying that I was drinking while pregnant?

It got worse. Get your box of tissues ready...

Moe claimed I forced him to put his career on hold because he was the primary caregiver.

We were married for two years. We were in college at the same time.

A couple paragraphs down he said, "The mother completed nursing school and began working August 1, 2012. The father continued going to school where he later graduated on June 1, 2013."

Completely blind to the irony. Yes, I was working and completing my last year. We graduated at the same time. We had pictures together graduating. Did nobody around him question or call him out on anything he said?

He claimed I told him to go to rehab, and that it was going to be the start of us reconciling our marriage.

No, I asked for a divorce. The story continued, while he was in rehab, I ended up with sole custody alluding he didn't have the chance to fight for them.

Yet, in reality, Moe told the mediator the girls would be better off with me and gave me sole custody. This was just the first page. Lie after lie after lie. Page after page they rolled out. Sometimes, he would admit a half-truth but then ball them inside a ball of lies.

Parts of it read as confessions where he would fully admit his bad deeds but then provided an excuse. For example, he admitted to engaging in inappropriate conversations with a minor but stated it was because he had played so many hours of Xbox with him, he viewed him as an adult.

He continued saying he was in a depressed state of mind and because of that he lacked judgment and made poor decisions. The deeper I read, the more he admitted or bragged. He said he had a sexual relationship while he was a minor with his best friend's mom.

He made sure to note in all caps he only tested positive for LEGAL marijuana. He stated the exact date when he stopped using corporal punishment on the girls. There were a lot of weird comments like he claimed how he had to sneak into the girls' preschool to see them. He always carried ChapStick to mend Kay's lips, that he would talk to Diana in a playful manner, that Cecilia is a Christian church member, and firefighters gave Mallory a red plastic fireman hat.

Moe also included hundreds of pages of Talking Parents messages, his files on all of the men I had dated, including Facebook posts they posted predating when I knew them, and pictures of my art.

Dr. Bedlam called me for the exit interview. He led with all those little things corporate people say to wrap up a conversation, except we didn't have a conversation. He then asked, "So anything else I need to know?"

I said a sentence or so before I paused because I could tell he wasn't really listening. "Okay, great, I'll be submitting the report…" My mind trailed off… was he trying to conclude the call already? I was confused. Did he not read what I read? And he had no questions?

"Are you sure you don't have any questions for me?"

That kind of threw him off. "Oh, uhh, hold on let me see, umm."

I could hear papers moving around. "Umm, tell me about your art."

"Art has always been a part of me. I am currently trying to put together a collection of ten pieces that, once completed, I can sell and hopefully donate the money to a charity."

Dr. Bedlam made no comment then asked me, "Tell me when Diana choked on a Hatchimal toy."

I explained Diana never choked on a Hatchimal, that the story was made up. I explained I had told the girls that they needed to put all their small toys away in a box because Diana could choke on them. From that, Moe made up this whole story claiming Diana choked, almost died, that 911 was called, and told the court he was going to drive to the firehouse and get the report because he had concerns about what happened inside my home. But none of that actually happened, it was all a dramatic fabrication that originated from me asking the girls to pick up their toys.

Dr. Bedlam again had no comments and asked, "Are the girls in school?"

"Yes."

The conversation was over, and Dr. Bedlam hung up.

That was weird.

Whatever.

I didn't put too much thought into it.

It would all be fine; he had all the information.

When I walked into my therapist's office that same afternoon, I explained what happened. He had also spoke with Dr. Bedlam. He told me to call him as soon as I received Dr. Bedlam's report. He had an odd inflection of concern in his voice, but I was so convinced the truth would come out that I brushed it off.

Man, why was everyone acting weird this week?

The next day, he emailed me his report.

30

YOU KNOW, IN THIS LIGHT, YOU SORT
OF RESEMBLE RICHARD GARDNER

APRIL 26, 2020

Dr. Bedlam's report was 125 pages long. Anyone that was accustomed to reading journal articles knows if you want to find out what they discovered, read the conclusion first.

I scrolled down. Ah, there it was.

> Mother was to have the children on the first, third, and fifth weekends, father had them the remaining other time.

Must be a typo. Dr. Bedlam must have accidentally switched mother and father, so I emailed him. He didn't respond. I kept reading. Mother should be placed on supervised visitation if any other abuse claims arise.

Wait… what? Another typo? I read on.

> Father should be the primary parent and children should move in with him at his parents' house and attend school in father's hometown.

Dr. Bedlam was recommending to completely reverse custody. This wasn't right. My hand was shaking so bad I could hardly read on. Mother was a danger to her children, and they should be removed from her.

No, no this wasn't right. I must be reading this wrong.

I printed out the report.

My finger carefully traced the sentence, in my expert opinion I believe the mother suffers from Munchhausen's by Proxy.

I screamed and called Tony. "He's going to take the girls away from me! He recommended reversing custody and said if any other abuse allegations come in that I should be placed on supervised visitation!"

I was talking so fast Tony couldn't make sense of it. "No, that doesn't sound right. He can't do that."

"He is! I'm going to lose the girls!" I started sobbing.

"There's no way he recommended the girls living full time with that whack job, you must have just read it wrong."

"I'm not reading it wrong, Tony, they're taking the girls." I felt like I was dying. "He said I have Munchhausen's by Proxy and that I am a danger to the girls."

"What? What's that?"

"It's a diagnosis that means I'm abusing the girls for attention like that movie *The Sixth Sense* where the mom is slowly poisoning the girl's soup to gain sympathy from the community."

"You're not f***** hurting the girls, and everyone knows that."

"I know, but that is what Dr. Bedlam is claiming, and he's recommending Moe be the primary parent, and the court is going to adopt his recommendations."

"No, way. They aren't going to do that. They can't."

"They can." I started sobbing again.

"I'm coming over." And Tony hung up.

My brain was desperately trying to make sense of what I just read. How did Dr. Bedlam come to that conclusion? If I was so terrible, what did Moe have? I don't remember reading anything about him.

I read over it more carefully. Nurses are great at their jobs because most of us can turn off our emotions, triage a situation, tackle the problem at hand, and do what needs to be done. My eyes scanned his words line by line as my entire left hemisphere went into full analytic mode.

First, who was this girl he kept naming in the first few pages that was not a part of our family?

Did Dr. Bedlam get his clients confused?

Moving on to the gut of his report.

Dr. Bedlam said that I scored slightly defensive, which he interpreted to mean that I was not legitimately well, leading him to his conclusion that I had Munchhausen's by Proxy.

Dr. Bedlam stated he supported his diagnosis of Munchhausen's by Proxy with three prongs which included: the April 2019 bite incident, the November 2019 incident, and Kay's therapist.

He indicated that I was attempting to triangulate Kay's therapist, yet, in his limitation of treatment section, he noted that he never actually spoke with her. However he claimed, if he did, it would not change his opinion.

Did I read that right? He never actually spoke with her, so he formulated an opinion that would not be swayed even if he did have a conversation with her? Is that not the definition of bias? Okay, I could toss that out as he had no supportive evidence to support that assertion.

Next, the bite. Dr. Bedlam stated that the CPS report concluded that the bite found on Kay was from a dog.

No, it wasn't.

I read the sentence again. Dr. Bedlam *quoted* the forensic medical examiner, but that's not what he said. That should be easy to clear up because I had a copy of the CPS report right here.

I skimmed through the whole thing again. That quote Dr. Bedlam stated in his report was nowhere to be found in the actual CPS report. So, he lied about what the forensic medical examiner said and wrote a falsified quote.

Something unhinged inside me, and I started laughing.

Did Dr. Bedlam not know that I knew exactly what the report said? No wait, I gave him the report. What a goon. Nowhere in that report did it ever say a dog bit her. In fact, it repeatedly stated, human bite mark.

Dr. Bedlam went on to say Moe and his family told him it was a dog bite, so he believed them.

Let me get this straight. Dr. Bedlam was intentionally rejecting the facts supported by a CPS social worker along with two medical physician reports and instead was using a litany of selective hearsay to endorse his claims?

Seriously? Who paid this guy? Oh, ya, Moe did.

Dr. Bedlam didn't even really say anything about his third prong… his main focus which was the bite. None of it made sense because Moe admitted to both the April and November incidents happening while in his care.

How did he conclude with Munchhausen's by Proxy then?

Dr. Bedlam claimed the only reason I took Kay to urgent care after she got bit was because I was trying to shore up my own insecurities. Really? I was trying to shore up *my* insecurities. How did he explain then the CPS report claiming medical treatment was necessary, and the urgent care physician ordering antibiotics?

I laughed again. "I told him I was an eight on the Enneagram test, right? He really should have known better."

Wasn't Munchausen's by Proxy a diagnosis of exclusion meaning one had to exclude any other plausible medical or psychological reason before concluding the diagnosis? Didn't this diagnosis need to have an overwhelming amount of evidence that suggested the girls had an inexplicable trail of illnesses that seemingly could not be explained by any doctor?

In 1995, by the time Jennifer Bush was eight years old, her mother Kathy Bush subjected her daughter over six hundred and forty (640) days in the hospital, undergone forty (40) medical procedures, and had one thousand eight hundred and nineteen (1,819) nonsurgical treatments according to investigators.

In Texas, Kaylene Bowen-Wright, 36, subjected her ten-year-old son to three hundred and twenty-three (323) doctor visits, and he underwent thirteen (13) major surgeries.

So, let me get this straight, Dr. Bedlam was accusing me of being like Dee Dee Blanchard from the story of *Gypsy Rose*, but he did not even ask to see any of the girls' medical records?

He was hinging his diagnosis on three points: a prejudicial opinion, a lie, and nothing?

Maybe it was my Italian side or maybe it was my Belfast blood boiling, but *he could shove that three-pronged devil's pitchfork right up his gluteal cleft.*

I imagined him on his oversized computer typing into goggle WedMD search engine. Female, check. Between the appropriate age range, check. Had medical knowledge, check. Eureka! Munchausen's by Proxy.

By Dr. Bedlam's standards, I guess every female nurse and doctor with children must also have the same affliction. Reading his report was like reading a Mad Libs game with psychology words. He tried to sound dubiously smart because his ideas lacked any logical framework. In another section, Dr. Bedlam made an absurd argument that because I work full-time (three, twelve hour shifts per week), I don't have time for the girls and so more custody should be granted to Moe due to the fact he had more free time.

What? Dr. Bedlam previously was a lawyer? What's the argument here? Only parents who are unemployed should have custody of their children?

Wouldn't the fact Moe couldn't maintain employment be a red flag? To link unemployment to mental illness or substance use problems would just be too far reaching. It's like they seemingly forgot how Moe was able to pay them.

I've met some unintelligent doctors in my day, but he took the cake.

Dr. Bedlam wrote that Moe was a shining star.

He really had to scrape the barrel to find praises worthy to sing about Moe, but somehow, he managed to do it.

Moe had gone to therapy, proved that he had overcome every hurdle in his path, and really was the victim he claimed to be.

Dr. Bedlam claimed I was too harsh and unfair for involving police and CPS back in 2016, yet I wasn't even the one that initially reported it; the court mediator did. But I was concerned that he thought reporting sexually inappropriate behavior between an adult and a minor was extreme, harsh, and unfair. Tell me you're a pedo simp without telling me you're a pedo simp.

He tried to protect himself on a different page by stating the actions taken in 2016 were appropriate at the time; so, which was it? It couldn't be both.

This was not some Schrodinger's cat argument, child abuser edition; proposing if a child abuser and a child were placed in a sealed room, one would not know if the child was abused or not until the door was opened.

You couldn't play both sides of the fence to safeguard your ass when you're already up to your neck in sewage. Yet, the fact that the words *extreme, harsh,* and *unfair* were used when I not only verbally explicitly told him what was said, but he had a hard copy of the entire conversation as well, was telling in itself.

I flipped through his report, and I stopped on a picture of Moe's bonding study.

Moe, Cecilia, the girls, and both of his parents were all in the picture.

I thought the bonding study was to observe us the parents with the girls. Why was Cecilia doing the games while Moe appeared to be sitting on the couch? This was weird. Dr. Bedlam did both of his parents' and Cecilia's interviews at the same time as the bonding study.

Was Moe also included in their interviews?

Then I read the section and compared it to my bonding study. Dr. Bedlam barely spoke of Moe in his bonding study. By contrast, he had a lot to say about me. So much so, he included a numbered list of things for my bonding study.

The weirdest thing was everything he said supported that I was a good mother, caring, nurturing, supportive. It directly contraindicated his conclusion and recommendations.

Around and around Dr. Bedlam went topsy-turvy like an insidious loop of never-ending contradictions. One didn't even need a college degree to read Dr. Bedlam's report and know it was full of sh**, but it didn't matter because a *doctor* said it, and everything he recommended was likely to be adopted by Judge Mazle Dina, and she didn't care.

I could file a complaint with the California State Board of Psychiatry, but it could take one to two years for them to investigate, and they had no sway in custody. Plus, 730 reports were seemingly seen as just the opinions of a psychologist even if they had the legal duty to take reasonable precautions to protect children that burden befalls onto the courts, so it's likely the California State Board of Psychiatry wouldn't do anything.

The reality of my situation weighed heavy with me. I could voice all the flaws, bias, and downright lies, but my voice wouldn't matter. I was not a "doctor," therefore, I was not qualified to speak on his report. Even if I was, the court wouldn't listen to me, anyway. Judge Mazle Dina didn't care about the girls, she had proven that ten times over. They don't matter to her. I was powerless. My job was to keep them safe, but instead, I would be forced to throw them into the fire and watch.

If I ran, they would find me. They would take the girls and put me in jail then on supervised visitation. If I screamed, they would gag me. In all scenarios, I lost the girls.

I was going to lose custody of the girls.

My thoughts raced down the tunnel, deep and dark they unfolded. Diana was going to be ripped apart from her sisters. Would they understand why they couldn't see Diana anymore? What would Moe tell them?

In that dark place, it hit me. If I was a danger to *two* children then wouldn't I be a danger to *all* of my children?

Moe wasn't going to stop here. He would call CPS and make sure I lost Diana, too.

I dunk deeper and deeper. Moe would be able to do whatever he liked now. With this diagnosis, I would absorb all blame of all possible future abuse as well. By way of this strategy, it was a trap to silence me from reporting abuse and punish me if I did.

How was I going to keep my job as a nurse with this diagnosis? I was going to lose my job, too. If I couldn't work, how was I going to keep my house? I was going to be homeless, childless, with no hope out.

Hope.

Out of the black void of despair I heard a whisper, *Your therapist told you to call him, remember.*

I walked outside to my driveway and let the warmth of the sun cover me. I called my therapist, and he wasn't completely shocked.

"I'm shocked that you're not shocked, why aren't you shocked?"

He explained he was genuinely concerned after his conversation with Dr. Bedlam. He felt Dr. Bedlam was asking leading questions, but he couldn't say anything to me at the time.

He said, "I tried to tell him that I knew Moe from your marriage counseling sessions, and that I felt he was abusive, but he cut me off and didn't want to talk about Moe. Dr. Bedlam wanted to know if you had a disturbed childhood or if you had been raped, to both I stated that neither had come up in our conversations." Dr. Bedlam went on to tell my therapist that he felt it would explain his hypothesis that I was projecting his invented rape theory onto the girls.

He said, "We got into a debate, and I argued again that you had never disclosed that you had been raped. The conversation quickly dissolved after that, and Dr. Bedlam suggested that we agree to disagree."

Disturbed childhood? Raped? This was all new to me. I had never been raped, but I was being accused of it to support his made-up theories. My mind flashed to a line Dr. Bedlam wrote in his report; he claimed to have asked Moe if he thought I had been raped.

Dr. Bedlam claimed Moe said, "I don't know, probably." Did it ever occur to this dullard's mind to ask me? Instead, he went to my therapist and accused me of being raped?

Rage welled up inside me. What if a woman *had* been raped? Would he then exploit her most vulnerable painful moment to prop up a theory that carried no weight. And for what? To put children in harm's way?

I curled up in my bed. I couldn't move. The thought of losing my girls was unbearable. I cried so hard, my eyes hurt, and I stayed in bed all weekend. I was sinking deeper and deeper into despair.

What day was it? It was Monday. The girls came back today. Tony went to get them. I had to get up. I couldn't let them see me like this—a crying mess, curled up in bed.

Everything was fine. Get up! You know this BS isn't true, just *prove* it.

My mind was racing.

That idiot falsified a quote he claimed he plucked from the CPS report. Losing the girls was *not* an option. Get a second opinion; ask for a 733. Get another doctor to review Dr. Bedlam's 730 report. Call that doctor *that I wanted* to go with originally. The one Judge Mazle Dina declined.

Get up!

I pulled myself out of bed, walked over to my shower, and turned the water on. I stared down at the drain. The hot water flowed over my head, through my hair, and swirled down the drain. I longed to go with it. They said all water flows back to the ocean. I was so numb inside; my skin barely felt the scalding hot water.

I let my emotions go with the outgoing tide.

On June 25, 2020, we had another court hearing. Mr. Bladderwort told me in the hallway if I don't drop the restraining order and give Moe unsupervised overnights then he was going to ask the court to hear Dr. Bedlam's report in ten days.

June 25, 2020, Judge Mazle Dina granted Moe unsupervised overnight visitation every first, third, fourth, and fifth weekends from 9 a.m. Saturday to 6 p.m. Sunday. The police report stating that Kay told police Moe touched her vagina was never addressed, and no additional counseling regarding appropriate behavior with minors was ever ordered. No review of any reports was done. None of these things seemed to matter. Just, here ya go. Family court was pushing Moe through from point A to point B despite the consequences of what happened to our girls or me. It was hopeless. What Mr. Bladderwort and the court weren't expecting was that I already knew I had the legal right to a 733, which was a second opinion of sorts. It allowed me to contest the findings and recommendations of a 730-child custody evaluation and created a buffer zone thwarting Mr. Bladderwort's plans. It was my only chance. The court *had* to order it if I requested it, so I did.

31

FELONS OF A FEATHER FLOCK TOGETHER

"Why haven't you answered your phone?" It was Jacques.
"I, uh."

Before I could respond, he said, "So, I did some digging." He was practically giddy with excitement.

I raised both of my eyebrows and respond flatly, "And…"

"Okay, so you're not going to believe this, and it might explain our she-devil a little bit. I was looking for some history like education, or rather I was looking for a lack of education. You know something that could explain the why. Why is she so terrible, and you'll never guess what I found."

Jacques' voice paused, waiting for me. I said, "Well, what did you find?"

Jacques sounded like he was three espressos in. "So, this guy's face kept popping up, and I was like who is this and why does his face keep coming up in my search? So, I found out who he was. This guy was a certain city's City Councilman, and on July 2, 2017, he goes to Arizona with I'm assuming, his wife. The news article said they were at BJ's tavern, a bar and restaurant, when she hugged someone there, and he became enraged with jealousy. Words were probably exchanged because his wife left alone and upset that he was mad at her for hugging someone. She walked about a half mile then called him to come pick her up. He was too drunk to drive, so he showed up in an Uber with some other female. The three of them leave together in this Uber. Just before they were dropped off at his house, he threatens his wife, *'just wait until we get home.'* He was still mad about the hug, and one thing led to another, and then next thing you know, he starts choking his wife. He strangles her to the point of unconsciousness. So, now his wife is now laying lifeless on the ground with her eyes open, and the other female jumped in. He told her something like *'stay the f*** out of it,'* then he pushed her against the wall and then starts strangling her, too! Someone, I think from inside the house, called the police. When police arrive, the wife regains consciousness and is crying on the ground. He made some comment to police like, *'anything she says is a lie!'* The police noted redness around the wife's neck, no petechia hemorrhage, yet her eyes were slightly yellow, maybe she is a drunk, too. The police arrest him for domestic violence aggravated assault, aggravated assault, and drunk disorderly conduct. He has guns in the house, but the police report stated they were *'not brandished.'* At 0135 now the next morning, he agreed to a breathalyzer and blew a 0.173… he was facing two felony counts and a misdemeanor."

"Was the other female the judge or something?" I asked.

"No, not likely. She was described as being five feet three inches, one hundred and thirty-eight pounds (138) which does not fit the description of your she-devil," Jacques said.

"Okay? So, why is this story relevant?" I asked.

"Because the wife is the judge's sister!" he announced.

"Yeah, but the judge isn't liable for what her family does."

"You are absolutely correct; however, I also found a public document that shows, *'The Arizona Strangler'* and his wife, the sister, co-own property with the she-devil herself."

"Was he really called the Arizona Strangler?"

"No, I took creative liberties, and you're missing the point," Jacques said.

"What point is that exactly?"

Jacques sighed. "Like I was saying The Arizona Strangler co-owns property with the Perverter of Justice. She wore shirts with his name supporting his campaign, they go horseback riding together, and she also personally swore him into office. These two are tight."

I imagined Jacques interlocking his fingers together. He continued. "He flaunts her on his social media like he won a county fair blue-ribbon. Can you guess who got all charges dropped? Him. The questionable part is this, if they co-own property and he's the breadwinner in the marriage, then it would not be financially conducive for your judge if he got charged with two felony and a misdemeanor. Judge Mazle Dina needs him to pull his weight and pay his half of their shared property, plus the potential bad press it might bring her. She needed it _all_ to go away, and she has a particular talent for burying information."

"Can you prove the judge had any connection to getting any of those charges dropped?" I asked.

Jacques said, "Well, no. But there's definitely a possible motive to. Plus, it gives us a peek behind the curtain; felons of a feather flock together, ya know."

Allowing what Jacques just told me to sink in, my eyes welled up. There was a long silence. Not the reaction he was expecting, I guess. He asked, "What's wrong?"

I told him about Dr. Bedlam's report. He listened as my painful words flowed from me. I then realized. "Wait. I've been so busy moving all the little puzzle pieces that I couldn't see the bigger picture."

The court had seemingly been cultivating unpredictability and keeping me in suspended terror, yet, I was good at recognizing patterns; enough randomized plots create a set of data that once coded could be easily visible like Koch snowflake fractal. A corrupt government may extend its control indefinitely by creating a never-ending series of problems. I saw her clearly in this moment, who she was, what she was pretending, and how she had been controlling the system.

The court was seemingly attempting to make me dependent on her by tying my hopes of freedom and prosperity to fear, as if proclaiming she was the only one with the power. She thought me daft and ignorant, but she was using the same toolbox as the abusers. Her tools may be more cunning and sharp, but they all originated from the same wheelhouse, power, and control.

The CPS report stated that the incident was not probable, yet inevitable, due to Moe's mental health issues and substance abuse issues. But, the judge said on April 4, 2018, that she didn't think either of those two things were relevant, dismissing both of them, making her potentially liable.

When I read the report to her, and she had no comments, she *was* stonewalling me. She hid in the shadows of silence of *no comment* on record attempting to conceal her intentions. Yet, through her actions of writing the court orders, she had made her intentions visible. She hadn't drug tested Moe since 2018 because then she could maintain an illusion that he was sober or at least deny that she wasn't aware he was still using. Yet again, the CPS report ruined her deniability because not only did Kay test positive, it contained Moe's confessions of using while supervising the girls during his unsupervised visitations. She needed to bury that report so far in the ground no one could find it. Then Mr. Bladderwort provided her with an alternative option. Blame me.

Remember, Mr. Bladderwort made that passive aggressive pseudo-threat that I agreed to settle with his client's request on July 25, 2019; I thought it ludicrous. Then on October 15, 2019, Mr. Bladderwort began by stating that they wanted a 730 evaluation.

"We think that a 730 evaluation in this particular case would be very helpful." He continued. "We believe that there are serious questions regarding the motivations in the approach the mother to take this case that are detrimental to the child. I think those are matters in which could assessed best by the 730 evaluations."

Yet, Judge Mazle Dina said, "I can tell you reading the reports that there are problems with the kids. I don't need a 730 evaluation to tell me that."

And she also stated, "I have no evidence that he needed a mental health evaluation." However, she ordered a request for a 730 evaluation anyway.

I could feel my anger beginning to rise. Then when I kept reporting the issues with Moe, I might as well have painted a target on my back.

Judge Mazle Dina said it herself, "Perhaps you should remove yourself from the exchange, so you don't have an issue with it anymore."

Basically, telling me to stop reporting abuse, play nice, make the girls more available to Moe, and turn a blind eye to the abuse like she was. So, why would Judge Mazle Dina order a 730 evaluation she previously claimed she didn't need? Because it was never intended for Moe nor for the best interest of the girls. She ordered it to have double assurance. She wanted me gone, so like some cliché mafia movie, she sent her hitman to make sure the job was done. She denied my psychological evaluator because Mr. Bladderwort already had a special one picked out. One that repeated his words *the mother's motives are detrimental to the children.*

Voilà, Munchhausen's by Proxy, and now the judge could *legally* take the girls away from me. All the while she was getting paid. Money flowed more freely if what was best for the girls was determined to be what was best for the judge's pockets.

Judge Mazle Dina was colluding with Mr. Bladderwort and Dr. Bedlam! And she chose this cheap charlatan whose diagnosis couldn't withstand even a whispering wind of elementary logical questioning to destroy me?

F*** her! I'm going to send her hitman's head back to her in a box!

32

CONVINCE THE COURT

D r. Bedlam's strategy was not original; this was some Gilded Age Era bullshit. We may be in the twenty-first century, but they were pulling the same tricks from the turn of the nineteenth century yet with a modern twist. Asylums and lobotomies were so yesterday. They've just rebranded "hysteria" to an array of terms that should make the hair on your arms stand straight up should you heard them. Regardless how they've re-packaged hysteria, it's all part of what's called the "alienation industry." In fact, reports of child abusers gaining custody occurred so frequently in family court that it prompted academic researchers to comb over their data.

In 2011, Dr. Daniel Saunders of the University of Michigan received funding from the US Department of Justice to conduct significant research to examine how successfully court officials, notably evaluators, responded to domestic abuse cases. Respondents to the survey included four hundred and sixty-five (465) custody evaluators, two hundred (200) judges, one hundred and thirty-one (131) legal aid attorneys, one hundred and nineteen (119) private attorneys, and one hundred and ninety-three (193) domestic violence program workers. "The Saunders' study found that even among professionals most concerned and interested in domestic violence, at least 39% of the judges and 35% of the evaluators do not have the training they need to protect children and their mothers.' He also found that, 'domestic violence is frequently undetected in custody cases or ignored as a significant factor in custody visitation determinations."[1]

So, the courts, which were meant to be *the place* to deal with domestic violence and child abuse, had personnel who were not trauma informed, were not trained in checking for risk assessment, domestic violence, post-separation violence, and the impact of domestic violence on children because that totally made sense.

A hospital wouldn't let a janitor, or a nurse or even an internal medicine physician perform open-heart surgery on a patient because they were not qualified. Even Pediatric medicine screens for possible issues concerning domestic violence because they know the adverse effects it could cause. The Adverse Childhood Experience (ACE) Study that began in 1994 by Kaiser Permanente and the Center for Disease Control (CDC) assessed the effects of child abuse and related adverse childhood experiences as a public health problem. Vincent J. Felitti, MD, published the ACE Study in 1998, finding that ACE prevention, such as abuse and neglect, could have a significant impact on our society's health. The ACE Study uncovered how childhood stressors affect a person's health and social well-being later on in their life. The cumulative negative exposures impaired the biological pathways that could give way to health risks, disability, disease, and early mortality. The greater the number of ACE's the child was exposed to, the more that child was at risk for developing significant health problems. In the same way the longer a person smokes cigarettes, the greater the odds that person risked developing chronic obstructive pulmonary disease (COPD). The CDC states, "ACE's are linked to chronic health problem, mental illness and substance abuse problems in adolescence and adulthood. ACE's can also negatively impact education, job opportunities and earning potential."[2]

If hospitals were implementing ACE screening tools within their pediatric offices, why wasn't the family court doing the same? ACE's are preventable. The ACE Study has been available for twenty-five years. To my knowledge, the Family Court System has not acknowledged or utilized the ACE assessment. This meant that some families were experiencing a second cycle of generational abuse, and the courts are not taking any action to recognize or stop it? I must be missing something. I read on.

In 2016, Geraldine Stahly, PhD, professor at California State University San Bernardino, wrote a research article called, "Protective Mothers, Endangered Children: Quantifying System Failure." Geraldine Stahly PhD and a group of interns analyzed data from a national survey of protective mothers who were involved in custody disputes from thirty-nine (39) states. The following statistics are for the one hundred and sixty-three (163) California cases, which comprise 40 percent of the total three hundred and ninety-nine (399) cases. Among the mothers from California, 82 percent of mothers started with primary custody; nearly all the cases had allegations of physical and sexual child abuse.[3]

However, when the mothers brought up the issues of child abuse, domestic violence, violations of court orders, criminal conduct, substance abuse to the attention of the courts, the judges ignored and minimized evidence of abuse and ultimately changed custody to the alleged abuser. Only a staggering 12 percent of these protective mothers had primary custody after court proceedings. At some time throughout the proceedings, more than half the mothers who were fighting to safeguard their children from abuse were restricted from any contact with their children, and half were ordered to be placed on supervised visitation. Over two-thirds of the children continued to report abuse, and over half of the mothers stopped reporting abuse for fear their contact with their children would be terminated completely. There was minimal difference in the outcome for California mothers and the mothers from the other thirty-eight (38) states. Eighty-six percent of mothers believe their children were still being abused yet believe they cannot protect their children. "73.5% of California mothers reported that family court judges and commissioners ignored, minimized or refuted evidence of child abuse, less often than non-California cases (81%.)"[4] Attorneys for both the California and non-California groups cautioned mothers that pursuing any form of legal action against the fathers may jeopardize their child custody rights, and they were counseled not to report child abuse or domestic violence to the family court.

Lawyers in California advised mothers 64.2% of the time not to pursue, 68.4% of mothers were advised not to mention abuse, 58.7% had medical or physical evidence of child abuse, 82.5% had other corroborative evidence of child abuse and 74.7% of the cases the children had positively identified the father as the perpetrator of the abuse.[5]

Most of the time the court requires mediation, in California 82.8% were court ordered to mediation (non-California only 44.1%) and 52.3% of the mediators ignored, minimized, or refuted evidence of abuse. "59.1% of California mothers reported that mediators who made recommendations to the court ('Child Custody Recommending Mediators') recommended that mothers, who had come to court to protect their children, should lose custody rights or all contact with their children."[6]

The study also examined various agencies that are currently set in place to protect children. When law enforcement was involved, unfortunately there was no benefit, and majority of California fathers were neither arrested nor prosecuted for their crimes. "When law enforcement does not take a case forward to prosecution, there is a tendency to assume that no crime has been committed. That is an incorrect assumption in many of these cases, since the District Attorney needs to meet a high criminal burden of proof for prosecution and often children are unable to testify due to the trauma arising from the crimes committed against them."[7]

Court ordered custody evaluators like Dr. Bedlam were among the worse; 73.1% of California custody evaluators recommended the mother lose parental rights. These evaluators assigned a high rate of non-scientific labels and exotic diagnoses to mothers, with the most common being, "Parental Alienation Syndrome" (PAS) at a staggering 42% for both groups, a non-scientific label invented by Richard Gardner MD "The label 'Alienator' was also used at close to the same rate for California (30.9%) and non-California (34.4%) mothers.

Unusual labels and exotic diagnoses such as "Delusional," "Munchhausen's Syndrome by Proxy" and "Folie à Deux" were assigned at about the same rate for mothers in both groups, none of whom had previously been diagnosed with any such condition." Sound familiar doesn't it. In California alone, 11.9% of the mothers in this study were diagnosed with Munchhausen's Syndrome by Proxy.[8]

PhD Stahly states, "Professionals appointed under Evidence Code 730 are not regulated nor are their fees capped. There is no requirement for them to have specific experience or in-depth training or expertise on child sex abuse. The role of an expert witness is to educate the court on a subject about which the court needs more information. To be deemed an expert in court, one needs have special knowledge, skill, experience, training, or education sufficient to qualify him as an expert on the subject to which his testimony relates. Expert witnesses are called in a trial or hearing to discuss their areas of expertise. It is unclear what area of expertise, if any, child custody evaluators have."[9]

Overall Geraldine Stahly Ph.D study found, "When mothers with custody brought concerns of domestic abuse to family courts and asked for protection of children, a counterintuitive denial of the documented epidemic of family violence took place across all systems. Mothers' reports of violent crimes were mostly ignored or minimized by professionals despite evidence of such abuse."[10] Almost all women in both groups said they felt discriminated against because they sought to protect their children and themselves from domestic violence and child abuse. "The Leadership Council on Child Abuse and Interpersonal Violence conservatively estimates that family (divorce) courts place about 58,500 children with abusive parents per year nationally, despite their having a safe parent able and willing to protect them. California comprises 12% of the national population, thus, its family courts are estimated to place over 6,000 children at risk every year."[11] Both domestic violence and child abuse are a United States national epidemic. Nearly all current systems in place failed to protect the children from continuing abuse. A safe, non-violent protective parent is refused custody in favor of the abuser in surprisingly most circumstances. Gender prejudice, cognitive dissonance avoidance, refusal to consider children's admissions of incest and violence, a purposefully formed and carefully maintained culture of denial in family courts, motivated by a desire for financial gain have all been proposed as reasons for such failures. Geraldine Stahly Ph.D recommended that the reasons for such extreme system failure be thoroughly investigated.[12]

In 2020, Joan Meier, a professor of Clinical Law and Director of the National Family Violence Law Center at the George Washington University Law School, then conducted a federally funded study published in the *Journal of Social Welfare and Family Law*, "U.S. child custody outcomes in cases involving parental alienation and abuse allegations: what do the data show?" In an article she wrote on December 2, 2021, Victims of Domestic abuse find no haven in family courts. She stated,

"Working with four other researchers, I conducted a federally funded study that reviewed all electronically published family court cases between parents in the U.S. between 2005 and 2014 related to custody or visitation that involved abuse or alienation claims.

"Among the results from this analysis of thousands of cases: Courts rejected women's claims of partner violence and child abuse by men, on average, roughly two-thirds of the time. They rejected mothers' claims of child abuse by fathers approximately 80% of the time. And they reversed custody from mothers alleging abuse to the allegedly abusive fathers at rates ranging from 22% – for partner violence claims – to 56% when mothers alleged both sexual and physical child abuse."[13]

This study analyzed over 15,000 cases over a ten-year period from January 1, 2005, to December 31, 2014, and then was able to code 4,338 cases that matched the criteria required in the study. "The Study sought to develop empirical measures of (i) the rates at which courts credit (i.e. believe) eight (8) different types of abuse and alienation allegations raised by either parent against the other; (ii) the rates at which parents win/lose the case, or lose custody when alleging any type of abuse against the other parent; (iii) the impact of alienation claims/defenses on (i) and (ii) above; and (iv) the impact of gender on (i), (ii), and (iii) above. That is, do the rates of crediting of abuse, wins, or custody losses vary for mothers and fathers when one accuses the other of abuse or alienation?"[14]

The findings back up popular criticisms of family court processes that place children in the care of abusive or dangerous parents. Overall, the data clearly indicated that mothers who accused a father of abuse—particularly child abuse—have a significant risk (almost 1 in 4) of losing custody of their children to the accused abuser. Even when courts found that fathers had abused the children or the mother, they still awarded them custody 13% of the time and in cases with credited child physical abuse claims, abusers still won custody 20% of the time. Again, discovering that allegations of alienation seemed to trump any allegations and proven evidence of abuse. Barry Goldstein an attorney said, 'For some reason, the avalanche of research from the most credible sources and horrific catastrophes that could have been prevented have not yet convinced the court system to create the needed reforms. If they do not believe the outside sources, the least they could do is create their own study or investigation to confirm or deny the concerns of so many credible sources. The failure to take these concerns seriously creates an appearance that they do not want to know they failed the children.'[2]

Chief Counsel Robert David Steele said at the ITNJ Judicial Commission of Inquiry into human trafficking and child sex abuse in 2018, "I have found in my research and in preparation for this court and all of the work that will follow that most organizations that end up being used to prey on children, Oxfam is a resent example. All of the United Nations organizations, the Boys Scouts of America, all of the child services agencies across the United States of America. They did not start out as organizations to prey on children, but they attract pedophiles, and ultimately pedophiles end up rising in the ranks, controlling those organizations. So that an organization that initially started out in the service of children becomes an organization that is in fact hunting children." [15]

So here's who they (the Family Court System) really do not want you to know, Richard Gardner, since it's not like our government would ever support someone who has a direct impact on children without properly checking their background.

So who is he? Before I go any further, you should know who he is and what he did. In the 1980s, Richard Gardner invented the term Parental Alienation Syndrome (PAS) to describe what he observed as an epidemic of child sexual abuse allegations in custody battles. To summarize, he argued that the vast proportion of mothers were just vindictive or insane and were lying about the abuse to obtain legal advantage. The more the child refused to go with the accused abuser, the more he asserted PAS was present. He claimed, "that 90% of children in custody litigation suffered from PAS." As hysteria had just been removed from the Diagnostic and Statistical Manual of Mental Disorders (DSM-5) his goal was to have PAS added to the DMS-5 and recognized as an official diagnosable psychological illness. However, his theory was rejected due to its lack or credibility and due to his "apologist attitude towards pedophilia."

"Gardner's views of sexuality were disturbing. He claimed that all humans sexual paraphilias, including pedophilia, sadism, rape, necrophilia, zoophilia (sex with animals), coprophilia (sex with feces), and other deviant behaviors 'serve the purposes of species survival' by 'enhanc[ing] the general level of sexual excitation in society.' (Gardner, 1992b, p. 20; see also Hoult, 2006; Dallam, 1998.) He also "argued expressly that adult-child sex need not be intrinsically harmful to children," (Gardner, 1992b). He viewed Western society as "excessively punitive" in its treatment of pedophilia as a "sickness and a crime" (Gardner, 1991, p. 115), and attributed this "overreaction" to the influence of the Jews (Gardner, 1992b, pp.47, 49). Gardner opposed mandated reporting of child sexual abuse (Gardner, 1992b, pp. 611-12; see also Dallam, 1998)." He wrote in his book, *Sex Abuse Hysteria: Salem Witch Trials Revisited*, "sex abuse is not necessarily traumatic; the determinant as to whether sexual molestation will be traumatic to the child is the social attitude towards these encounters." He continued and stated, "the child has to be helped to appreciate that we have in our society an exaggeratedly punitive and moralistic attitude about adult-child sexual encounters."

He even claimed "that woman's psychology and conditioning make them potentially masochistic rape victims" who may "gain pleasure from being beaten, bound, and otherwise made to suffer," as "the price they are willing to pay for gaining the gratification of receiving the sperm" (Gardner, 1992b, p.26)."[17] He said much more but you get the point. With no chance of getting his made-up diagnosis recognized by the medical community, he instead traveled across the United States and testified as an expert witness in over 400 cases within the Family Court System selling "parental alienation," (PA) or simply "alienation," the idea that one parent was trying to ostracize the other by making up lies of child abuse to gain leverage in court. The courts didn't seem to question its scientific validity, and it was now routinely used as a defense against child abuse. It had set "up a paradoxically disastrous dynamic: So long as an abuser can convince a court that the children's attitudes can be labeled 'alienation,' he can *benefit* from the very impact of his abuse."[18] "The perverse 'genius' of PA's deception has been the way it backs mothers into a corner, preys on her fears, and turns her maternal instincts to protect her children into a pitfall.... Due to PA's dominance of family court proceedings, a 'good mother' is now not one who is loving, caring, and responsible towards her children, but instead a mother who actively encourages contact with a father, whether he is violent or not.[19]" But how far does that notion go? Surely, they were not endorsing incest and pedophilia, right? In 2021 inside a family court room in Pittsburgh, Pennsylvania, the mother's lawyer, Richard Ducote, was questioning a professional witness, Robert Evans, who was there on behalf of the father. Here is their conversation:

Ducote: Can a parent inflict more damage by parental alienation to a child than the parent could inflict by, say, breaking the child's bones?

Evans: Conceivably, yes.

Ducote: How about, you have a four-year-old child, and the parent punches the child in the face and leaves two black eyes. Could in your opinion, parental alienation be worse for the child than that?

Evans: Potentially, yes.

Ducote: Okay. How about if you have a 4yr old, and the father forces the child to perform fellatio on him. Could that be less harmful to the child than parental alienation?

Evans: Potentially, yes.

Ducote: How about the father actually fully penetrates his four-year-old daughter's vagina with his penis. Could that be less harmful to the child than parental alienation?

Evans: Potentially.

…Evans, needing to protect his source of income, unashamedly sticks to the grift, maintaining an appalling commitment to the idea that lack of normalised contact with a father is what is truly damaging to children, regardless of how much violence and abuse is inflicted on them."[20]

This is the work of Richard Gardner, and it has infested the entire Family Court System. "Due to the way legal processes build on precedents, once his ideas had worked their way into the justice system they were easily able to multiply and fortify themselves. The legitimacy of PAS in the eyes of the judges and other legal associates stemmed solely from the frequency by which it was used, rather than the validity of the concept itself." When custody decisions are decided based on immoral reprehensible deceit without beneficial scientific support, the consequences can be catastrophic.

Agencies like the Center for Judicial Excellence have been tracking the murder of children where judges have knowingly placed them in harms way. The Family Court System uses predatory practices to prey on vulnerable situations, utilizes gender bias against women, has commodified children, and upholds this political fallacy that male physical, sexual and emotional violence is just in their biology therefore they should face no consequences for exerting it.

I sat back in my chair, so I basically had almost no chance, the courts were run by predators, child abusers and incest apologists. Who can I even report this to that's not corrupt? These reports have been out for decades… they're aware, they just choose to do nothing. Addressing this issue necessitates accountability, which implies that the courts would have to be answerable for damages. If we look at other organizations like the Catholic Church for example that have been held accountable for child abuse and they paid well over $3 billion in settlements for roughly over 8,600 cases… imagine how much the family courts would owe. These people are not dumb, they know that it may cost them billions if not trillions to rectify. They seemingly have no ethical morals, but when I look at the state of even our highest Supreme Court, am I surprised? So what can I do? Do nothing? Screw that! Nemo me impune lacessit, that is, no one attacks me (or my daughters) with impunity!

The first thing I needed was a lawyer. Yet seemingly every lawyer in the area knew the odds, but fighting back was my only option. Finding one who even wanted my case or whose first words weren't "we need to settle" proved difficult. Settling wasn't an option. If the 730 report was not contested, it opened the door for any foreseeable abuse to occur then automatically transferred onto me. A 50/50 custody arrangement would not be in the best interest of the girls, but all of this was a moot point anyway because Moe wanted it all now. Moe read what Dr. Bedlam recommended, and he was refusing anything less; he agreed the girls should be removed from me, placed into his parents' house, transferred to a different school, and he wanted me on supervised visitations. This unholy trio, Judge Male Dina, Attorney Bladderwort and Doctor Bedlam, created a new monster.

33

HIDE AWAY
WHERE YOU'RE SAFE

To fight a 730 report was an uphill battle with many obstacles, and it was also a very isolating experience. I soon realized by sharing my experience or what I had read, most people had very little understanding of what was truly occurring within the Family Courts, unless they had gone through it themselves or knew someone who had. Some people seemed skeptical of my claims. Some suggested that perhaps I was the one hurting my children, or that I could use this time to work on myself, as if justifying the false accusations made by Dr. Bedlam. Some simply expressed sympathy for my situation, "Sorry that's unfair," but could not offer real help. Suspicion, blame, and pity; it made me feel sick. The people that wanted to help had no power, and the people that had power to change this were sitting idly by. No one wanted to come out and take accountability for these problems besides the world had other bigger problems right now. The coronavirus (SARS-CoV-2) had just hit, which ironically was a good thing for me right because the courts were nearly shut down thus no trial would be happening soon. Yet that didn't mean Mr.

Bladderwort didn't try; he pushed to have the trial as soon as possible. The hospital was imploding. I don't need to explain to you what it was like being a nurse during COVID-19 because it was on the news every day, all day.

Our ICU quickly converted into "The COVID Unit," and everyone was afraid; afraid of COVID, afraid of our unit, and afraid of us. I watched a report on the news of an ER doctor having their child visitation removed from them because they worked on the *frontlines*. That was what I was terrified of, and Moe, being opportunistic, wasted no time inquiring about my patients' diagnoses. I was already staring down that tunnel, and I didn't need new reasons I might lose the girls. By this time, I was a *grey rock* communication pro. Responses devoid of emotion, short and stick to the facts. For example, *Per hospital policy I am not allowed to disclose that information.* Done. Moe's messages made me want to gouge my eyeballs out. Moe stated several times that I should review the 730 report by Dr. Bedlam, so I could better understand my issues. "I urge you to read the evaluation again, to see why Dr. Bedlam made the evaluation he made."

I had to prioritize my fights. Moe was just a distraction, and Dr. Bedlam would have to wait, too. I was now a family court leper; no attorney wanted to touch my case. One of them told me, "You should settle with him 50/50, otherwise, he is going to get the girls, and can you imagine what that would be like; can you imagine what he would do to them?" He worked on me in this fashion for a good long while, trying to get me to settle until I snapped. "No, that cannot happen. That *will* not happen. I don't have Munchhausen's by Proxy. The girls and I cannot afford to allow this to go uncorrected. I can't settle."

He was out. This... I don't even know what to call him... shameless lawyer already knew Moe's unwavering stance, too. It was mentally taxing having nearly everyone tell me I had an 80 percent chance of losing custody. A legal assistant tried to... I don't know, one up my situation thinking maybe it would make me feel better. "Your case isn't the worse I've seen... I once saw a case where the toddler (they proceed to tell me the graphic details of the sexual abuse) and the courts still forced the mom to give the toddler over to him." That didn't make me feel better, I just felt incredibly sad.

Dr. Bedlam's report felt like I'd been handed a terminal illness, and I had less than a year to live. Trying to cherish every moment yet already mourning that every moment might be our last. This might be my last summer with the girls before they were taken away. This might be our last photo, kiss, hug. Doing this while also trying to maintain a smile was crushing. Then I had to walk into work where everyone died. Nearly every patient that was transferred to ICU died. I was losing track of how many bodies I'd put into bags. I couldn't process the pandemic because my mind was too preoccupied with the thought of losing the girls. The 733 report was going to cost at least 10K and the lawyer for the trial probably another 10K. I needed money. In attempts to cut costs, I switched the girls out of private school to public school, assuming COVID was going to pass by the fall. What a wishfully ignorant thought that was.

From Monday to Friday, I was now also a teacher for kindergarten and first grade. I don't know how parents were doing it. During the girls' parent-teacher meeting online, I asked when she expected the kids to be able to return back in-person to school.

She replied, "Oh, they've extended the online learning until at least December 2021."

"What? Next year, too?"

"That's what I've heard," she said.

There's no way. The private school announced that they were going to have in-person learning starting January. I would sell a kidney if I had to. I didn't tell her, but this online learning was garbage. The fundamentals of kindergarten and first grade were not designed to be absorbed through a screen, and I was not going to have them struggle through the remainder of their schooling because they didn't get the essential building blocks. Perhaps I was being a tad extreme with the kidney. I could refinance my house instead.

So, I did.

I found a lawyer, but she wanted a ten-thousand-dollar retainer upfront, and I was told the 733 would be costing more. Good thing I pulled money out during the refinance. Trying to explain everything to her in an hour consolation while mentally capped was probably not me at my best; *she thinks I'm crazy*.

However, she knew Dr. Bedlam. They apparently went to law school together. She said, "He was a bit of an odd duck." When I repeated some of the things Judge Mazle Dina had said, she looked confused. With what I perceived as great suspicion, she took my case. I don't know why she agreed to take me on, but she did, maybe she just wanted to read what the odd duck wrote.

The psychologist that I previously wanted, Luke Mazzini, PhD, had over thirty years of experience in criminal forensic neuropsychology. His college age secretary greeted me and asked if I would like some water.

"No, thank you. I have a water bottle in my purse, but thank you for asking."

His office was in the shape of an upside-down L, her office on one end and his office on the other with the long lobby stretching to the door.

"He'll be right with you," she said, and she turned back to her desk.

Both their doors were left open, but I could just see the tip of his desk from where I sat.

A couple minutes later, PhD Mazzini came out to greet me. He had a curvature in his spine that made him walk slightly hunched over with a limp. He offered me a seat in his office as he made his way back to his desk. Behind my chair was a wall of books. After pleasantries, he began asking questions. His eyebrow raised as I told him about my experience, and that Bedlam had conducted the interviews with the father's parents and Moe's wife during the bonding study and with Moe present. PhD Mazzini had written the book on how to conduct a proper bonding study. I noted all the inconsistencies, and that Bedlam never asked me for any medical records prior to coming to his diagnosis. I sensed that PhD Mazzini didn't want to say too much without first reading over Dr. Bedlam's report. We concluded our conversation, and he had me meet with his secretary again to go over payment before I sent him the 730 report by Dr. Bedlam.

Weeks later, PhD Mazzini called me astonished; he asked, "What is this whole section about rat pups about?"

"I have no idea. I assumed it was normal psychology psychobabble."

"Very strange," he said.

PhD Mazzini questioned how Dr. Bedlam made the correlation from "'testing defensive' to you are not legitimately well?" I didn't have an answer.

He said, "I will need to request all of Bedlam's notes… He conducted the entire bonding study improperly. Why would he have Mr. Malvado's entire family present during his bonding study? It is intended to be a controlled study between Mr. Malvado and the children. I have several serious concerns that Dr. Bedlam did not conduct his report in accordance to local Rule of Court 5.225 and testing in critical areas relevant to you cases such as domestic violence analysis, substance abuse assessment, an assessment of sexual deviance, and an assessment of child abuse potential were all missing. I need to review the notes, I will call you back once Dr. Bedlam sends them to me."

Apparently, Dr. Bedlam was scheming more than I knew because it appeared that he took my data and compared it to an improper sample group in order to make my results appear higher than they were. PhD Mazzini explained to me on the phone that if my results had been compared to the sample group in which I belonged to then being "defensive" was not uncommon, basically, I tested normal. Dr. Bedlam had seemingly only included favorable information about Moe and excluded information favorable about me. As PhD Mazzini read on, he seemed outraged that Dr. Bedlam was seemingly deceptive with Moe's test results by omitting that Moe had aggressive impulses and paranoid thoughts.

PhD Mazzini said, "There is a preponderance of evidence, that was even previously supported by the court, that the minor children were at risk of harm by the Father."

He seemed confused why Dr. Bedlam did not seem to even consider the long-term effects of methamphetamine and found no mention of Moe's high scores of Thought Dysfunction with possible psychotic thinking. Critical items in Dr. Bedlam's notes suggested Moe had significant issues involving a pattern of denial of substance abuse with again concerns regarding aggression.

PhD Mazzini blurted out, "The possibility of dual diagnosis when mental health and drug addiction are present was seemingly never mentioned by Dr. Bedlam prior to his recommendations, which, as the CPS report noted would have inevitable abuse outcomes. More appalling is Dr. Bedlam failed to consider any other alternative hypotheses before arriving to his conclusion that you had Munchhausen's by Proxy when there was a myriad of legitimate concerns about the father."

He went on. "Your presentation of test results indicates in Dr. Bedlam's own words, *'mission-minded, social and conscientious.'* These qualities are positively associated with positive attachment and healthy parenting. Structure is an attribute of positive parenting. Yet, Dr. Bedlam does not note this in his report. Whereas Mr. Malvado's score was elevated on the Turbulent Scale on the MCMI-IV. This suggests that his behavior may be extreme, reckless, erratic, and he has a manic-like pattern which could lead him into a state of depressive exhaustion. His results are a pattern of unpredictable behavior, scattered thinking, brash and impetuous actions characterized by outburst of anger and fearful anxiety."

Hearing the words of PhD Mazzini was like taking off my N95 mask after a twelve-hour shift, and that seeming 80 percent chance of losing the girls felt less heavy. The truth would come out.

I read over Dr. Bedlam's report again. Dr. Bedlam claimed Moe told him Kay ran into his arms after she got bit by "a dog." Dr. Bedlam attempted to connect this story as an example of a secure attachment system. Claiming that a five-star restaurant chef and a fast-food worker had the same culinary skills was like saying an apple was the same as an orange because they're both fruit. Connecting these two was like saying David Dunn and Mr. Glass from the movie *Unbreakable* were the same, when they were on opposite sides of the spectrum. A traumatic incident was literally the nemesis to a secure attachment system. He continued saying that Moe told him he let the girls jump on a trampoline to which Dr. Bedlam expressed demonstrated Moe's ability to promote autonomy. He erased all of the previous court findings, all the years of motherhood I had already provided and in essence he was erasing me.

And there tucked away, Dr. Bedlam provided himself with a loophole. The devil was in the details.

He used D.W. Winnicott's theory of the "good enough mother," omitting the word *mother* of course. Claiming the perfect parent did not exist. He then implied that a parent generally (not always) needed to be able to give a safe place and solid base only around 30 percent of the time.

But it was the use of the words *generally (not always)* that were key.

Generally, but not always, I kept repeating. By way of those three words, a parent didn't even necessarily need to meet that 30 percent threshold; thus Dr. Bedlam was saying he didn't think a parent needed to be safe or provide a solid base. He could give the children to whomever he liked, and the worst part was Dr. Bedlam was protected by qualified immunity. He could say and do whatever he liked, and our government protected him.

Meanwhile, Moe was like this ever-annoying mosquito buzzing around looking for blood. He wrote to me on January 5, 2021, saying, "And things very well may change as far as where the girls live.

What exactly is your purpose of changing schools and putting them back in a private school knowing things might change?"

I don't have the time nor the energy to explain when he was only trying to gloat that the girls were going to be living with him soon.

A meet and confer hearing to discuss extending the trial date was set for January 6, 2021. The timing couldn't be worse: the hospital was at max capacity drowning in COVID-19 patients, and they were dire for nurses. I was assured by my attorney my presence was not needed at this hearing as it was just a formality, and the only purpose was to discuss what was scheduled on the calendar.

I went to work, and my attorney called me upset. Of course, Moe had expressed his disapproval in court. "I am not comfortable with them attending school on campus. Whether or not they have 'safety guidelines' for in campus learning." My attorney explained Moe wanted to pull them out and instead practice homeschooling. I shuddered. Mr. Bladderwort pushed that Moe's visitation should be extended because his client *deserved* to have custody. So, I don't think it should come as a shock to anyone that even though it was not on calendar to be discussed, Judge Mazle Dina changed Moe's visitation, extending his time *again* by adding an additional overnight. My attorney stated that she was adamantly opposed to modifications to visitation and was surprised that Judge Mazle Dina deviated from the calendar. I didn't doubt she did. I bet she was astonished Judge Mazle Dina didn't even respect her voice or concern. She probably thought to herself, "Well, screw me."

While she was beside herself in shock, I, however, was not surprised by Judge Mazle Dina's decision at all. Then it became apparent Judge Mazle Dina likely didn't respect any other women. To her, women probably were manipulative, dishonest, irrational, inept, unintelligent, but she was exempt because she was superior to other women and on a par with, if not higher than, the top males of her profession.

She also seemingly did not care at all that we were in a pandemic, f*** nurses, this ruling felt like she was giving me the middle finger.

Judge Mazle Dina stated during the hearing, "I understand your client's position and I am going to extend his time, but I'm not changing primary custody."

Judge Mazle Dina went on to explain how unfair that would be.

Oh, how gracious she was.

Never mind, the fact that changing primary custody without reviewing first the 733 that she ordered while also deviating off calendar was, oh, I don't know, illegal.

I mean, isn't it? Who knew here. She continued to explain both girls had "exhibited trauma and you know I'm familiar with the case."

Was she seriously pretending to be benevolent to gain admiration while she had directly contributed to their trauma?

My attorney said, "She also at the end informed me to prepare your client for changes to come in regard to custody," alluding to the pending trial that she intended to change custody.

I asked, "What did she say exactly?"

Judge Mazle Dina said, "Neither one will eventually be the primary parent. That word needs to leave their vocabulary."

"How can she speak on the outcome of pending trial that hasn't happened yet?"

My attorney had no answer.

Judge Mazle Dina already had a copy of Dr. Bedlam's report, but she was completely unaware of PhD Mazzini's report, the nuke that was about to land in her lap.

January 6, 2021, Court Orders

Pending futher hearing, father's weekends with the minor children shall be from pick up from school at 3:00pm on Friday until 6:00pm on Sunday. - The EC 730 report shall be released to Dr. Mazzini. - All other orders not modified

```
shall remain in full force and effect. - Hear-
ings: trial setting conference set for April 19,
2021, at 08:30 in Dept. S53 action
```

Moe was like a pendulum swinging in the wind. On March 10, 2021, he wrote it was not the school he disapproved of, it was the lack of stability. "I do not disapprove of 'the private school' at all, my only concern was them being on campus full time and they have been in roughly four different schools in five years, which is a lack of stability."

Yes, Anna went to a different preschool after all the drama at the other preschool and children typically age out of pre-school. I would have never even considered public school if I received more than two hundred and seven dollars for both girls in child support, but I don't say any of that.

Moe continued. "Maybe they will enjoy other schools as well." Wait what? I thought he just stated them attending different schools reflected a lack of stability?

It was like he forgot the arching plan was to remove the girls from me and relocate them into another school closer to his parents' house. The sheer stupidity hurt my head. Moe continued to tell me how he had paid for half of all of their tuition. Please provide any receipt, I'll wait. Was he high or so disconnected from reality that he resided in an alternate reality?

He needed a new angle, so on February 7, 2021 Moe told me on Talking Parents that Anna was being bullied in school. "I was bringing this up to your attention so that you can handle it." He went on and on in great length despite the school reporting no issues. On February 11, he said, "Bullying happens all the time in school, and nothing is ever done. That's why kids become depressed and harm themselves."

Now a month invested and not seeing the results he wanted on March 10, Moe claimed Anna was in a fight at school. "Anna got into a fight at school and got in trouble."

The school reported no fight occurred. He continued and stated, "It's clear the school isn't doing what they should to rectify this situation going on."

I told him if he had any concerns to feel free and call the school. Moe continued to make assertions that Anna was being bullied at school despite the school still reporting no issues. His goal, the girls needed to switch schools because bulling lead to depression and self-harm.

On March 12, Moe asked me whom he should get to pick up the girls for him for his visitations. Yes, you read that right. Of course, I didn't respond.

Sometime later, Moe sent, "I have drafted and sent a letter to my lawyer to address this issue as you refuse to even communicate with me on this matter. You ignore me, that's fine. We will have a trial like you want."

How do you explain to people this level of insanity? Whenever trying to explain Moe's actions or comments it made me appear crazy because he was so over the top. I realized when explaining Moe, I had to maintain a narrator voice like you see on the animal documentaries, "Here you see Moe a small cumbersome mammal asking a ridiculous question, who should I get to pick up the girls for my visitation? Moe is easily irritable and is an irrational beast. When he doesn't seem to get what he wants he throws a fit, yelling and spinning about. Moe perceives everything as a threat. So, he barks with the hope of scaring off (camera zooming in closer) what appears to be a flower, as he retreats back into his burrow."

On April 16, I communicated to Moe that Anna was missing one day of school because she had a cough but no other symptoms. Moe insisted he knew that Anna really missed five days of school.

I don't even know why I try to keep up this charade the court calls *co-parenting*. This was counter-parenting-insanity.

Moe then claimed Anna was "immunocompromised." What was he even talking about? Did he even know what that word meant? These idiotic conversations were meant to be all consuming, and he never grew tiresome. In 2018, Moe sent me five hundred and eight (508) messages. In 2019, he sent me five hundred and sixty-seven (567) messages. The messages usually were never just one sentence either, they were paragraphs upon paragraphs, I called them novellas. Utilizing this shotgun bombardment to distort and twist his false narrative to showcase, "I have tried relentlessly to effectively co-parent with Ms. Malvado and every time I am ignored and dismissed."

I agreed he was relentless but in no way was he attempting to co-parent.

The sheer volume of times Moe had mentioned the word *co-parenting* on Talking Parents had to be into the thousands within the last few years. Perhaps he perceived the more he stated it the more credible he seemed. Saying something frequently does not equate to that thing being true.

I could climb on top of my counter in the kitchen and yell, "I'm the best free climber the world has ever seen," every morning but that didn't make it true, that just makes me weird. What Moe was doing was repetitively telling others he was trying to co-parent to make it seem like I wasn't but in reality he was being manipulative, deceptive and abusive.

A few days later, April 19, 2021, we had another court hearing; a conference to discuss the trial dates.

I was sitting in the hallway when Judge Mazle Dina walked in. I cringed as she awkwardly lumbered down the hallway wearing what looked like a forced facade of femininity, a plain white stained t-shirt and pleated pink skirt.

I imagined her grabbing the shirt she was wearing from the pile of clothes thrown in an oversized chair in her room, "this will do" as she looked at the stain. A stain from the A1 sauce she used to slather

her well-done cooked porterhouse steak from last night's dinner. "My black robe is going to cover it anyway, who cares."

In the courtroom, Judge Mazle Dina derailed off calendar again, giving Moe center stage.

Moe spun into his alternate reality now claiming I had been withholding school information, that I refused to give him the girls' school schedule, refused to tell him who the girls' teachers were, and that the school was aiding me by also refusing to give him any information. He yelled, "I'm not sure the girls are even in school at all!"

Due to the fact none of today's lies that were being guzzled down by Judge Mazle Dina were on calendar again, I was not given the chance to refute what he accused me of. Yet, if I had time to prepare for this ridiculous argument, I would have pointed out on Talking Parents January 6, 2021, Moe sent, "I just looked online, their school ends at 12:30 on Friday. That's when I will be picking them up at the school says Friday's TK - 8th grade get out at 12:30."

Plus, the fact that I had provided him the names of the teachers on March 10, 2021, "All the school information is accessible on their website, but if you're having trouble their teachers are 'Mrs. A' & 'Mrs. B.'"

Regardless, Judge Mazle Dina granted Moe extra time because, arguably, the truth didn't matter only the predilection for double-dealings and deceit mattered in this court.

My attorney tried, but Judge Mazle Dina mowed her over.

She was beside herself and couldn't wrap her head around what just happened. "She really doesn't like you."

I think she thought I must have done something; nope, what you saw in there was just abuse.

It's still going to be okay. This treacherous train would be coming to a full complete stop once PhD Mazzini's report hits.

April 19, 2021 Court Orders

```
Proceedings: Action came on for trial setting
conference. 09:20 Witness - Both parties are /
is sworn and examined. After testimony and due
consideration by the court: - The court sets
court trial and trial readiness as set forth
below. - The court orders from now until June
4th, if there is any off-track time for the
children then father shall have that time with
the children. - Trial estimate is 2 days -
```

The court just deprived me of my voice again and gave me these ridiculous vague orders that, undoubtedly, Moe was going to misuse again.

Moe wasted no time. The following Monday, the school had a teacher in-service day.

"Judge Mazle Dina said anytime they are not in school they are to be with me. I will have them from Friday after school, they get out at noon until Monday evening at six. We will be getting the transcripts and filing ex parte if need be." This month alone, Moe had threatened to take me back to court at least five times.

He took the girls.

Police were confused by the order. Inevitability the police said, "This is a civil matter, you're going to have to deal with this in court."

There's nothing I could do.

A month later, on May 18, 2021, Moe wrote on Talking Parents, "Seraphine I wanted to discuss Memorial Day weekend with you. I was thinking I'd pick them up from school Thursday, May 27th and drop them off Monday May 31st at 6pm at the same drop off location as normal. They get out of school at 2:30 and I am hoping you'll just allow me to pick them up at that time."

On the surface it passed but I'd learned that right beneath the surface a monster lurked. I didn't reply with yes or no but rather "Let me get back to you."

Moe wrote, "As for the schedule, I get them for that four-day weekend. So, what is there to get back to me with?"

A request that did not allow the reply *no* was not a request, it was a demand. The challenging thing to explain was that sometimes Moe may appear to ask civil requests by tagging in polite words, but the undercurrent was full of maligned venom that did not allow the recipient (me) to decline his requests.

If I declined, retaliation would ensue.

Example: I declined a different irrational request. Moe notified me that he told the girls *the truth* about me, he was referring to Dr. Bedlam's false diagnosis of Munchhausen's by Proxy. He continued. "I have discussed this situation with my therapist, and many other situations along this line. I will not lie to our daughters anymore. I will not lie to them to protect their image of you." Things unfolded slowly, the girls said things to me like "Daddy said you loved me more when I was sick." But I know the court would not hear any of it, claiming all this was just hearsay. There comes a point in family law that if you travel far enough you begin to tread water while its systemic undertows drift you back from any safe resolve and instead straight toward certain death.

34

SHE CAN'T IGNORE ME

June 6, 2021

On June 6, 2021, Moe withheld the girls and refused to return them. Moe informed his attorney that he was going to take custody of the girls for the balance of the summer vacation until the start of the trial June 23, 2021, as evidenced per Mr. Bladderwort's email on June 7, 2021, 04:50 p.m. stating, "It has been our client's instruction to me that I was to request all the vacation time between now and the time of trial."

My attorney wrote a letter to have Kay and Anna immediately returned as Moe was violating court orders.

Moe refused, claiming Judge Malze Dina said he got them, and since he's getting custody anyway, he's just going to take them now.

I drove to his house and called the police.

Three hours later, police showed up. With court orders in hand, they asked Moe to return the girls.

Moe adamantly refused and started yelling at the police to arrest me for trespassing on his parents' property.

Police told me there's nothing they could do because he refused, they couldn't force him.

Again, the matter would have to be dealt with in court.

On June 9, 2021, Moe filed an ex parte on himself, yes, you got that right, like that drug dealer who got robbed then he called the cops to proclaim "someone stole my drugs."

In court, Judge Mazle Dina dismissed the matter. "This is not emergency."

My attorney had to remind Judge Mazle Dina that he still needed to return the girls. To which Moe claimed he couldn't return the girls because they're camping with his family.

Judge Mazle Dina turned in her chair, rolled her eyes, and asked, "Where is your family camping at?"

Moe responded, "About sixteen miles away."

Judge Mazle Dina waved her hand as if shoeing us out of her court. "Return them when the camping trip is over, by the end of this week. Is June 11, Friday, good?" Mr. Bladderwort nodded, and we were motioned to leave by the bailiff.

One week later, on June 20, 2021, Moe withheld the girls again. My attorney couldn't believe it. "He's sabotaging his own case." This time he told police he had "secret court orders between him and Judge Mazle Dina" that she just hadn't signed yet. Instead of driving to his parents' house, I waited the three hours at the local police station.

To no surprise, the police reported to me Moe was extremely argumentative with them and adamantly refused to return the girls. Again, there was nothing I could do except go back to court.

After I left the police station, Moe immediately drove to the police station demanding the secretary give him a copy of the police report. I returned the next day to pick up a copy, and she said, "Oh, you're that girl from yesterday, right?"

"Yes," I said. She began to tell me how Moe came in right after I left, and when she explained to him she couldn't provide him with a copy of my report, he became enraged and began yelling at her. She said he was so disruptive that she had to inform the watch commander and had to ask him multiple times to leave.

She still seemed shaken up over the whole ordeal.

"I'm really sorry," I said.

She said, "No, I'm sorry you have to deal with all that. Here is your copy. I hope things work out for you."

Three days later, on June 23, 2021, our trial started. With Moe essentially kidnapping the girls not once but twice right before the trial and told police he had "secret court orders" between him and the judge was like committing trial suicide.

Moe still hadn't returned the girls. Judge Mazle Dina walked out of her chambers wearing grey fuzzy slippers. My attorney notified the court that Moe had taken the girls again and what he told the police. The fact the police wrote in their report that Moe said he had "secret court orders" between him and the judge made her upset. She began the trial with a long-winded speech about how she was not biased.

If you have to give a speech about how you are not biased, you are most likely biased. But nice try gaslighting the situation; your effort is noted.

Apparently, she's never heard Aesop's fable of the farmer and the viper. Judge Mazle Dina had been coddling Moe. Nestling him close in her breast pocket. The viper then bites the farmer in the neck leaving him for dead.

Now, Judge Mazle Dina was upset that Moe betrayed her, and she wanted to act surprised? That's what happens when you coddle a viper. The fable was supposed to remind the listener not to befriend vipers because, at some point, they will bite you. The moral being when one engages in unethical behavior, he or she was not immune to harm.

She verbally told Moe to return the girls by 7 p.m. today and said I would be getting the time he withheld the girls back. Judge Mazle

Dina and our two attorneys spent almost the entirety of the first day of our trial in the judge's chambers privately discussing off record.

I was then informed that Judge Mazle Dina had already made a tentative decision and wanted us to settle on it. Judge Mazle Dina's purposed plan was: joint legal custody, joint physical custody, with Mother's residence primary for school purposes. The parents shall have week-to-week visitation. Moe was furious because that's not what Dr. Bedlam recommended. Expecting his parents' house was going to be the girls' primary residence for school, Moe whined to Mr. Bladderwort.

Mr. Bladderwort cleared his throat. "Um, Your Honor, my client rejects the week-to-week visitation stating it's too much in gas to drive the girls every day to school." Moe couldn't pour water out of a boot if you told him the instructions were written on the heel.

Judge Mazle Dina looked perturbed; this was not the intended grateful response she was expecting. She literally handed 50/50 custodial time to him on a silver platter, and he refused it.

Mmm, maybe because this was never about the girls, it was about power and control.

She was forced to alter her plan. "During school, the father must get the children to school on time, and if the father was late or tardy to school 3 times in a month, then his visitation time would revert to every first, third, fourth, and fifth weekends from Friday 6 p.m. to Sunday 6 p.m. Father is not to consume drugs during his custodial periods."

Judge Mazle Dina wanted us to think it over tonight and then come back tomorrow with a final decision. Of course, she wanted us to agree to her settlement idea then she could avoid the trial, burying Dr. Bedlam's report, avoiding record of PhD Mazzini's review of Dr. Bedlam's report, and use me as the fall-guy, "well she agreed to it."

This was a waste of time because we already knew Moe was never going to settle, he wanted verbatim what Dr. Bedlam recommended. This was the problem when you enabled an impulsive, irrational,

entitled, abusive viper. Moe's uncompromising behavior was so pre-
dictable, I won't need to say anything tomorrow.

Day two of our trial. We sat back and let nature take its course.
Mr. Bladderwort said, "Your Honor, my client does not agree to the
settlement."

Judge Mazle Dina tried to hide her aggravation. She pretended to
be ultra-calm, but her jaw was clenched, and she maintained tense
eye contact. My attorney's voice came out small as if she were walking on eggshells to delicately remind the court that she ordered the
733, that I had paid a ten thousand retainer, as well as an additional
twenty thousand for the 733 evaluations to prepare for this trial and
politely requested the court hear the trial out.

This was ridiculous. My attorney was over here asking pretty please
do not enforce your proposed settlement against my client without
first listening to the testimony of PhD Mazzini that you ordered. If
only there was some legal amendment or procedural civil process for
the family court to follow. Perhaps my attorney wouldn't have to be
so careful not to "offend" or "upset" our omnipotent judge.

Judge Mazle Dina begrudgingly agreed to continue the trial and
asked Mr. Bladderwort who he would like to testify first.

I was called first to testify. My attorney informed me ahead of
time that either of us could be called up to testify today, so I was
prepared. She also instructed me to perhaps wear a dress instead of
a suit as if that might change Judge Mazle Dina's bias against me. I
played along.

I took my place on the stand. I wore a cardigan, with a floor-
length long plain black dress and my hair pulled up into a clean
formal bun like usual.

I placed my hands in my lap. There was a part of me that wanted
to wear the white *Gone with the Wind* Southern belle ball gown to
court... *"Is this enough lace to not be treated with bias, Your Honor?
Missouri court would have told Scarlett O'Hara, 'please cover your
forearms.'"*

Both psychologists were set to testify on their reports, so I was advised to just focus on the questions that I was asked, implying not to say anything about the reports. Leave that to the professionals.

My attorney told me the day before that Mr. Bladderwort said, "I don't think either of our clients are going to testify well."

To which my attorney responded, "Speak for yourself."

Speaking in court had become no different to me than reporting to an ICU attending, surgeon, or nephrologist. If I couldn't effectively communicate to doctors day in and day out my patient's entire history that I just received that morning, then he had no idea what he was in for.

I answered Mr. Bladderwort's poorly prepared questions while he seemed to dig his client a hole so large, I wondered how he was intending to get Moe out of it. "But there was nothing prior to CPS report in 2019 that would warrant concern of my client having custody?"

"Umm, actually, in 2015, your client admitted to using methamphetamine, on September 29, 2016, the court ordered your client to complete a boundaries with minor course (I recant line by line Moe's messages) that again was suggested by the court last year 2020 for Moe to take again. Then on December 7, 2017, there was the domestic violent restraining order that the court granted where the judge found there to be sufficient evidence of domestic abuse, and she was concerned for the probability of future abuse occurring. Oh, and there was the incident on October 16, 2018, where your client overdosed our then three-year-old Anna with Benadryl, then of course, April 2019, the human bite mark and marijuana found in Kay, and then there's the continued court violations persistently made by your client, and there's the countless times I had to call the police. Do you want me to list those as well?"

"No, that's not necessary." He tried to push on fumbling through his papers. He asked more questions, each time I met them with dates, times, and quotes.

During the cross examination, I informed the court Moe's continued threats to take me to court, his threats to call CPS and police as retaliation, that I had to stop dating for the last two years because Moe would question the girls about my personal life causing them undue stress, and that Moe would bombard me with relentless messages.

Judge Mazle Dina acted a gasp, like she was not aware any of this was going on. "You should have informed me so that I could have put a stop to it." She looked over at my attorney. I realized in that moment that my attorney had become my witness.

Judge Mazle Dina asked, "Does he message you every day?"

I responded, "Nearly. Sometimes they are every other day and sometimes they are every ten hours."

Judge Mazle Dina said, "Well, you should have informed me."

I felt like saying, *You're the one that literally ordered to respond to messages on Talking Parents within ten hours of receipt.* Instead, I just looked at her.

"I'm going to order that he is not to message you more than twice a week."

This triggered Moe, and he ripped his mask off. I left the witness stand. As I passed Moe, he was visibly upset. His face was red and wet with tears and snot. He dragged his arm across his face.

The bailiff walked over and asked him to put his mask back on.

Moe pointed at Judge Mazle Dina. "She's not wearing a mask! Why do I have to wear one?"

My jaw almost hit the floor. I was not sure why I was so shocked; this wasn't the first time he'd yelled in court, nor was it the first time he'd shouted at the judge.

Moe yelled that he had important medical questions that needed to have responses, and I was not allowed to ignore him.

Judge Mazle Dina then responded, "If the message warrants a response then I'm sure she will reply. However, she can ignore you if she wants to."

Moe exploded and screamed, "She can't ignore me! She can't ignore me!"

Judge Mazle Dina replied, "Sir, she can ignore you if she wants to."

Moe just kept yelling, "She can't ignore me! She can't ignore me!"

Mr. Bladderwort attempted to hush him and hurry him out of the courtroom, but Moe was going berserk and threw a wadded-up piece of paper.

I had my eyes on Judge Mazle Dina to see what she was going to do about this scene.

Moe leaned over to my lawyer and muttered, "F****** lowlife."

She said, "Excuse me? Did you just hear what he called me?"

Judge Mazle Dina just shrugged her shoulders. She was already walking off the stand and made no comment as she continued through the door to her chambers.

Mr. Bladderwort was practically pushing Moe out the courtroom doors.

My attorney and I were left standing there. What just happened?

I guess that concluded the second day.

We walked down the hallway to the back elevator, down to the first floor, and stood down the hall from security to talk.

As we debriefed, we heard a commotion coming from the elevator. When the doors opened, it was Moe and Mr. Bladderwort.

Moe was screaming at Mr. Bladderwort who swiftly moved past us. Moe never stopped screaming.

We just stared at them.

Moe was so deranged I don't think he even saw us.

Mr. Bladderwort walked out of the courthouse and across the street. We could still hear Moe screaming.

I almost felt bad for Mr. Bladderwort. I figured he must be really desperate for money if he would tolerate being screamed at like that. What a sad sap.

Then I thought about all the times Moe probably yelled at him, all the crazy irrational emails Moe probably wrote, all the pictures of our girls Moe emailed to him, and how many times Moe told him he wanted to take me to court. There was no conceivable way Mr. Bladderwort wasn't aware of the abuse. He was Moe's gatekeeper. He knew Moe was abusing the girls, yet he continued to defend him, dismissed the abuse, and attacked me.

My mind ran back to when the girls acted out during Moe's supervised visitation, and Mr. Bladderwort told the court, "Does that fall on dad's side? I think it's a child who—if the child is raised 90% of the time in moms' home, needs to have some more built-in control."

F*** him.

35

DEAL WITH THE DEVIL

Since COVID-19 hit, none of Moe's family members had been permitted in the courtroom. Moe returned home telling his family that I confessed to all the things he claimed I had done. Not that it really changed anything, they would believe whatever he said present or not. He could have told them he was the next messiah and they would have bowed and began worshiping him singing, "glory, glory be Moe's name." His parents continued to enable his behavior and with no gainful employment for years, they allowed him to live with them. Their willful denial of what was happening to their grandchildren had long since stepped into purposeful ignorance while they actively contributed to the abuse.

Moe and Dr. Bedlam were expected to testify on the third day of the trial; however, due to a COVID-19 outbreak in the courthouse, that day was canceled. Arrangements had been emailed to both the court's secretary and Mr. Bladderwort to ensure an additional day would be made available for the unexpected cancellation of Dr. Bedlam and Moe's testimony.

August 5, the fourth day of the trial, PhD Mazzini was scheduled to testify. I greeted PhD Mazzini at the courthouse. Per family court policy, he had to sit outside the courtroom in the hallway until Judge Mazle Dina called him in. They had no idea what they were in for; the bomb of information PhD Mazzini was about to deliver to the court was going to destroy them. Judge Mazle Dina wouldn't be able to get out of this one. I walked in the courtroom.

Judge Mazle Dina started by saying, "Let's address the elephant in the room." She explained how she was transferring back to criminal law. Judge Mazle Dina said, "I've never mis tried a case since I've been over here in family law. That's something, I guess, as crazy enough as it sounds, I do take some pride in, because I know other Judges that have, and it's not right especially when somebody's well prepared and ready to go forward. I know you both are extremely well prepared and have witnesses ready to go. I know that for a fact. So, I can work something out. Probably, you'll have to come across the street. So, it can be done." She continued. "The devil you know versus the devil you don't." She laughed. "That's the saying right?"

The bailiff chimed it. "Yeah, I think you said it right."

My attorney asked Judge Mazle Dina if she'd had the opportunity to read PhD Mazzini's report.

She replied, "I've not had an opportunity to review it."

Mr. Bladderwort asked if they could discuss the matter in her chambers.

My attorney, Mr. Bladderwort, and the judge disappeared again into her private chambers. I walked out and updated PhD Mazzini.

Over an hour went by.

Eventually, my attorney walked out. "Let's go talk in here."

She led me into a private conference room. My attorney's face was tense. "Judge Mazle Dina informed me to tell you that you that she is going to adopt PhD. Mazzini's report into evidence without his testimony. If you want him to testify today she is going to mistrial your case. She said you can either take her judgment today, which is joint custody, or you can have your case heard in front of a different Judge and pay an additional fifteen thousand or more and they'll probably order the same thing. I'm just repeating what she said."

"I don't have that kind of money. I refinanced my home and pulled out money, all to pay for something she isn't even going to read?"

I sat there trying to process what was happening. In the past four years, from January 31, 2018, to today, August 5, 2021, I had been to 35 court hearings. She had been financially draining me for years. I had spent more money on legal expenses than I had on student loans. She didn't care if she bankrupted me, none of them did.

Mr. Bladderwort had been given a copy of PhD Mazzini's report prior to today. He knew what it said. My attorney explained that Mr. Bladderwort was very upset that the judge was going to submit PhD Mazzini's report into evidence because she said he wanted it tossed out. My attorney was kinda thinking out loud at this point. "If I was Moe, I'd be upset I never got to testify."

She didn't get it. They couldn't risk putting Moe on the stand. You don't question an explosive ticking time bomb; you toss it so far out to sea, so you don't get blown up. They're burying the body and hoping no one finds out. They couldn't have either doctor testify for risk of exposure. Of course, Mr. Bladderwort was upset, Judge Mazle Dina had absolute immunity, she wasn't going to take the fall, and he knew it. Judge Mazle Dina knew I didn't have the money, and she was forcing me into a settlement.

What were my other options? There were none, it was pay or get out. I didn't anticipate this. I didn't know she could just refuse to hear evidence. What do I do?

I walked out of the room and found PhD Mazzini sitting on the bench still. I told him, "The court doesn't want to hear your testimony. She said she's just going to submit your report into evidence, and if I choose to have you testify, then the court is going to mistrial this case."

He said, "I'm not sure I understand. Your attorney emailed the court and arrangements were made. Didn't you just tell me she was agreeable to make accommodations to hear Moe and Dr. Bedlam's testimony?"

"She doesn't want to hear them, either."

He scratched his head. "That's odd, but she knows I charged you five thousand dollars to be here today."

I responded, "Yes, the attorney told her. She doesn't care. She said I could go with the devil I knew versus the devil I'd have to pay at least an additional fifteen thousand (15K) dollars to. She knows I don't have the money, so she's forcing me into a settlement."

PhD Mazzini said, "I've never had a court behave like this, the court knows I have been waiting out here for over an hour. Then to just waste my time and your money when she had already agreed prior...."

I interrupted. "I'm very sorry."

PhD Mazzini said, "There's something off here."

"I know." He talked a bit more before he headed back to his office with his assistant.

I walked back into the courtroom.

Judge Mazle Dina smirked as she read her final judgment. "The Court modifies the visitation as follows; to permit father more time with the minors, to handle the educational needs of the minors, the father will now receive the minors on the first, third, and fifth weekends of the month."

This was what she was planning the entire time.

"He's advised not to keep secrets, not to tell the children to keep secrets from their mother."

I stared at the pen mounted to the table in front of me.

She continued. "There was talk at the last hearing that father has overused Talking Parents, so he understands now that he's limited by way of subject matter to two per week, if needed."

I wondered how far I would get if I pulled that pen off and tried to stab her in the voice box.

"One last thing," she said. "The Court does not adopt any factual finding or factual representations made by Dr. Bedlam or PhD Mazzini in their reports that were submitted and/or lodged." Judge Mazle Dina closed with, "Good luck," and she walked out of the courtroom.

She could wait to screw me with her stogie wiener. *("Stogie wiener" was the online alias username she went by.)* She knew she was eliminating my right to appeal.

Maybe that was just how trials were in family court, no questions, none of the facts mattered, no law applied, no seeming logic applied either… the judges just got to do whatever they wanted and with every court access portal update less and less information is publicly displayed, systematically burying the trails of evidence.

The father's rights to have access to the children surpass the child's rights for welfare, health, and safety.

As Judge Mazle Dina made her grand exit out of family court and back into criminal court, I couldn't help but wonder if she was going to convict actual criminals or prosecute people she transformed into criminals?

That's when I noticed she hadn't written any orders on June 9, 2021, or June 23, 2021, because she didn't want the next judge to ask why joint custody was granted just a month after the father withheld the daughters not once, but twice. She was covering her tracks. I kinda felt dumb, I mean she told us what she was going to do on January 6, 2021. Laws weren't going to stop her; she *is* the law.

The true malice was what she did to our daughters. The Oregon subcommittee of the State Family Law advisory committee wrote "Custody and Parenting Time: Summary of Current Information and Research," by Scher & Vien in March, 2011, "Children under age ten are particularly vulnerable because they have not yet developed the internal coping skills or external support systems that would help them navigate family conflict. Relevant to this discussion are findings that delineate situations in which joint custody and care is problematic or contraindicated. Where domestic violence, mental illness and high levels of inter-parental conflict exist, joint custody and care result in poor outcomes for children and parents alike."[1]

They also stated, "Notably, the research finds that joint arrangements entered into willingly by parents were two and a half times more stable than their counterparts over time. Of considerable concern are the findings that shared parenting time compelled by a legislative presumption appeared to perpetuate higher levels of inter-parental conflict that increased over time and appeared to increase children's reports of feeling caught in the middle."[2] She systematically increased Kay and Anna's ACE scores; with higher scores comes a higher risk of poor health outcomes.

Former Surgeon General of California, Nadine Burke Harris, explained it like this:

"the brain and body's stress response system that governs our fight-or-flight response. [Works like] well, imagine you're walking in the forest and you see a bear. Immediately your hypothalamus sends a signal to your pituitary, which sends a signal to your adrenal gland that says, 'Release stress hormones! Adrenaline! Cortisol!

And so, your heart starts to pound, your pupils dilate, your airways open up, and you are ready to either fight that bear or run from the bear. But the problem is what happens when the bear comes over and over and over again, and it goes from being adaptive, or life-saving, to maladaptive, or health-damaging. Children are especially sensitive to this repeated stress activation, because their brains and bodies are just developing."[3]

Whether her intent was to cover up her negligence or to cause me harm, she was willing to sadistically bring harm, anguish, and despair to children to win her goal. Judge Mazle Dina fed off violence and fear. Perhaps family court just wasn't violent enough for her appetite.

I imagined Judge Mazle Dina returned back to her old chambers in criminal court. Her desk covered in pictures of victims; stabbed or shot. Her engorged fingers thumbing through the grotesque pictures as she paused on one, her finger circling the wound. The reality of it is it's worse than that, she now oversaw petitions to terminate registered sex offenders.

36

PERVERSION OF JUSTICE

felt like there was nothing else to say or do. I walked out of the courtroom and down the hall. I went into the same room where I had talked with my lawyer earlier.

I needed to catch my breath. *"Accountability and compassion make judicial power worthy of our respect." A tyrannical court has no authority here. She wanted to name herself "the devil." Well, the devil has no ownership here; whatever was done in darkness shall be cast into the light.*

I was not sent into the fire so I may burn. He knew I could withstand the flames for I am living fire. I have been sent to dispel the shadows of darkness. I am not the one who should be afraid.

I hear a slow clap behind me. "Jacques? What are you doing here?"

"It's about time. Don't be afraid."

"I'm not. Time for what?"

"Time you realized your power. I have been watching you since you came into your mother's womb. I came down for you. You have more power in your fingertips than they have in their entire bodies. Cast them into the light. I am here to protect you."

I looked down at my hands.

Jacques said, "use them to write." He continued "There has been an outcry of outrage, za'akah and tza'akah, from these lands. I have been watching for quite some time now. I have laid ruin to lands that were inhospitable to people, had a perversion of formal justice, and who perpetrated sexual crimes. I see no difference to those lands and this. Even in your nation's highest court, they have perjured their way to the top to expel suffering and torment. I have come to gather a first-hand account of what is going on."

I sighed wearily. "What been happening here is bigger than the Catholic Church scandal. Family Law seems to be practicing Gresham's law; bad parents have driven out the good. The family court system is shoving abusive parents into the column of good co-parents like the big banks in 2008 gave high-risk loans a AAA rating. All the while arguing domestic violence doesn't exist, it's just as believable as them saying the housing market was stable. Yet, instead of families losing homes, children are losing their lives. Between 2008 and 2021, the Center for Judicial Excellence discovered eight hundred and nineteen (819) child murders in the United States by parents when divorce, separation, custody, visitation, or child support was mentioned in news coverage. Yet cases like mine don't make the news. Children are losing the security of their safe parents and are being ripped apart from their siblings. If the children resist, transporters will take them and put them into reunification camps. The number of *these* cases is unknown."

Jacques said, "There are many children missing. Robert David Steele said, 'The working assumption yet to be proven is that the totality of the children disappearing worldwide is toward eight million people, toward eight million children. In the United States of America, the acknowledged number, not counting the children being bred without birth certificates, not counting the children being imported without documentation, is between six hundred and eight hundred thousand a year."[1]

"That's so many…" I start calculating, "If Dr. Bedlam saw one family each month for three years: that's thirty-six (36) families. If each family had three children, that's one hundred and eight (108) children. Then factor how many cases Judge Mazle Dina would see in a week, a year? This is one judge and one court evaluator. This problem is found in every court, in every city, in every state."

Jacques said, "Yes, abuse is rampant."

I said, "So, they will continue to allow children to suffer because they don't want to own up to their mistakes?"

Jacques said, "They will suppress and resist all desires to change the system due to fear of exposing it. Children have been dehumanized to pawns, weaponized to exploit money out of the protective parent, and used collectively gathered money from the abuser to exert power and maintain control over their victims. Grant Wyeth called it the *'repugnant market.'* He explains in part in his article, "How the Family Court's purpose to Protect Children Became Inverted." The Family Court System's duty per its own legislature, family code section 3020 subsection A, "finds and declares that it is the public policy of this state to ensure that the health, safety, and welfare of children shall be the court's primary concern in determining the best interests of children when making any orders regarding the physical or legal custody or visitation of children. The Legislature further finds and declares that children have the right to be safe and free from abuse, and that the perpetration of child abuse or domestic violence in a household where a child resides is detrimental to the health, safety, and welfare of the child."[3] Yet the courts have shown the derogation of their own laws by the results of Joan Meier, Daniel Saunders, and Geraldine Stahly, research studies alone. The courts have committed dereliction of that duty and more egregiously no change to course correct their behavior."

"I don't get it," I said, "if medical professionals practiced like this, they would be sued for medical malpractice, yet the Family Court System has protected itself by incasing their constituents with the veil of qualified immunity. Officials who don't even know the difference between the digestive and reproductive systems have the audacity to criminalize physicians for performing necessary healthcare procedures are the same that assert a system with a rudimentary understanding of domestic violence pass blanket laws for 50/50 joint custody rather than reform the system. It's understandable why our legal system hates science, education, and books. The family court system has been utilizing pseudo-science garbage to discredit child abuse and incest for decades. If 'alienation' is an arguable defense then so should I guess my astrological birth chart be used as credible legal defense. Can you picture it...? *Your Honor, my sun sign is in Cancer, my moon is in Sagittarius and my rising sign is Aries, therefore, it can't be what you're accusing me of. Besides, Mercury was totally in retrograde, and the timing of your accusations was not in alignment with Mars.* I thought the medical field had issues! At least, overall, they're trying to progressively push toward the future by applying research that might improve patient outcomes. But our legal system is seemingly trying to turn back the hands of time. Imagine if doctors began yelling, let's bring back the leeches! And the sad thing is the information for the family courts to improve themselves has been out for decades. They just failed to course correct preventable abuse. This logic is like have the capability to use anesthesia for surgeries but refusing to use it."

Jacques was just looking at me.

"Sorry, I'm just really angry."

Jacques said, "There will be a gathering soon of others like me to voice our findings. Many were dispatched to collect information. One in Polk County, Iowa, was talking with a teenager, another was sent out to at least eight women in Clark County, Jeffersonville, Indiana, few are in Idaho, Ohio, Missouri, and many more were sent to Tehran, Iran. Share your voice and speak for those who cannot. Help those who can't see, to see. Defend the weak and the fatherless; uphold the cause of the poor and oppressed."

With that, he was gone.

37

CONSENT IS JUST
A SEVEN LETTER WORD

August 5, 2021

N ot even six hours after the trial, Moe threatened to take me back to court.

Go ahead, I don't even care anymore. Of course, I didn't say that. Few days later, he demanded he was entitled to have them for three days because it was his birthday; the last of my scheduled time before school starts. They had been at his house for a whole week and he was going to have them again the upcoming weekend. The day before retuning them he notified me he's going to cut Kay's hair short in fifteen minutes. He claimed that Kay told him she desired to cut her hair short. However, I had just had their hair trimmed ten days earlier, and she did not want her hair cut short.

The fifteen-minute notice was given to make me panic and compel a response from me. Also, enough time for me to call my lawyer, who called Mr. Bladderwort, who called Moe. Moe told Mr.

Bladderwort, "I'm only going to trim it. Two inches at most. Kay told me she wants it."

Mr. Bladderwort relayed that he told Moe my expressed desire not for him to cut her hair, and that Moe told him he was just gonna get it trimmed.

My message of, "please don't cut her hair" nor Mr. Bladderwort's conversation had any effect on him whatsoever.

Moe started sending me moment-by-moment pictures of Kay getting all her long hair cut off. He cut off all of her beautiful hair and gave her a bob. As I held my phone crying looking at the final picture, Moe wrote, "You know I'm supposed to have them on my birthday. Kay loves her new haircut." "She asked for it." "She absolutely loves it Ms. Soyla." "The great thing about hair is that it grows back."

Despondent I said, "Legally that is not my name and Kay has never voiced any of that to me."

Moe replied, "Well it should be." "If there's nothing else, I'm ending the conversation. I'm going to go spend time with our daughters. Seraphine, Kay is so excited to show you her hair. Her exact words were 'I can't wait for mommy to see my hair, she's going to love it.' All I ask that you be happy for her. Also, again I ask that you allow me to have them from Sunday to Tuesday for my birthday. It's already court ordered that I have them on my birthday. Thank you."

I was told legally there was no order that stated he couldn't cut her hair, but morally, it was wrong of him to make the unilateral decision to cut all her hair off.

I never let Kay see that I was upset about her hair. "You look beautiful, baby." I kissed her on the forehead.

Cutting off a significant portion of a female's hair was not trivial or insignificant. It was relevant to her autonomy. But there's nothing seemingly I could do. I'm told, "It'll grow back."

Moe writes, "I got a letter from your lawyer. I sent the pics from

2019 where is shows we only trimmed Kay's bangs because you jacked them up by cutting Kay's hair yourself. We fixed her bangs. Again, we keep having the same problems with you twisting the truth to your narrative. If you would stop your lies, we'd have less problems. Have a good day." He blabbered on and on. Moe ignored the court's two message a week order. One morning I received twenty-two messages before 8 a.m.

Moe messaged me, "For Christmas vacation, which is from December 20–January 3rd, but actually starts on the 17th, I would like them from the 17th to the 30th. I would like them for Christmas Eve and Christmas, as you know we have a huge family and family traditions."

He had no shame, twisting the knife that most of my family was deceased, but I kept the messages even, "What you are requesting is unreasonable." He carries on and on over the next month about how he is entitled to both Christmas Eve and Christmas day.

About two months later, because I didn't tell him our bunny died, he cut Kay's hair again with the message, "I'd like to remind you that you're not to encourage the girls to keep secrets from me. Nor do you to keep secrets."

The girls began telling me, "Mommy, you're not fair. Daddy said he should have us for seven days, and you should have us for seven days so it's fair. Daddy only has us for four days, and you have us for ten days, and that's not fair."

They explained how they could go to school at his house for a week and then return to school here the next week.

I had to explain they couldn't be enrolled in two different schools. I was not sure they understood. Every week another new thing popped up. "Daddy said you don't like him" or "Daddy said Tony knows not to step on his lawn otherwise he would break both of his legs."

I redirect their questions. "How was school?"

It was Kay's eighth birthday. A wave of sadness came over me. Where had all the time gone? Instead of being able to focus on them, I'd been embroiled in court proceedings.

Judge Mazle Dina's decisions allowed for all of this to happen. On September 24, 2021, Moe instructed me that he would prefer that I change my name. "We have been divorced for quite some time now, I'm remarried. You've been engaged a time or two, who knows. Usually when two people divorce the woman goes back to using her maiden name. Which I would prefer you to do, seeing as how we are divorced And it's clear you're not keeping the last name because it's the same as your kids since your youngest has Tony's last name. If you can go by Soyla on social media platforms then you can go by it legally. I will refer to you as Ms. Soyla, it's not inappropriate, rude or anything else. It's your name Seraphine. Or I could speak to you about it seeing as to how you're my coparent not the school. But again, that would involve you to actually want to make things better between us as for coparenting and you just don't want to. I'll contact the school. Your lack of involvement, it's just swell."

Except I didn't have my maiden name on any of my social media platforms, so I said, "I do not have any social media platforms which you are claiming. Demanding me to change my name because 'you'd prefer it' is unreasonable."

Moe responded, "Tinder but let's just forget the important stuff? As far as Facebook 'Seraphine Anonymous.' A woman of many names you are. You go by Seraphine Soyla at work, Tinder, Instagram. Your Instagram name isn't 'themaldavoartcorner' now is it? Would you like pics? That little Tinder video you deleted off Instagram. You haven't dated for two years but that doesn't stop you from being on Tinder. I couldn't care less about what you do with your personal life. But the fact that you deny that you go by

Soyla on social media, to your friends and family, and work just baffles me. Again, why do you insist on keeping my last name?"

What a sad, deranged human. Over the years, I have had to delete my accounts and use different names because Moe would always find them. This was his way of telling me he found all of them again.

How would he know what people at my work called me? Was he calling my work now as well? Obviously couldn't trust the court to do anything about this, so I let it roll off my back.

I called my attorney when Kay came home for the second time with facial swelling raised about a half inch, red dots covering nearly half of her face, and a swollen eye.

Again, nothing I can do; the court would claim it was just coincidental.

It's hard not to cry when your child was in pain. I drove her to the urgent care where the doctor stated they thought it was an allergic reaction to something.

Moe argued saying it wasn't an allergic reaction, it was just eczema.

Kay didn't have eczema. Moe went on. "I believe it's a flare of her eczema that she was diagnosed with when she was about one. Weather changes can cause a flare in eczema." When she was one he was using meth. Moe said he was going to schedule an appointment with her dermatologist, that she didn't have, for the eczema, that she was never diagnosed with. I told Moe I took Kay to urgent care. Moe stated, "I don't believe that you took her to urgent care." The pendulum then swung the other way. Moe said, "You don't want to fall back into your diagnosis." Did he really accused me of first not taking Kay to urgent care then followed it up with don't fall back into the diagnosis of Munchhausen's by Proxy?

Numb nuts over here didn't seem to comprehend his hired gunman's diagnosis very well.

He continued. "Your behavior is not conducive to our daughters, nor your relationship with them. I've had to set a lot of things straight with them. I'm asking you to stop making things up. It doesn't suit you. I dare not tell you what it makes you look like." Thinly veiled insults with a layer of malevolent child manipulation.

Halloween was coming up. Moe agreed to let me have the girls since he had them last year, only to withhold them the day of because I didn't agree to his holiday schedule where he had them the entire time. He said, "This is my weekend with them, and we have no holiday schedule until November 15 when we go to court." Yup, we're already going back to court. We had a new judge now, but the rumor was that he was worse. I didn't even know how that's possible.

Day of court, November 15, 2021, he gave us temporary orders to last through the end year before he sent us to mediation.

I walked into mediation, and a woman ushered us back to her tiny office. I sat closest to the door, and Moe sat on the back wall in front of the window. She sat directly across from me.

She had a little TV tray-like stand that she used for her laptop. Before she even opened her laptop Moe explained to her how sick and tired he was with me. "We've been doing this for years now, we had a 730 done, and she was diagnosed with Munchhausen's by Proxy. She's a liar, and you shouldn't believe anything she says! She's a liar!" He's already foaming at the mouth and pointing at me.

The mediator stopped him. "Those kinds of comments are not allowed and please do not direct any comments directly to her. Since you filed to go to court, let's go over what you proposed first."

We slowly worked our way through each holiday. It was painstakingly slow because he was so argumentative. To my surprise for Christmas, he was now stating he wanted 12/24 noon to 12/25 noon.

When the court had decided on November 15, 2021, to split the Christmas break evenly.

Moe had disagreed afterward claiming, "I didn't make an agreement, the judge made an agreement until mediation" then demanded prior to mediation to keep them from 12/17 to Christmas Day 5 p.m. and have them again from 12/31 to return of school 1/3. So why now was he agreeing to what I had been saying the whole time?

We moved on to the topic of Christmas break. Moe stood up, walked across the tiny mediation room, and hit the calendar on the wall. He demanded that he be given a three-hour dinner and face-time calls during the time I would have them.

I explained the historical issues with the face-time calls. (How he abused the court order, called me incessantly, yelled at me during the calls, inappropriately used them to talk to Diana and when asked to stop, he didn't.)

Moe shouted, "Damn right, I'm gonna call her as many times as it takes to get MY ten-minute call!"

The mediator attempted to move on and asked Moe to sit down.

"Why? I'm making her nervous?" He laughed and went back to his chair. "So are you approving my calls or not?"

She responded, "Absolutely not, I am here to set you up for success and by what I can see during this mediation allowing phone calls would surely not achieve that goal."

Moe started ranting again. She redirected him several times not to talk to me directly and not to get up out of his chair.

He yelled, "I didn't even touch her! Me getting out of my chair makes her uncomfortable?"

He again demanded he got a three-hour dinner midweek.

I said, "I feel this request is unreasonable and historically I have had two DVRO due to exchange conflicts. I want to limit as many exchanges as possible."

She agreed and had to explain to Moe that I had the right to disagree to his request.

Moe said, "Well, you as the courts can make her do it! You can go above her head and make court orders and make her do it!"

Her face soured. She explained that was not the intended purpose of the courts, and her job was to try to come to an amicable resolve.

Moe relentlessly disagreed. "Make her give me the three-hour dinner by placing the order."

I mean can we blame him? Up until now, all he'd had to do was snap his fingers, Mr. Bladderwort and Judge Mazle Dina would get him whatever he wanted.

After much back and forth, I think he short-circuited his brain because what happened next was just puzzling.

We were now discussing Thanksgiving and Moe seemed to be glitching. He just kept repeating "the girls get out on Thursday and so I think the holiday should be observed to Thursday."

She attempted to clarify what he was trying to say but he kept repeating "Thursday."

"Yes, I understand Thanksgiving is on Thursday, are you asking for the whole week?"

He snapped. "I wasn't done talking! I was trying to read what I wrote! If you would f****** let me speak!"

She lowered her voice and stated very calmly, "Again, I am trying just to understand what you are requesting."

Moe shouted at her, "Are you going to f****** let me finish! Like I was saying." He just repeated the completely nonsensical statement he'd been saying over and over.

She tried to frame her question a different way. "What time do you propose?"

Moe shouted, "Thursday!"

This went on for probably five more minutes. The mediator attempted to seek clarity and Moe just blurted out Thursday!

After they both seemed exhausted, I asked her, "Would it be okay if I told you about my idea for Thanksgiving and maybe he will agree."

Before she had a chance to answer, Moe yelled, "I don't agree!"

I stated several times over the course of the mediation that I was uncomfortable with Moe yelling and his behavior. I told her that he withheld the girls in June twice and again during Labor Day and Halloween. I also brought up the length of his unreasonable demands, and I thought he was cyber stalking me.

She informed me that I could file something with the court if I felt it necessary.

Moe laughed. "If she does, I'm going to take her back court again for child support." The mediator concluded our time and walked us out. We waited for the report. When her report came back, I was surprised when she didn't make a single note of his behavior or any of my concerns. She only wrote the schedule and nothing more, giving the new judge a total misrepresentation of what really happened.

I mean you read this report, and we appeared buddy/buddy. Moe used this to his advantage in court and asked the court to give him a now four-hour dinner midweek and two phone calls a week. If she would have just written one sentence on how that was not a good idea, I wouldn't be rehashing this request.

Luckily, the judge didn't want to hear it and just dismissed his request. However, as soon as we left court, Moe continued to demand I give him what he wanted, and if I didn't, he'll take me back to court again.

I reminded him of what the mediator said, and he responded, "If any of what you just said was true, why wasn't it in the report? I highly doubt she'd leave all that out."

I could punch a wall; the entire family court system was useless.

The negative reviews were stacking up on Dr. Bedlam's Google reviews. Apparently, he was triggered by one woman's review where she claimed Dr. Bedlam had no professional integrity and stated there was a support group for his victims. Like any rational professional, Dr. Bedlam not only attempted to join the *Victims Against Dr. Bedlam Group*, but feverishly took to his Google reviews.

He felt it was necessary to reply to each one of his negative reviews, citing the exact number of hours he provided on each case, details about each case (violating HIPPA), and even provided me with a new diagnosis of "alienation." The same day, May 17, 2022, he wrote the woman that upset his delicate constitution a cease and desist email, threatening to sue her if she didn't dismantle the support group against him, assuming she made it. You know with a guy like Dr. Bedlam, there will be other women, there always is. I found them.

One mother started the victim support page against Dr. Bedlam. He had also falsely diagnosed her with the same thing, Munchhausen's by Proxy. He also implied she had been raped to support his projection theory. With a national average of one in four, I guess he thought he had good odds.

She wasn't so lucky though, and she lost her children.

Another mother, same diagnosis, lost two out of the three of her children. Her older son chose to stay with her, rejecting the court's order.

With Munchhausen's by Proxy typically being such a rare diagnosis, it sure was common in these parts. Dr. Bedlam had unearthed an entire coven it seemed.

I found a case on January 27, 2021, of another mother, again same diagnosis, who had four boys ages 20, 19, 17, and 12.

Three boys were from one father and the youngest from another. There were five CPS reports alleging the youngest was being subjected to general neglect, sexual abuse, emotional abuse, and physical abuse by his father.

On one incident, the mother claimed the father took their son against his wishes for a weekend. Afterward, he attempted suicide by jumping out of a moving car. He was only nine years old at the time.

The father's defense, accusing the mother of parental alienation. Dr. Bedlam submitted his report in August 2019 stating the abuse was not by the father but rather the mother. "A result of her own history of untreated trauma."

Dr. Bedlam said the boy was "broken and damaged, and the mother was doing it to gain the "status of the suffering saintly mother."

Again, Munchhausen's by Proxy was his official diagnosis, and the courts gobbled it up.

In the review, the mother claimed her primary language was Spanish, but Dr. Bedlam denied her right to an interpreter.

Dr. Bedlam stated the mother's other three boys and her other friends all believe "lock, stock, and barrel" the youngest boy was being abused by the father.

Dr. Bedlam noted the boys had an intense bond with their mother, he claimed to only be a trauma bond, and on October 1, 2019, he had all four boys taken into protective custody.

He diagnosed another mother as delusional. She unfortunately buckled under the stress and relinquished control of her children to her ex. However, she didn't go down without a fight. She was the one who stated he had no professional integrity. Dr. Bedlam came after her in his comment of her review with intensity stating, "I consider this to be libelous and defamatory per se. Mother here asserts fact that are objectively untrue. I am asking that this particular person cease and desist with false statement about my professional integrity. I would never put children in danger. Ms. (Blank)'s complaint against me was resolved against her. The court itself agreed with a settlement the parents appear to have reached based on the report. Mother's blanket admonition to others to avoid me evaluating their case fails to recognize that every case is unique and decided on its own merit—Mother's her included. It is always my effort to protect children from anything that undermines or threatens their health, welfare, safety, or development in any way. The 50/50 sharing agreement with the children was an appropriate recommendation in this case. I know because I had to review the case several times after it was submitted. I wonder why Mother would blame me for what the court decided and why she would persist in her attacks on my professional integrity almost three years after submitting the report. I suspect she continues to get bad results in court—I looked up the case and saw there is a hearing coming up in July 2022 that was filed on in March 2022. She had also set a review of the evaluation last year which I assume did not go her way either. It seems to me that Mother, in reckless disregard of the truth refused to read the evaluation in good faith—there was no bias against her, but seems to continue to blame me for her coparenting issues which persist along the lines I predicted if things did not change. I continue to hope the best for Mother and her especially for the children. It is always my goal to better the lives of the children which is in fact affected by their parents when they are stressed, upset or abuse. I repeat I would never knowingly place a child in danger and I have not done so in this case. I would also never allow an abuser to have custody order that did not protect the protect the children from abuse. I hope Mother's attacks against my professional integrity stop. They are in my opinion untrue and actionable. Dr. Bedlam."

To her defense, I updated my review to add, "To claim his professional integrity was under attack while currently violating HIPAA rights does not adhere to the fundamental standards of professionalism. Yet neither does blatantly lying in my court ordered report demonstrate integrity or align to CA rule 5.220. Dr. Bedlam made a new diagnostic claim of 'alienation' against me in his public comment that was never mentioned in the original report. A report where he deliberately fabricated a false diagnosis of Munchhausen's by Proxy (MBP) against me with no supportive evidence. I have no history of mental health illness or did Dr. Bedlam review my or our daughters' medical records, so it stands to reason it is seemingly more plausible Dr. Bedlam is a greedy charlatan who is morally bankrupt." Perhaps realizing his impulsive grave error, Dr. Bedlam deleted all of his comments three days later, but I had screenshots.

Two months later, Anna asked me if she could ask about something she heard.

Apparently, the whole time we were in mediation, Anna was in Moe's car waiting with Cecilia. Anna told me she knew about our meeting. "Daddy said he couldn't talk because she was crying so much, he couldn't speak."

She said she asked him if Mommy was the one crying. He told her no, "The lady they put in the meeting to make sure Mommy and Daddy did not fight was crying."

Anna was confused and didn't really believe him. She asked, "Were you crying, Mommy?"

"No, baby."

She asked why the mediator was crying? I told her she did not cry, either.

She paused and then asked, "Why did he say that?"

"I don't know, baby," and then I changed the topic.

A couple months later, it was, "Mommy, why is pussycat a bad word?"

"It's not."

"Daddy said pussy means vagina, and it's a bad word. I also know what dick is." She ran off.

I emailed my attorney, but even I knew it's just gonna be "he said she said," and no one was going to believe me. I should just title my emails to my attorney "cathartic diary entry #289" because that is all they were at this point.

Every month or so, he sent out something. One month, he would demand for my personal cell phone number, threatening if I declined, he would take me to court. "If you force me to file it will be for much more than just information Seraphine."

Next month, it's 'we should go to every parent-teacher conference together.' Next, he's demanding to attend every doctor visit with me.

When I voiced I would rather not be in a room with him, he said, "I have every right to be there, Seraphine, and if you cancel, I will take you to court."

Joint custody eliminated my ability to express consent; whether or not I asked him not to show up to doctor's appointments, his "right" to be present superseded any of my rights. He showed up to my house. He showed up unannounced to a school fieldtrip he never signed up for or paid for. Ignoring him didn't work. Walking away didn't work, either. At the last fieldtrip, while I attempted to walk away Cecilia grabbed Anna's arm and tried to pull her away from me. I was told I had to tolerate it.

America has normalized male violence to such a degree that joint custody with an abusive man means to the family court system abusers have implied consent. I cannot complain that Moe abusive as it is just his nature.

And if you're wondering if even a near-death experience of our child would change Moe; no, it didn't. In January 2023, Anna had difficulty breathing and had to be placed on life support. His presence at the hospital was a performance, like look at me. Afterward, he claimed it was not fair that Anna got sick for two weeks during his Christmas vacation time. Again, stating he should be given make-up time during my time. Besides, in his mind I owed him. When Anna was still in the hospital, he didn't want the parental responsibility of taking Kay to school, so I offered to do it for him... yet, in his mind, he "allowed" me to have her. Because I disagreed to the extra time, on his next visitation, he made the girls watch *The Black Phone*. A rated-R movie about a child serial killer who kidnaps a thirteen-year-old boy and puts him in his basement where the boy begins talking to the dead ghosts of children the man murdered to help him escape. I couldn't say anything because if I voiced my disapproval, Moe would double down, and I feared would make them watch it repeatedly like *Coraline*.

Two weeks later the school called me concerned about Anna. I rushed there worried she was having a complication from her lengthy hospital stay. She appeared lethargic and said her chest hurt. I raced her to the ER. They said she had pericarditis and admitted her. As I was helping her with breakfast Moe walks in, "You gonna leave so my wife, her step-mom, can come in? They only allow two visitors."

I said, "No."

He threw a small tantrum. "I know Tony was just here."

I said, "No, he wasn't, no one has been here."

Anna said, "I saw Tony..."

Moe interrupted her sentence, "Oh, yeah, when did you see him? Where was he? I knew he was here."

She tried to say that she saw him the last time she was in the hospital, but Moe continued. "You know your mommy gets confused with the truth sometimes."

Upset, I said, "That's enough!"

He continued. "Maybe you should go take a break... maybe go outside and take your meds."

I said, "You will not disrespect in front of Anna."

He smiled. "Respect is earned, not given." I bit my tongue not to say anything else in front of Anna but I could hold back the tears of frustration that were welling up in my eyes. Moe smirked and video called Cecilia, and they began talking with Anna. The nurse stepped in, and I was so upset I stepped outside the room. With her in the room he told Anna, "Your mommy won't allow Cecilia in. Your mommy needs to understand that Cecilia is my wife and your stepmom. I'm sorry your mommy is so mean." He used the girls to obtain revenge on me, making decisions based solely on his own interests, failing to consider their needs, using manipulation, coercion, and exploitation to gain control.

People may think only rich powerful men get pardoned for all their misdeeds, but once you go through the system, you learn even unemployed men that still live with their parents, do drugs, and abuse children get pardons, too.

The biggest lie the family courts have sold is that they are here to protect children.

"The reason you haven't heard my story and thousands of others like it is because our children are still alive, and the Family Court System has destroyed, and continues to destroy, all hope for escape.

Our Family Court System would rather terminate hope than terminate the parental rights of an abusive father."

— Kerry Hernandez

EPILOGUE

How can a system that is heavily rooted with patriarchal values, white supremacy, and has tremendous religious power be threatened by divorce and how did Richard Gardner's insidious theories dominate the United States legislative framework?

Divorce can provide women with the opportunity to gain economic independence, which undermines patriarchal systems that rely on women's economic dependence on men. Historically, women's financial reliance on their husbands has perpetuated power imbalances and limited women's options for autonomy. Divorce signifies an assertion of agency and self-determination for women, as it allows women to make choices regarding their own lives and relationships. Patriarchal systems often prioritize male authority and control over women's lives. When women choose to end a marriage, they challenge this patriarchal authority and reclaim their right to determine their destinies. A woman's success historically was in terms of their marital status, and by rejecting societal pressures to remain in unhappy or abusive relationships again challenges patriarchal expectations. Thus the choice to divorce can be seen as a threat to systems that uphold patriarchal values due to its potential to disrupt gender roles, promote economic independence, assert agency and self determination, and redefine societal notions of success for women. In response, the system might employ male backlash to harm women, aiming to maintain control and reinforce patriarchal norms. This backlash could manifest through various means, including social ostracization, economic retaliation, legal obstacles, religious condemnation, and even physical violence, all aimed at silencing women and discouraging them from exercising their agency and pursuing independence.

When we look at what is wrong with the Family Court System, we have to look at the #MeToo movement and rape culture because they are closely intertwined; they have a dual mindset. Rape culture is pervasive and is embedded in how we speak, think, and navigate through our society allowing sexual violence to be normalized and justified. On January 4, 2021, Jenifer Kuadli posted *32 Shocking Sexual Assault Statistics for 2021*, here are some of them:

- An American is sexually assaulted every 93 seconds.

- Rape Statistics show that less than 20% of rapes are reported.

- For every 1000 rapes in the US, 995 perpetrators will go unpunished.

- Over 40% of women in the US have encountered sexual violence. Around 20% of American males have been the victim of sexual violence.

- In Florida alone, a staggering total of 1,477,000 men have been victim to sexual assault.

- During 2019, 13% of all women in California were victims of rape.

- 7.2% of all children surveyed in 2019 had been victims of sexual assault.

- The majority (90%) of rape victims are female.

- Approximately 70 women commit suicide every day in the US following an act of sexual violence.

- 69% of rape victims in the US are women aged between 12 to 34 years old.

- Girls and women between the ages of 16 and 19 are 4x more likely than girls and women in other age groups to be assaulted or raped.

- A quarter of male victims of sexual assault were under 10 years of age.

- Almost 95% of child victims knew their sexual attacker.

There are many factors that have also contributed to the normalization of sexual violence in America including: a culture that values men over women, a culture that objectifies and sexualizes women, lack of education about consent and healthy relationships, lack of accountability for perpetrators, including lenient sentencing for those convicted of sexual violence, and lack of support and resources for victims. Victim blaming is an attitude that suggests a victim rather than the perpetrator bears responsibility for an assault.

In 2021, Francios Momolu Khalil raped a woman, and the Minnesota Supreme Court unanimously overturned the third-degree criminal sexual conduct charge by stating the rape victim was *"voluntarily intoxicated"* at the time because she had made the decision to drink, and therefore did not meet the threshold for mental incapacitation under state law (Morales, 2021 NYTimes).

Basically, the Minnesota Supreme Court is supporting the fact if someone voluntarily gets drunk and then gets attacked, the attacker will not be held accountable for anything that they may do to your unconscious body. This decision sends a damaging message to survivors of sexual violence, suggesting that they are responsible for the crimes committed against them. Perhaps they should ban alcohol in Minnesota if this is their response. Laws that should be protecting victims are instead claiming it's the victim's fault for voluntarily drinking alcohol, and no consent is necessary.

They weren't even denying Mr. Khalil raped a woman, they were arguing over the verbiage of Minnesota law. It's apparently a loophole in their legislation, and what's worse is that they said it has been a problem for years.

Years?

The Minnesota Supreme Court ruled that the state's definition of *"mentally incapacitated"* does not include voluntarily inebriated victims. Even more chilling it was noted that similar *"law loopholes"* are applied in about forty (40) states.

"The reported facts are horrifying," said Jill Hasday, a law professor at the University of Minnesota. "think it highlights the need for legislative reform (NYTimes)."

It would seem our courts are currently supporting rapists more than the victims of this crime.

Just as rape culture shifts the blame off the rapist and onto the victim, the Family Court System will persecute and attack the safe parent and in-turn justify and ignore the actions of the abuser. Both *"rape culture"* and *"pro-contact"* use tactics of victim blaming. This is what victim blaming might look like within the Family Court System:

- Blame the victim ("They married them!" "They asked for it." "They chose to have children with them." "They must have known they were violence before they married them.")
- Trivializing domestic violence
- Tolerance of abusive behaviors
- Inflating false abuse report statistics
- Publicly scrutinizing a victim's motives, mental state, and history
- Gratuitous gendered violence in movies, TV, and media
- Defining *"Fathers"* as dominant, behaviorally aggressive, irreplaceable, emotionally callous

- Defining *"Mothers"* as submissive, behaviorally passive, all slightly insane, gold diggers

- Assuming they must be lying about the abuse as leverage in court

- Refusing to take abuse accusations seriously

- Teaching victim how to avoid getting abused

- Teaching children they must live with or like their abuser because they are their parent

- Re-unification therapy

- Assuming child is lying or was told to lie about abuse

- Denying incest

An example could be that "Parent B must have provoked Parent A into being abusive. They both need to change." This then assumes that the victim is equally to blame for the abuse, when in reality, abuse is a conscious choice made by the abuser. Or perhaps that Parent A must have known that Parent B was abusive before they got married and had children, therefore, it is Parent A's fault.

This is not sound logic.

By engaging in victim blaming this emboldens the abuser because it reinforces what the abuser has been saying all along; *"that it is the victim's fault this is happening, and they are the 'true victim.'"*

Domestic violence is not about the victim's actions some misconceive as the victim's way to incite the abuser to hurt them, but rather it's the abuser's sense of entitlement to do whatever they want to the victim. When victims of domestic violence turn to the Family Court System to seek freedom for them and their children from their abuser, they instead find the courts are *"pro-contact"* and it seems a "good parent" is defined as one encouraging children to have a relationship with the other parent even if that parent is abusive. In cases where abuse is present, the victim or advocate may have legitimate concerns; however, another issue that arises almost immediately is that the couple might get labeled as *high conflict,* again denoting that they both are at fault instead of identifying a domestic violence abuse case. "Court professionals are taught to use 'high conflict' approaches by which they mean the parents are angry with each other and act out in ways that hurt children. The research establishes, however, that a large majority of these cases involve the most dangerous abusers who are using custody to regain control over their victims. They are the most dangerous because they believe she had no right to leave, but professionals looking only for the most severe physical assaults fail to recognize the danger. (Goldstein, 2017)"

This pattern of behavior that intends to exert power or control over someone by eroding their self-autonomy is known as coercive control. Identifying abuse or a power and control dynamic is key analysis that can provide context when gathering information. "For example, a mother who avoids phone contact with an abusive former partner might be seen to be neglecting her duties for information sharing about the children's activities; however, within the context of spousal violence, this same behavior can be understood as an attempt to protect herself and her children from further harassment and abuse (Jaffe, Crooks, Bala, 2005)."

Alyce LaViolette M.S. Psychology Psychotherapist, Consultant, and domestic violence expert has extended the framework of researcher Michael Johnson who has argued for delineation of different patterns of spousal violence and developed "The Continuum of Aggression and Abuse."

CONTINUUM of AGGRESSION and ABUSE *by Alyce LaViolette*

Exacerbating Factors: Family of Origin Issues – Substance Abuse - Age (Younger)
Previous Abusive Relationships – Psychological Issues

Common Couple Aggression	High Conflict	Abuse	Battering	Terrorism / Stalking
• Aberrant act • Remorse • Does not cause fear, oppression or control • No serious injury • Comes from escalating arguments • Could happen in any family	• Do not solve problems well • Anger is an issue in family • May have remorse • May have sporadic physical aggression and/or destruction of property • Not emotionally abusive • No fear • Comes from escalating arguments	• Sporadic physical aggression • Name-calling, but not character assassination • Verbal abuse, but not psychological • Development of apprehension • May be remorseful • Threats of abandonment • Threats of getting custody • Aggression takes place without witnesses	• Monopolization of perception • Generally more regular physical abuse, but may occur without any physical abuse • Threats to victim's support system • Isolation • Name-calling that attacks character • Threats to kill self or others • Jealousy • Putting down of family and friends • Destruction of property • Self-absorbed • Sexual abuse • Change in victim's personality • More generally violent	• Monopolization of perception • Insidious psychological abuse • Well-thought out threats to kill—very specific • Torturing pets • Extreme isolation of victim by perpetrator • Generally more regular physical abuse, but may occur without any physical abuse • Sexual humiliation and degradation

Mediating Factors: Connection to community – Job that has meaning – Age (Older)
Participation in abuse intervention program
Participation in recovery program

If we view abuse with the perspective of a spectrum ranging from common couple aggression to more severe forms like stalking and terrorize, then it is easier to spot the differences between the lines of high conflict and abuse. If abusive characteristics are identified, then methods to prevent harm can be implemented. It is well know in domestic violence crisis centers that the most dangerous time for a victim is when they leave their abusers.

Abusers that need to have control and power after divorce may engage in what is referred as Post Separation Abuse. If court officials fail to recognize the tactics of post separation abuse, then this is much like a doctor failing to see the signs and symptoms of a disease that could lead to catastrophic effects. Coming from a medical background, I think of analogies that make sense to my brain. Post separation abuse is much like renal failure to me.

There is a spectrum of renal failure from acute onset, acute kidney injury (AKI), to slow gradual failure known as chronic kidney disease (CKD). In the individual that has a sudden acute onset of kidney injury (AKI), this can occur over days or weeks typically caused by low blood volume, or the heart is pumping out less blood than normal, and/or the use of certain medications.

Let's equate this to the time nearest the date of the divorce. The tension is high, the arguments are frequent, and the relationship is not functioning well. Typically, these two situations are hopefully reversible. The kidneys hopefully return to a normal healthy function just as two parents can divorce then eventually can co-parent well. This is the ideal situation, *a separated or divorced couple that can set aside their differences* and *shift their primarily goals to the best interest of their child.*

Chronic kidney disease has a slow onset that spans over months or years that can be caused by a number of various factors like diabetes or high blood pressure for example, just as abuse usually stems from many contributing factors. Chronic kidney disease typically doesn't result in end stage renal disease overnight, it takes a while to develop; however, the damage done to the kidneys is often irreversible and/or permanent.

Just as abusive relationships typically don't begin violent, and over time, the abuse becomes more frequent or more intense. The longer the abuse spans the less likely the abuser is going to stop. Just as doctors are not shocked when their CKD stage 5 patient enters into renal failure (ESRD), criminal detectives are not shocked when investigating murders when months usually years of violence precedes the final crime. The Family Court System doesn't seem to have a good handle on diagnosing *"chronic kidney disease" aka "post separation abuse,"* how to treat it and/or how to manage it in the long run.

www.theduluthmodel.org/wp-content/uploads/2021/10/Post-Separation-Power-and-Control.pdf

For a doctor to push IV lasix on an ESRD then get upset that that patient is not producing two liters of urine in a day is equivalent to Family Court System pushing the idea of co-parenting when one parent is abusive then getting upset that conflict continues to arise. Both are unrealistic and are likely to cause more damage than good. Understanding the distinctions between varying kinds of violence is essential for determining if a certain post-separation parenting arrangement are suitable.

The power and control wheel was developed by the Domestic Abuse Intervention Project in Duluth, Minnesota, in 1984, to help describe the experience of victims of violence and the tactics that abusers used. The Duluth model includes an umbrella of abuse: using threats, harassment, stalking, coercive control, intimidation, emotional abuse, isolation, economic abuse, legal abuse, using male privilege, using the children, abusive parenting, counter parenting, alienation allegations, minimizing or denying abuse, and blaming. This abuse is targeted directly at the other parent or at the children or boarder community with intentions of hurting the safe parent.

The abuser may use counter parenting tactics such as undermining the parenting capabilities and judgments of the safe parent, deny or refuse to agree to provide care for a child's medical issues, prioritize punishment and hatred for their ex over the well-being of the child, and to spite the safe parent, tries to instill opposing beliefs in the child. The abuser may use neglectful or abusive parenting tactics such as exposing the children to potentially harmful material, situations, or persons and may use violence, intimidation, threats, manipulation, and humiliation to win the compliance of the child to cause stress and panic in the safe parent.

The abuser may also attack the safe parent too by painting a false narrative, spread rumors or lies to ruin their reputation, cyberstalking, bombard them with messages typically abusive in nature, gaslight them, criticize them, or generate a fearful atmosphere that penetrates every aspect of the safe parent's life. The abuser may deny access to bank accounts, withhold child support, or even use the court to deplete their finances or further harass the safe parent. The abuser will typically not follow court orders and might even attempt to gain custody only to punish and emotionally harm the safe parent. It seems most of this abuse goes completely unchecked by the court system and post-separation abuse is rarely recognized.

However this research has been out for nearly 40 years, so the questions I have are: is this truly a lack of knowledge? Is the system itself intentionally designed to coercively control women by silencing them and discouraging them from exercising their agency and pursuing independence? Are the children in these cases just collateral damage? Has our system ever cared about the children or is it purposeful incompetence to exploit them for financial gain? Or are they in so deep that the cost to extricate themselves away from Richard Gardner's perverted theories is one they are not willing to pay? We live in a time where it is easier for a rapist to rape a woman, obtain custody of the child, and abuse the child then it is for victims to ever see justice.

Change requires a cultural shift. One that challenges the deeply ingrained attitudes and beliefs. It also requires us to work together, as a society, to create a culture that values and respects the rights of all individuals, and that holds perpetrators accountable for their actions. By taking these steps, we can begin to build a Family Court System that truly protects victims and supports survivors.

THE CONVERSATION

Warning: contains explicit language

MINOR CHILD　　　　　　　　**MOE**

Can you possibly take me to pick this girl up

> when

pretty soon I'm asking her right now if she is coming or not

> Let me know cuz I'm a chicks pad on the Mesa.

> I'm just chilling, she's on her period.

> So I'm not getting any tonight

Never mind she's coming over tomorrow though

Gay.

Tell her to shut the fuck up, I will pick her up.

You can eat her out.

It's happening tonight and your gonna make her cum.

Or not, I've been drinking.

I will give you 2 rubbers. Use them wisely my young padaewon.

I got a tittie pic right now

I don't believe you.

(Minor boy sends Moe pictures of minor female)

Ok. I believe you. But I don't need them on my FB. That's kiddie porn. Duck. Dick.

Just delete the message.

Hahahaha.

Deleted.

Good for you though. They are nice.

FEBRUARY 1, 2016

R u up

yeah

I'm coming for my yogurt

ok

I fucked her in the ass

lucky

yup. The door is locked.

Dude I might get to fuck my girls friend.

At the same time?

No but her friend wants to lose her virginity and my girl knows what's up and I'm trying to hook it up.

Fucking young ass girls.

If she was 18 I'd take her to the moon hahaha lol jk.

Hahah straight up
hey Germany friend ain't bad dog

Her friend

Send pic

(Minor boy sends Moe pictures of minor female)

Oh she's super cute dude.

I asked my girl if we could have a threeway with another chick and she was li,etc I have a friend that want to lose her virginity and I was like hey hook it up. And I might have two chick to fuck all the time.

She wants older dick.

Who?

Me

Haha yeah right.

lol

Omg Moe your ridiculous.

If I laid a finger on or in one of those girls a few things would happen.

1) they would be sprung on this dick

2) they wouldn't want your inexperienced ass anymore

3) my be behind bars lol

Haha probably all 3 would happen.

I just want to taste virgin pussy again lol jk.

Who wouldn't can't blame you.

Hahahahaha butterscotch. Gorilla rape.

—————— 9 PM ——————

(Moe sends picture of female to minor)

Ohh shiit you gonna fuck

yup

lucky I want to bang her too

Y would I share if your not gonna share

You can't have it even if I did share

Damnit.

Neither can you for the same reason lol

Nah that's different

Nope... Stat rape is stat rape

FEBRUARY 4, 2016

Come get a match of bots fag

Ok fucker.

I just got home. I had Kay and Anna today.

I'm gonna get a bottle of booze beforel come over homo suck stick

Haha ok ima get dabbed out before you come

You should be calling your gf and finding out when you can put your dip stick in her oil pan

I've been messaging her and she won't answer

I told you...

You wait too long she will find someone else to fill her hole.

She thinks all you wanted was to fuck and cuz you won't go fuck her again she's got a new dick

uh uh uh she could have came over last night but she didn't feel good

of course she didn't. Cuz she couldn't walk cuz banged her til she couldn't walk straight

not even

FEBRUARY 17, 2016

Are you still taking me to get a bong

Tomorrow. I got to pick up my aunt from the airport

FEBRUARY 29, 2016

You coming back to finish the match?

(Moe sends minor a closes up picture of a female vagina)

that pic was sent to me a lil bit ago.
That's the fatty I don't tell no one
about lol. No I'm home and in bed. I
got to be 'at the hospital' by 9:30 am.
I have a doctors appointment.

MARCH 1, 2016

call me fucker.

I'm trying to see if you want
to make some money bitch

yes I do

Chapter 17

1. Mary Frances Mullins, "Cannabis Dabbing: An Emerging Trend," *Nursing* 51, no. 5 (2021): 46–50. https://doi.org/10.1097/01.nurse.0000743108.72528.d8.

1. verywellmind.com

2. Jiries Meehan-Atrash, Wentai Luo, and Robert M. Strongin, "Toxicant Formation in Dabbing: The Terpene Story," *ACS Omega* 2, no. 9 (2017): 6112–17. https://doi.org/10.1021/acsomega.7b01130.

3. Alan J Budney and John R Hughes, "The Cannabis Withdrawal Syndrome," *Current Opinion in Psychiatry* 19, no. 3 (2006): 233–38. https://doi.org/10.1097/01.yco.0000218592.00689.e5.

Chapter 22

1. Jane K Stoever, "Firearms and Domestic Violence Fatalities: Preventable Deaths," Family Law Quarterly 53, no. 3 (2019): 186. https://www.jstor.org/stable/27007852.

2. Jane K Stoever, "Firearms and Domestic Violence Fatalities: Preventable Deaths," Family Law Quarterly 53, no. 3 (2019): 201. https://www.jstor.org/stable/27007852.

3. Jane K Stoever, "Firearms and Domestic Violence Fatalities: Preventable Deaths," Family Law Quarterly 53, no. 3 (2019): 186. https://www.jstor.org/stable/27007852.

Chapter 24

1. Peter G Jaffe, Claire V Crooks, and Nick Bala. "Making Appropriate Parenting Arrangements in Family Violence Cases: Applying the Literature to Identify Promising Practices," Government of Canada, December 28, 2022. https://www.justice.gc.ca/eng/rp-pr/fl-lf/parent/2005_3/index.html.

2. Ibid.

3. Ibid.

Chapter 32

1. "Using the Saunders' Report- Part One," National Organization for Men Against Sexism, August 22, 2022, https://nomas.org/sanders-report-part/#:~:text=The%20Saunders'%20study%20found%20that,protect%20children%20and%20their%20mothers, 6.

2. "Fast Facts: Preventing Adverse Childhood Experiences |violence Prevention|injury Center|CDC," Centers for Disease Control and Prevention, April 6, 2022, https://www.cdc.gov/violenceprevention/aces/fastfact.html, 6.

3. "Protective Mothers, Endangered Children: Quantifying System Failure," https://
    irp-cdn.multiscreensite.com/0dab915e/files/uploaded/2018%20article%20on%20
    survey%20Protective%20%20%20%20Mothers%2C%20Endangered%20Chil-
    dren%20April%2027%20copy.pdf

4. Ibid., 13.

5. "Protective Mothers, Endangered Children: Quantifying System Failure," https://
    irp-cdn.multiscreensite.com/0dab915e/files/uploaded/2018%20article%20on%20
    survey%20Protective%20%20%20%20Mothers%2C%20Endangered%20Chil-
    dren%20April%2027%20copy.pdf

6. Ibid., 10.

7. Ibid., 17.

8. "Protective Mothers, Endangered Children: Quantifying System Failure," https://
    irp-cdn.multiscreensite.com/0dab915e/files/uploaded/2018%20article%20on%20
    survey%20Protective%20%20%20%20Mothers%2C%20Endangered%20Chil-
    dren%20April%2027%20copy.pdf

9. Ibid., 17.

10. Ibid., 15.

11. Ibid., 16.

12. "Protective Mothers, Endangered Children: Quantifying System Failure," https://
    irp-cdn.multiscreensite.com/0dab915e/files/uploaded/2018%20article%20on%20
    survey%20Protective%20%20%20%20Mothers%2C%20Endangered%20Chil-
    dren%20April%2027%20copy.pdf.

13. Joan S Meier, "Victims of Domestic Abuse Find No Haven in Family Courts," The
    Conversation, November 15, 2022, https://theconversation.com/victims-of-domestic-
    abuse-find-no-haven-in-family-courts-159192, para. 6.

14. Joan S. Meier, "U.S. Child Custody Outcomes in Cases Involving Parental Alienation
    and Abuse Allegations: What Do the Data Show?" Journal of Social Welfare and Fam-
    ily Law 42, no. 1 (2020): 92–105, https://doi.org/10.1080/09649069.2020.170194
    1, 94.

15. https://commission.itnj.org

16. Joan S Meier, "Parental Alienation Syndrome and Parental Alienation: A Research
    Review," vawnet.org, September 2013, https://vawnet.org/sites/default/files/materials/
    files/2016-09/AR_PASUpdate.pdf, 3.

17. Ibid., 3.

18. Ibid., 9.

19. Ibid., 9.

20. Grant Wyeth, "How the Family Court's Purpose to Protect Children Became Inverted," Medium, October 28, 2021, https://medium.com/equality-includes-you/how-the-family-courts-purpose-to-protect-children-became-inverted-d300871553d0, para. 22.

21. Grant Wyeth, "The Facilitating System of the Family Court," Medium, November 18, 2021, https://grantwyeth.medium.com/the-facilitating-system-of-the-family-court-cf4ee5a3b30b, para. 6-15.

22. Barry Goldstein, "The Question for Family Courts: How Can You Give More Influence to a Pro Pedophile Theory than Scientific Research from the CDC and U.S. Justice Department," Barry Goldstein, May 8, 2017, https://www.barrygoldstein.net/articles/the-question-for-family-courts, para. 34.

Chapter 35

1. "Custody & Parenting Time," Oregon Judicial Department : Custody & Parenting Time : Children & Families : State of Oregon, n.d., https://www.courts.oregon.gov/programs/family/children/Pages/custody-parenting-time.aspx, 6.

2. "Custody and Parenting Time," Custody and parenting time | Oregon State Library, n.d., https://digital.osl.state.or.us/islandora/object/osl:25683, 8.

3. NPR/TED Staff, "Nadine Burke Harris: How Does Trauma Affect a Child's DNA?," NPR, August 25, 2017, https://www.npr.org/2017/08/25/545092982/nadine-burke-harris-how-does-trauma-affect-a-childs-dna.

Chapter 36

1. https://commission.itnj.org/

2. Grant Wyeth, "How the Family Court's Purpose to Protect Children Became Inverted," Medium, October 28, 2021, https://medium.com/equality-includes-you/how-the-family-courts-purpose-to-protect-children-became-inverted-d300871553d0, para. 3.

www.ingramcontent.com/pod-product-compliance
Lightning Source LLC
Chambersburg PA
CBHW070905120626
46546CB00001B/143